William James Linton

European Republicans

Recollections of Mazzini and his friends

William James Linton

European Republicans
Recollections of Mazzini and his friends

ISBN/EAN: 9783337218676

Printed in Europe, USA, Canada, Australia, Japan

Cover: Foto ©ninafisch / pixelio.de

More available books at **www.hansebooks.com**

EUROPEAN REPUBLICANS

RECOLLECTIONS OF

MAZZINI AND HIS FRIENDS

BY

W. J. LINTON

The Republican Party is not a political party: it is a party essentially religious.
Foi et Avenir.

LONDON:
LAWRENCE AND BULLEN,
16, HENRIETTA STREET, COVENT GARDEN, W.C.
1892.

RICHARD CLAY & SONS, LIMITED,
LONDON & BUNGAY.

PREFACE.

My acquaintance with Mazzini, the chief of the Republican Party in Europe, dates almost from his arrival in England in 1837. I first heard of him from my brother-in-law, Thomas Wade (the poet), then editor of *Bell's New Weekly Messenger*. His friend George Toynbee, a young literary man of considerable talent, who had studied medicine under a brother of Thomas Wade, was one of the very first persons known by Mazzini in England. By George's brother Joseph (the aurist) I was introduced to Mazzini. The opening of his and other exiles' letters at the English Post-office in 1844 brought us more closely together: the active part in calling public attention to the outrage and in bringing it before the House of Commons being intrusted to me. From this time we were intimate friends. It was in days which he spent with me at Woodford, rambling through Hainault Forest with me (and with my artist friend Thomas Sibson, then living with me), that I heard from his own lips the story of the Bandieras. In 1848, a few days after the three days of February, I took to Paris the first English congratulations, from a public meeting chiefly of working-men. Mazzini traveled with me, and we shared rooms together during my fortnight's visit. Up to the hour of his death there was no diminution or shadowing of our friendship.

So much I ask leave to say, not without pride,

in part warrant of my undertaking to be his biographer and interpreter. I have also under my eyes at this writing his special authorization (given to me on my going to America) to explain his views, and to act for the Republican Party. I feel, therefore, that I am at once fulfilling a sacred duty, and carrying out his own wishes in the work [1] to which this is preface.

It may be that my memoir may be deemed partial. But how shall the "impartial" be fairly appreciative? Who shall speak with sufficient authority of a man, unless it be one loving him and loved, so qualified to read his soul, so abled to judge the man and his acts from intimate knowledge of his principles and character. I profess not to be impartial, but in all I would be true: hiding nothing out of fear of belittling my hero, saying however admiringly only what I know caring most to give a faithful presentment of one indeed dearer to me than a brother, whose superior in all that constitutes an accomplished and heroic manhood I do not find upon the scroll of History. I desire also to present to Englishmen and Americans a clearer idea than I have found elsewhere of the aim and purpose of his life, the Republicanism, as understood and preached by him, which, I believe, has yet to regenerate the world.

I add such brief notices as I have had opportunity to collect (much from personal knowledge) of the men who were nearest to Mazzini in his aims and in his work.

New Haven, Conn., U.S.A. 1892.

[1] Written in 1876 for a series of *Brief Biographies* in course of publication at that date. Not willingly have I waited until now, twenty years since my friend's death, for the publishing of my words.

CONTENTS.

	PAGE
MAZZINI	1
YOUNG ITALY	3
YOUNG EUROPE	31
MILAN	65
ROME	96
THE PARTY OF ACTION	130
RUFFINI AND THE BANDIERAS	165
LAMENNAIS	191
PESTEL AND RYLÉIEFF	223
HERZEN	241
AUTOBIOGRAPHY	243
VIVOS VOCO	271
KONARSKI—DARASZ—STOLZMAN—WORCELL	305
APPENDIX—A BASIS OF ORGANIZATION	343

MAZZINI.

"In exile because I have loved righteousness and hated iniquity."
Words of Gregory VII.

YOUNG ITALY.

THE FORMATION OF A NATION IS A RELIGION.

"Italy is a single nation: her unity of manners, of language, and of literature ought, at a period more or less remote, to unite her inhabitants under one government."—NAPOLEON, *at St. Helena.*

1814—NAPOLEON was fallen. Whatever hopes yet remained to the peoples whom he had crushed beneath the wheels of his ambition were buried with him at St. Helena. The "Holy Alliance" of king-vultures, single and double headed, was proclaimed, and they had again fixed their talons in the throbbing heart of Europe. Peace had come, and the Treaty of Vienna had but to arrange the new map—to last for ever. Italy was returned to her old masters, Austrian, Bourbon, Papal, and Savoyard,—the last permitted to share by grace of the greater Kaisers, to keep out France, whose restlessness was still feared. Seven rulers cut up the land, seven rulers, some better, some worse, so dividing the spoil the more easily to keep possession, held down the Peninsula. Excellent arrangement, but Italy, the birth-place of Brutus and of Dante, was not content. Ere seven years had passed there was an insurrection, the war for Italian liberty resumed.

GIUSEPPE (Joseph) MAZZINI was born on the 22nd of June, 1805, in the Strada Lomellini, Genoa, in which city was then living his father Giacomo Mazzini, physician and professor of anatomy. His mother, Maria Drago, is said to have been of great personal beauty, quick and vigorous intellect, and strong affections. The child Joseph, one of several children, was during his earliest years delicate and fragile,—"nearly six years of age before he could walk firmly." Incapacitated in consequence for the ordinary amusements of childhood, his mind became precociously active, and study was at once the employment and the pleasure of his days. This physical weakness, however, he entirely outgrew. At the age of thirteen he entered the University of Genoa, where he remained for five years, distinguished for assiduity and good conduct, for the gentleness and generosity of his disposition, for a notable ascendancy over his fellow-students, and for an indomitable uprightness and resolution of character.

During this time at the University occurred the Piedmontese insurrection of 1821. The defeated revolutionists fled to Genoa, where the people sympathized with them, and where they looked for means to pass into Spain, at that time hopeful of revolutionary success under the leadership of Riego. One April day as the lad Mazzini was walking with his mother and an old family friend, Andrea Gambini, they were stopped by one of these unfortunates, who held out a white handkerchief towards them, saying only—" For Italy's proscribed." " That day," writes Mazzini, " was the first in which was confusedly presented to my mind, I will not say a thought of Country and Liberty, but a thought that one might and therefore ought to struggle for the liberty of one's country. I was already unconsciously educated in the worship of Equality by the democratic habits of my parents and the identical manner used by them toward the people or the patrician : in the individual they looked only for the man, and the honest man. And the aspirations toward liberty, natural to my soul, were nourished by the records of a recent period, that of the republican French war, often repeated from the lips of my father and the friend before named; by the histories of Livy and Tacitus which my Latin master made me translate ; and by reading of some old journals which I found among my father's medical books, among them some numbers of the *Chronique du Mois*, a Girondist publication of the early days of the French Revolution. The idea that there was in my own country a wasting evil against which one must have to struggle, the idea that in that struggle I might have to take my part, flashed before me in that day, never more to leave me.

"The image of the proscribed, many of whom afterwards were my friends, followed me everywhere by day and was before me in my dreams. I would have given I know not what to follow them. I sought to gather names and facts. I studied as I best could the story of their generous attempt and the causes of their defeat. They had been betrayed, abandoned by those who had sworn to concentrate all their forces on the endeavour; the one Italian king, Carlo Felice of Savoy, had called in the Austrians. . . . The sum of all the details I was acquiring led me to think—was it possible, then, if each had done his duty, to have conquered? Why then not re-attempt? This idea took almost constant possession of me, and the impossibility of perceiving in what way I might attempt to translate it into deeds darkened my soul."

These thoughts continued to haunt him during his stay at the University, even in the hours of study; he was sombre and distraught, and in his boyish fanaticism dressed himself in black in mourning for his country. That habit he continued through life. His friendships, always warm, with the Ruffinis, Campanella, and others, lifted him out of the gloom, helped also by his literary tendencies and the hope through them of some practical outcome. For a time, it seems, he thought of following his father's profession, but was deterred by his inability to overcome his first disgust in the dissecting-room. On that account, on leaving the University he applied himself to the study of Law, was appointed Avvocato, and began to practise, not without promise of popularity and success from his devotion to the cause of those poorer clients for whom alone the youthful advocate had the opportunity to plead.

Toward the close of 1826 his first literary essay, on Dante, sent by him to the *Antologia* of Florence, but rejected there, was printed in the *Subalpino*. Just then the fight between the Classic and Romantic Schools was beginning: the former composed of Academicians, professors and pedants, mere unpatriotic literati, lifeless and tyrannical assertors of the false doctrine of art for only art's sake; the latter represented by young men purposeless and lawless (arbitrariness as ever opposed by mere wilfulness of rebellion), basing their literature only upon individual fantasies. To Mazzini, even in those young days, it seemed that something more was needed: that neither literature nor art could be real and vital without freedom and object; wherefore the first question to be resolved was, not what should be the form of Italian artistic or literary production, but was there to be an Italian nation, anything at all Italian? A little later such thoughts, moved at first by the sight of the proscribed Piedmontese, logically led him to abandon even the seductions of pure literature, toward which his taste impelled him, for the rougher field of politics. Only the necessity of the time and the generous shame he felt at his country's abasement forced him, as our own Milton had been forced before, into the path he would not else have chosen. This, he himself says, was his first great sacrifice.

There was at this time in Genoa a little journal of mercantile advertisements called the *Indicatore Genovese*, published by one Ponthenier, and, according to the rule then in force, limited to such matters. Mazzini persuaded the publisher to add to his announcements of books for sale some few lines descriptive of the subject, and to employ him to write them. This was the beginning of his career as a critic. Little by little the mere description grew into a review. The Government, not more awake than the country, either did not see or did not heed. The *Indicatore* was transformed into a literary journal not without political significance. In the eyes of Mazzini and his young friends the fight for romanticism was only a skirmish with the outposts of Authority, and already the young reformer was laying his parallels, thinking where and how to attack, and perceiving with marvelous sagacity for one so young that all roads lead to Rome, that he must look upon all sides, understand all things, in order to succeed in the one great object from which all else was to follow —the establishment of Italian freedom. In time the Government saw, and became alarmed; and when, at the close of the first year, an enlargement of the journal was announced, a governmental prohibition put it down. A certain amount of repute however had been already obtained for the publication, so that when it was suppressed by the Piedmontese Government at Genoa, it was revived at Leghorn under the title of the *Indicatore Livornese*, the political purpose scarcely disguised. It was the first struggle with the foreign dismemberers of unhappy Italy. Guerazzi and Carlo Bini were contributors with Mazzini. They spoke of Ugo Foscolo, who, both by his acts and his writings, had insisted on Literature as the minister of Patriotism; they spoke of the *Exile*, a poem of the proscribed Giannone; of the poems of Berchet, then aflame with true Italian passion; they spoke so daringly that at last even the less tyrannical Tuscan Government was roused, and ordered the discontinuance of the journal. But the two attempts had done their work. The vibrating chords were struck in youthful hearts; and, which was of yet more importance, it was shown that the best of the Italian Governments were deliberately averse to all progress, and that even intellectual freedom was not possible without their overthrow. Such was the politico-literary beginning of the struggle for Italian emancipation. And now Mazzini was initiated among the Carbonari, the only political association then known.

In 1830 came the new French Revolution of July, and hopes with it for Italy. A few days later young Mazzini was arrested; and after some preliminary detention in the city barracks was sent to the fortress of Savona, on the western shore of the Gulf of Genoa.

To his father, inquiring as to the reason of his arrest, the Governor answered that it was sufficient that he was thoughtful and reticent, fond of solitary walks by night, and the Government "misliked young men of talent whose thoughts they did not know." There being nothing to be proved against him except his having initiated a certain person (a Government spy not convenient to produce) into the second rank of Carbonarism, he was after some months released on condition that he must not reside in Genoa or on the coast, in Turin, or any other city of importance. His location was prescribed for him, in Asti, Acqua, Casale, or any other little inland town where he could do no mischief, under pain of banishment during the royal pleasure. As this really meant inaction and uselessness under the watchful eyes of the police, he preferred activity in exile.

It was in prison that he received the news of the Polish Revolution. His friends could not see him, but his mother secretly conveyed to him the two words—*Polonia insurrexit.* His first inquiry upon coming out was—"About Poland?"

During the months of his imprisonment at Savona he conceived the plan of the GIOVINE ITALIA, the association afterwards formed by him which was destined to be the lever of Italian unity. In those months, to quote his own words written in 1861, "I meditated upon the principles on which to found the organization of the party and its openly-declared purpose. I thought of the manner of implanting it, of those whom I would call to initiate it with me, of the possible linking our labour with the other revolutionary elements in Europe. We were few, young, without means, and in influence yet more restricted; but the problem seemed to me to consist in grappling with the truth of instincts and tendencies yet mute, but pointed out by history and the presentiments of the heart of Italy. Our force could only proceed from that truth. All great national enterprises have been initiated by men unknown and of the people, without power except that of faith and the will which regards neither time nor obstacles. The influential, the men of name and means, come in afterwards to invigorate the movement created by these first, and too often to mislead it from its aim.

"I need not say here how the instincts and tendencies of Italy, such as they appeared to me across the path of history and in the inner social constitution of the country, led me to the prefixing of UNITY and REPUBLIC as the intent of the imagined Association. . . . Only I may state that even then the generating thought of my every design was not mere political thought, was not the idea of bettering the lot of the one people which I beheld dismembered, oppressed, and held in contempt, but a presentiment that Italy in rising would be the initiatrix of a new life, of a new and potent unity for the nations of Europe. However confusedly and against my will fascinated by the fervid words, as of a directing conscience, then uttered by France amidst the general silence, my mind was stirred with the idea, expressed in after years, that a void existed in Europe, that Authority, the true, the good, the Holy Authority, the search for which, ay! always, confessed to ourselves or not, is the secret of the life of us all, irrationally denied by those who confound with it a phantasm, a false Authority, and think to deny God when they are only denying idols, had vanished from, was spent in Europe; and that thence there lived not in any people the power of an initiative. This idea years, studies, and griefs have irrevocably confirmed in my mind and changed into a faith. And if but (though I may not think it) it were given to me, Italian unity once founded, to live a single year of solitude in a corner of my land, or in that where I am writing and which affections have made a second country for me [England], I would attempt to develop and bring out the consequences, more important than seems thought by others. Then it was enough that there flashed upon me, as a star in my soul, an immense hope: Italy reborn, at one bound the missionary to Humanity of a Faith in Progress and in Fraternity more vast than that of Old. I had in me the worship of Rome. Within her walls had been twice elaborated the One life of the world. There, whilst other peoples, a brief mission completed, had disappeared for ever, and none had twice guided, life was eternal, death unknown. Over the potent vestiges of an epoch of civilization which had, anterior to the Greek, its seat in Italy, and whose external action the historic science of the future will show to have had a wider scope than the learned of our day suspect, was superposed, blotting that into oblivion, the Rome of the Republic, concluded by the Cæsars, that behind its eagles' wings furrowed the known world with the idea of Right, the source of Liberty. Afterwards, when men were bewailing her as a sepulchre of the living, she rose again grander than at first, and hardly arisen constituted herself, with the Popes, holy once however abject to-day, the accepted Centre of a new Unity, which, lifting the laws of earth to heaven, superimposed upon the idea of Right the idea of Duty common to all, and therefore the source of Equality. Why should not arise from a third Rome, the Rome of the Italian People, of which I seemed to see the indications, a third and yet vaster Unity, which, harmonizing earth and heaven, Right and Duty, should speak, not to individuals, but to Peoples, a word of Association, teaching to the free and equal their mission here below?

"These things I thought of in my little cell at Savona; these things I think of to-day [1861], with better logic and a clearer foundation, in the little chamber, not larger than my prison, in which I am now writing. And during my life they have availed but to bring against me the charge of being an Utopian and a fool; and outrages and disillusions which made me often look back with longing and regret to my little cell at Savona, between the sea and the sky, far from the contact of men. The Future will say if I prophesied or dreamed. To-day the revival of Italy confided to immoral materialists, extolled as great by the ignorant and corrupt vulgar, condemns my hope. But what is death to other peoples is only sleep to us.

"From these ideas I gathered that the new work ought to be before all things moral, not narrowly political; religious, not negative; founded upon principles, not on theories of interests; on Duty, not on well-being. The foreign schools of materialism had pained my soul during some months of my University life; History and the intuition of conscience, sole criterions of truth, reconducted me rapidly to the spiritualism of our fathers."

Through Savoy, which the Moderate Party had not yet sold to France, he crossed over Mount Cenis to Geneva, there visiting and friendlily received by Sismondi. Thence he went to Lyons, where were some two thousand Italian exiles planning an invasion of Savoy, their preparations public, the French Government parading its sympathy, Louis Philippe hoping so to frighten his fellow-kings into recognition of his dynasty: that or revolution throughout Europe offered for their choice. Admitted as a member of the royal gang, the patriots were betrayed. It was the third kingly betrayal under Mazzini's eyes; the first that of the Carbonaro prince, Charles Albert; the second that of Francis the Fourth, Duke of Modena, who had first protected the conspiracy organized in his name by Ciro Menotti, and then had carried the same Menotti prisoner to Mantua and hanged him when the Austrians restored the ducal power. Now was the traitorous turn of Louis Philippe. The expedition was prevented, and an exile-hunt began. Some of the Italians were thrust into French prisons, some driven into England; some made their way to Corsica, Mazzini among these, hoping in Corsica to organize another expedition. There Mazzini waited until the last opportunity for action was gone with the succumbing of the insurrectionary Bolognese.[1]

[1] The "Bolognese insurrection" began on the night of the 2nd of February, 1831, at Modena, at the house of Ciro Menotti, a young man of fortune, but devoted to the cause of Italian freedom. There thirty-one conspirators, surprised by the ducal soldiers and summoned to surrender, answered with musket-balls, and withstood for hours the troops that surrounded the house. Cannon was brought and leveled against this improvised fortress of new-born liberty; and it was the sound of this cannon which awoke Bologna. She rose in the night of the 4th. When the next sun set, Imola, Faenza, Forli, Cesena, Ravenna, the whole of the Romagna, were in arms. Modena, recovered from the momentary stupor of Menotti's defeat and capture, drove out on the night of the 5th the Duke, who dragged with him as his prisoner the wounded Menotti. On the 7th Ferrara rose under the eyes of the Austrian garrison, which withdrew from the city. On the 8th Pesaro, Fossombrone, Fano, and Urbino expelled their Austrian governors. On the 13th the insurrection triumphed at Parma. Later Macerata, Camerino, Ascoli, Perugia, Terni, Narni, &c., &c., emancipated themselves. Ancona had to surrender to some companies of soldiers and national guards commanded by General Serçognani. All this was the impulsive action of the people, without need of chiefs. Old men and women all joined in the work. By the 25th of February the

Returning to France, he resumed at Marseilles his design of founding the Association of "Young Italy," the place being well suited for his purpose, refugees from Modena, Parma, and the Romagna having resorted thither to the number of more than a thousand, among them Celeste Menotti (the brother of Ciro), Nicola Fabrizzi, and Lamberti. With these he began the Association.

At Marseilles he wrote and published his first purely political writing, his *Letter to Charles Albert*, the Carbonaro prince of 1821, who in 1831 had succeeded to the throne of Piedmont and Sardinia. "Not that I believed then any more than I now believe [so writing in 1861] that it was possible for Monarchy to come to save Italy, that is Italy as I understand and as we all understood it but a few years ago—One, free, strong, independent of all foreign supremacy, moral, and worthy of her proper mission ; . . . but in writing to him what he ought to have found of himself to do for Italy, I intended simply to write to Italy what he failed to do."

Still the *Letter* was true to its open purpose, that of inciting patriotism in a royal breast. Eloquently Mazzini points out the choice the King should make, urging him to prefer the nobler path toward his

---

cause of Italian freedom had been embraced by two millions of Italians, a noble beginning. But the isolating policy of the chiefs, who, fearing to attempt too much, dared not invoke the whole of Italy to support them, rendered all of no avail. The insurrection was suppressed.—*Monthly Chronicle*, 1839.

country's freedom, warning him of the consequences of error. Referring him to the words of Napoleon at St. Helena—" I have offended the ideas of the age " —the *Letter* concludes—

" Sire ! I have told you the truth. Freemen look for your answer in deeds. Whatever it shall be, be sure that posterity will proclaim you the First of Men or the Last of Italian Tyrants. Choose !

"AN ITALIAN."

The *Letter* went into Italy, was read by the King : of course with no effect except that a mark was set against the writer, and in its influence on the minds of those who read the Italian reprints.

Accepting Mazzini's hope and scheme, the Association began its work, its first object the education of the people. Carbonarism, only revolutionary, had failed ; the endeavour must be regenerative. With this idea the founders of " Young Italy " saw themselves at an immense distance from all who had preceded them. They had to turn their backs on the theory of materialism, leading in politics to individualism, impotent to found nationality or association, and to recur to the synthetic spiritualistic Italian philosophy of the sixteenth and seventeenth centuries, to revive the faith which alone could implant in Italian souls the conscience of the nation and its destinies, and by means of this conscience to re-endow them with courage, devotion, constancy, and harmony. They had to combat the fractional spirit, and to pave the way for unity, by principles

C

embracing all the manifestations of Italian life, applicable not only to politics, but to philosophy, to the science of law, to literature, to the fine arts, to everything. It was a wide task: but they believed that it was enough to have caught a glimpse of it to render it their duty to pursue it, whatever time might elapse before the enterprise could succeed.

Hence the double motto of *Young Italy*, asserting the necessity of the twofold life, special and general, national and humanitarian. Mazzini heads the statutes of the Association with the words

LIBERTY—EQUALITY—FRATERNITY

and underneath them

INDEPENDENCE—UNITY:

the first three words indicating a general belief for all nations, the last two expressing the peculiar needs of Italy herself.[1] So it stood forth first among political associations to include in its conceptions all the branches of national activity, seeking from a religious stand-point to cause them all to converge toward one object in accordance with the idea of a mission imposed upon mankind.

---

[1] His translator (*Life and Writings of Joseph Mazzini*, London, 1864), printing the words in one line, misses altogether Mazzini's purport. So repeatedly he has suffered in the house of his English friends, the fulness of his thought not comprehended. Indeed, he has been so often insufficiently rendered in English that I have learned to understand Harriet Martineau's remark to me: "I can not sometimes tell what Mazzini means."

The Association was organized in a very simple manner. Reckoning upon the effect of their principles rather than on the power of mystery and symbols, it rejected all the complex machinery of the Carbonarian hierarchy, and all the pomp which was only calculated to hide the absence of real purpose. It had a central committee abroad to keep upreared its standard, to form connections with foreign democratic associations, and to direct the general enterprise; it had also committees in Italy directing the practical conspiracy, established in the important provinces, and corresponding with the centre; agents to preside over work in the cities corresponding with the provincial committees; and below the mass of members, all equal except that only those believed to have the necessary prudence were allowed to introduce new members. It had the formula of a declaration of political belief; a method of recognition, especially for the envoys of the association; a branch of cypress for symbol, in memory of the martyrs, and suggestive of the constancy to which all were pledged; and the words *Ora e sempre* (now and ever) for motto. Looking for success from other elements than its predecessors, having at heart especially to banish distrust and scepticism, and to call forth in the souls of the young enthusiasm, devotion, and that faith which does not exclude the observation of facts, but which will not allow itself to be subjugated by them—having besides to initiate a work of education—the Association decreed secrecy only so far as prudent necessity required it, that is for its operations in Italy; with respect to its existence, its object and hopes and principles, it challenged publicity. A journal entitled *La Giovine Italia*, was established at Marseilles, the situation being favourable for communication with Italy. Another secondary journal, more particularly intended for Lombardy, was established in the Swiss Canton of Ticino. There the exiled members of the Association developed their doctrines and their ideas on the prospects of Italy. Others undertook to render these familiar to the people under forms of dialogues and catechisms. The object was to spread all this throughout the Peninsula. This was effected by means of considerable outlay of money and through the devotion of a valuable class of men, the merchant sailors, for the most part eminently Italian. These men were tried, and accepted their mission with enthusiasm. By actively organizing relations in Italy at every point where communications were frequent, regular transmissions were effected; the packets were confided to devoted youths, who braved every danger to carry them to their destination; they were finally distributed throughout the country, and in spite of espionage, severe penalties, and a thousand acts of imprudence, their circulation was immense, and their effect also.

Such almost literally is Mazzini's own account [1]

---

[1] Given in letters on the state and prospects of Italy, in the *Monthly Chronicle*, London, 1839.

of the beginnings of Young Italy. In later autobiographical notes he supplies yet further information of the progress of the Association, and of the methods employed to circulate its writings.

"Committees were rapidly organized in the principal cities of Tuscany. In Genoa the Ruffinis, Campanella, Benza, and a few others, who accepted the office of spreading the Association, were almost unknown, very young, without fortune, or means of acquiring influence. And nevertheless, from student to student, from youth to youth, the brotherhood extended much more rapidly than was to be hoped for. Our first writings supplied the want of personal influence. Those able to read them fraternized with us. It was the victory of ideas substituted for the power of names and the fascination of mystery. Ours had found an echo, apparently answering to an inspiration until then unconscious, dormant in the hearts of the young. And this was enough to encourage us and to mark out the duties which in truth we, that little phalanx of precursors, fulfilled, so far as unwearied work and sacrifice were concerned. Except the association of the St. Simonians, in which the simple pretence of religion inspired for the moment a greater power of sacrifice and love than was in all the purely democratic societies of those times, I have not seen a knot of young men with so much mutual affection, with such virgin enthusiasm, such readiness for toil every day and every hour, as that which then applied itself with me.

"We were Lamberti, Usiglio, one Lustrini, G. B. Ruffini, and five or six others, nearly all Modenese, alone, without calling, without journeymen, immersed the day through and greater part of the night in our duties, writing articles and letters, interrogating travellers, affiliating sailors, folding printed sheets, tying up bundles, alternating between intellectual occupations and the functions of the workman. La Cecilia, then upright and good, was compositor; Lamberti, reader; another literary porter to save the expense of the parcel-carriage. We lived in truth as equals and brothers, with one sole thought, one sole hope, one single worship of the ideal in our souls; loved, admired, by foreign republicans, for our tenacity of purpose and faculty of continuous labour; often (for we had no funds except our own) in miserable straits, but rejoicing on our way and smiling with a smile of faith in the future. There were, from 1831 to 1833, two years of young life, pure and gladly devoted, such as I would desire for the rising generation. We had a sufficiently dogged warfare and dangers, but from enemies from whom we expected them. That miserable, saddest warfare of grudges, of ingratitudes, of suspicions and calumnies, from men of our own country, and often of our own party, the unmerited abandonment by old friends, the desertion of the Banner, not on account of new convictions, but from weariness, offended vanity, and worse, by almost a whole generation, in those years vowed with us, had not yet, I will not say, laid bare or withered our souls loving as in that day and believing still as then, but had not taught us few 'the forced and desperate calm,' the labour without comforting of individual hope, from simple reverence for cold, inexorable, barest Duty.

"The smuggling of our papers into Italy was a vital question for the Association and a grave one for us. A young man named Montanari passing to and fro on the Neapolitan steamers as agent for the Company, and others employed on the French steamers, helped us wonderfully. And until the anger of the Governments was converted into fury, we trusted to these men our parcels, content to write on the parcel destined for Genoa the address of some unsuspected commercial house at Leghorn; on that for Leghorn an address at Civita-Vecchia; and so on: withdrawing in this manner the parcel from the scrutiny of the custom-house officers and police at the first point stopped at, the parcel was kept by the friend in the boat until one of ours, apprized, received it on board, where he could dispose of the papers by concealing them about his person. But when attention was awakened and vigilance increased, when rewards were offered to whoever would sequestrate our writings, and tremendous threats pronounced against the introducers,—when the war grew fierce as Charles Albert by edict signed by his ministers menaced with two years of imprisonment and a fine whoever did not denounce, promising the informer half the fine and secrecy,—then began between us and the petty Governments of Italy a duel which cost us heavy labour and expense, but which we prosecuted with good success. We sent the bundles in barrels of pumice-stone, afterwards in the middle of pitch-barrels, filling them at night in a little warehouse hired for the occasion. These barrels, ten or twelve, numbered, we sent by means of commercial agents ignorant of their contents to equally ignorant commission agents in different places, where one of our friends, advertized of their coming, presented himself to buy the barrel indicated by the number that it bore. I give this as one of the many stratagems of which we thought. . . .

"This organization spread rapidly from Genoa along the coast, into Piedmont and to Milan, from Tuscany to the Romagna. Committees were multiplied. Secret communications, regular and tolerably secure, were established even on the Neapolitan frontier. Travellers coursed frequently from one province to another, to infervorate men's souls and to transmit our instructions. The thirst for papers was such that, ours not sufficing, clandestine presses were planted at two or three points in Italy, reprinting our articles or issuing brief publications inspired by local circumstances. *La Giovine Italia*, accepted with enthusiasm, became in less than a year the predominant association in Italy. It was the triumph of principles. The bare fact that in so short a time a few young men, sprung from the people, unknown, unprovided with means, publicly opposed in their doctrines and their actions to those who by the popular vote and recognized influence had till then led the political movement, should find themselves chiefs of an association so powerful as to provoke the trembling persecution of seven Governments, was, methinks, enough to prove that the banner they had lifted up was the banner of the True."

It was indeed a success. The national instinct was awakened. The formula of *Republican Unity* was accepted with enthusiasm by the youth of every province of Italy. The creatures of tyranny wrote ferociously against it, only thereby procuring it more friends. Metternich saw the importance of the new apostolate, and sent to Italy for so many volumes as were published, not without expression of impatience for farther issues. Other Italian societies merged themselves in *the* Association. The scattered remnants of Carbonarism bowed to the faith and the direction of Young Italy. In France, Buonaroti, the chief of those whose names before the time of Louis Philippe had been given to Carbonarism, and who was the revered correspondent of all the secret societies in Germany, entered into close and fraternal communication with the young Italian. So also did Godfrey Cavaignac and Marrast and the more ardent men of the *Tribune*, and Armand Carrel and the more politic men of the *National*. Lafayette had words of encouragement; and the Polish Emigration (the democratic majority) was surely with them.

In Italy, where there were no avowed "Moderates," Gioberti congratulated the Mazzinians as "precursors of a new political Law, the first apostles of a renewed Gospel." . . . "I announce to you," he wrote from Turin, "a good success for your undertaking, since your cause is just and compassionate (*pietosa*), being that of the people, and holy, being that of God. . . . It is eternal, more lasting than the antique form of Him who said *God and your neighbour*, but who now says through your mouth and that of the age *God and the People.* . . . We will close round your banner to the cry of God and the People (*Noi ci stringeremo alla vostra bandiera e grideremo Dio e il Popolo*), and we will study to propagate that cry. . . . We will combat those false lovers of liberty who, short-sighted and unjust, would have it without the people and against the people, those haters of the old aristocracy who in making revolutions intend to transfer power to themselves, standing aloof instead of identifying themselves with the people and restoring to them their ravished rights,—who vilify the people with depreciatory and abominable names and ill-treat them with imposts and outrageous injuries, aggravating their yoke with the same hand with which they would protect themselves from that of the nobles and the tyrants . . . I frankly promise you a constant disposition and a lively desire to die with you, if need be, for our common country." [1]

---

[1] This letter, in which Gioberti so forcibly condemns his own after conduct and that of the Moderate Party, was published in the sixth number of *La Giovine Italia*, signed *Demofilo*. It was afterwards reprinted over his own name. Here also may well be

But this very success was sufficient to provoke persecution. And it began on the part of the "liberal" Government of France, moved by the desire to keep on politic terms with the rulers of Italy. It was of course first directed against the Association in Marseilles, with a view to destroy the journal, or at least to deprive it of the facilities of transport there available. A governmental decree expelled Mazzini. He published an indignant protest, and remained. Concealing himself from the police, he went on with his work. His companions, compositors, supposed contributors, were threatened, watched, expelled. French compositors took their places. A citizen of Marseilles, Vittore Vian, became responsible editor; the contributors kept at a respectable distance; the printed copies were dispatched in secret. Then (again in Mazzini's own words) "began for me the life I have lived for twenty out of thirty years—voluntary imprisonment within the four

---

appended the names of others who before the bribes of place or princely or public favour had seduced them, or weariness and doubt had sapped their vitality, associated themselves to the higher hopes and destinies of Young Italy. Guerazzi and Pietro Bostogi (Minister in 1861) were at the head of the Tuscan Association in Leghorn. In Bologna Farini outdid his associates with violent speeches. Carlo Poerio, Leopardi, and others in Naples, had their corresponding organization ready to act under the same programme. The Marquis Roveredo and others of the nobility, with Lorenzo Pareto (afterwards minister), joined the party in Genoa. Depretis (afterwards prime minister) and many others of rank were also in that day admirers and abettors and associates of Mazzini.

walls of a little room. They did not find me. The precautions with which I eluded them; the double spies who served at once the Prefect and myself, bringing me the very day copies of the instructions given on my account by the authorities; the comical manner in which one day, my asylum discovered, I persuaded the Prefect to let me leave without scandal or disturbance, watched by his agents, then sent to Geneva in my place a friend who personally resembled me, whilst I passed through the detectives in the uniform of the National Guard,—these things come into the story I here write (*Autobiographical Notes to his Political Writings*), not to feed the curiosity of idle readers, but to serve as historical indications and examples to my countrymen. Enough that I remained a whole year at Marseilles, writing, correcting proofs, corresponding, face to face at midnight with men of the Party coming from Italy, and with certain of the leading republicans of France."

Unable to get rid of him by other means, the French Government tried the effect of calumny. They published in the *Moniteur*, the official newspaper, a forged document pretended to be a report of the proceedings of some secret tribunal (Young Italy of course) decreeing the assassination of certain individuals for having written against the Society, and signed by Mazzini as president. Unable publicly to meet the slander by an action for libel, Mazzini could only protest by denial, which denial the

Moniteur would not insert.[1] The scoundrely manœuvre failed. Young Italy's work went on.

[1] The true story of the French business was given very clearly in the *Westminster Review* (by the editor, Mr. W. E. Hickson), when Lord Aberdeen in 1844 unburied it in the English Parliament.

"On the 31st of May, 1833, two spies of the Duke of Modena, Lazzareschi and Emiliani, who had been sent to mix among the political exiles and worm out their secrets, were killed in a quarrel at Rodez (Aveyron) in the public road, in open day, by an Italian named Gavioli. The deed naturally brought much odium upon the whole of the Italian exiles, and to damage them still farther advantage was taken of it by a secret enemy to connect it with the name of Mazzini. The next week (June 8) there appeared in the non-official part of the *Moniteur* (without any introductory preface or explanation) a forged document purporting to be the decree of a secret revolutionary tribunal pronouncing sentence of death upon Emiliani and others, and signed *Mazzini*, president, and *La Cecilia*, secretary. As Mazzini was then lying concealed at Marseilles, this was looked upon by his friends as a *ruse* of the French police to induce all honest French citizens to assist in discovering his retreat. The badness of the style and composition, the half-French expressions, the numerous grammatical errors, of the pretended document, proved that it could not have been written by an educated Italian, much less by a man of high literary reputation like Mazzini; who however at once denounced the forgery, in the columns of the *Gazette des Tribuneaux*. The subsequent trial, Nov. 30th, 1883, of Gavioli before the Cour d'Assizes of Aveyron satisfied the public that no such secret tribunal existed. *The document was not produced in evidence;* and the jury, convinced that Gavioli had no accomplices, and that the crime committed did not amount to murder with intent, returned a verdict of *homicide sans préméditation*. Gavioli was sentenced to *les travaux forcés;* and farther, to show that the French Government perfectly well understood all the facts of the case, we may add that La Cecilia, whose name was coupled with Mazzini's in the forged document, was at the time openly living in France, where he still remains

(1844) supported by the grants of the French Chamber for exiles; and was neither arrested nor once interrogated on the subject.

"In 1840 the story was revived by Gisquet, the ex-prefect of police, in his published memoirs, afterwards translated into English. Mazzini thereupon brought an action against him for defamation. The action was tried before the *Tribunal Correctionnel* of Paris, in April 1841; but owing to the impudent but ingenious character of the defence set up, a verdict was given for the defendant. Gisquet met the charge by asserting that there was more than one Mazzini in the world; and that Mazzini, the prosecutor, being a man, as all admitted, of the highest moral integrity, he could not possibly be the Mazzini in the paragraph quoted from the *Moniteur*.

"Here, it might be supposed, the matter would have ended, but the tale of slander was yet to serve the cause of absolutism; and so it was circulated anew in England to damage Mazzini with the English Government, and afterwards repeated by the friends of the latter to justify the secret espionage of Lord Aberdeen."—*Westminster Review* of September 1844.

The forged document is given at length in the *Review*, but is not worth reprinting here.

YOUNG EUROPE.

By the beginning of 1833, the organization, not two years old, was strong enough to think seriously of action : the very need of action also becoming urgent, lest the conspiracy should be prematurely crushed. Genoa and Alessandria were chosen for the starting-places of the movement: partly because of the difficulty of concerting measures with the Neapolitan patriots, partly because an insurrection only in Central Italy would have left Charles Albert free to co-operate with Austria and close Lombardy to the revolutionists; and also because those two cities were the two points at which the Association was most powerful, and the revolution in Piedmont, if it carried the army with it, would supply material and moral resources not to be obtained elsewhere.

The exiles were to invade Savoy, not only in order to divide the royal forces, but to open the road for help from the French republicans then preparing an insurrection of the working-men of Lyons. The Piedmontese army had been sounded. The superior officers held generally aloof, though even some of them promised to join at a later period if a good beginning should be made; the inferior were well-disposed. Communications had been established with nearly all the regiments, active centres of revolt in some. The most intimate relations were with the artillery in charge of the arsenals at Genoa and Alessandria. A general plan was agreed upon and the different affiliations informed; means also were ready. Meanwhile the Piedmontese Government, though aware of the network in which it moved, was vainly seeking the chiefs among the higher classes, or among the old leaders of the Carbonari. Everything seemed propitious. An accident overthrew all. Two artillery-men quarreled about a woman. One was a member of Young Italy, and had proposed to the other to join. They came to blows, and were separated by some carabineers, but not before angry words of menace had been uttered, which were noticed and remembered. These gave a clue, and the Government, already suspicious and on the look-out, lost no time in following it. A search in the knapsacks of the artillery brought out some of the publications of the Association. The owners of the knapsacks were arrested; then their friends, then any who seemed to take interest in them. A little time was allowed to elapse, so that it might appear that some had confessed and denounced their comrades. The arrested were kept apart from one another, in close confinement; and no means were left unused to extort confessions from them, to implicate others. Three soldiers and one civilian were cowardly enough to betray their associates. Others confessed for their own part, but would give no names; none the less their known friends and acquaintances swelled the list of the imprisoned. This at Genoa. At Turin, Chambery, Alessandria, the prisons were also filled with the suspected. At Nice and the smaller towns, Cuneo, Vercelli, Mondovi, the same course was pursued. Everywhere was terror. Some fled; some hid themselves, waiting for the storm to blow over, partly because they saw that the Government had not discovered much, partly because they feared if failure should follow now they might be accused of having hastened the movement to shield themselves.

Amidst these waverings the opportune moment was lost, and the insurrection became impossible. Precautions were taken everywhere by the Government. All intercourse between soldiers and citizens was prevented; and official calumny yet further divided them by pretending to have found papers proving the conspirators to be atheists and incendiaries, ready with torch or dagger, with powder or poison, to destroy all that was respectable or sacred: Turin was to have been devoted to the flames, and new Vespers were to have rid the Genoese of the Piedmontese soldiers.

So what is called "the public" was kept down. And against the prisoners, guilty of patriotism or not, was let loose the unbridled ferocity of a Government

D

doubly cruel because it had felt fear. Only the pen of a Tacitus, says Mazzini, and that pen dipped in blood, could write this page of the story of the Savoyard Monarchy: a story "to be read again and again by all men who need to renew in their souls the abhorrence of tyranny, and which mothers should repeat to their sons to teach them the possible lot of a land not free."

Within the prison walls terrible were the scenes enacted, in order by extorted confessions to discover the leaders, and so haply crush the dreaded Association. Bribes for some, terror for all. *Atropos belladonna* was mixed with the prisoners' drink to weaken their minds, and render them easier victims of their inquisitors. To the timid they said: "Your guilt is known, your sentence is already pronounced, but you may yet save yourselves by giving up the names of your accomplices." To others of more robust virtue: "You have erred, but with good intention; we know it, and we pity you: you thought you were engaged in a work of devotion, and you have confided in traitors unworthy of your sacrifice; you think by your silence to save faithful friends, but you are destroying yourselves and your families for the sake of cowards who have already denounced you: here is their evidence against you. Now will you, confessing, rejoice the hearts of your dear ones by your restoration to them, or will you, persisting in silence, perish miserably?" And they laid before them a confession and denunciation with a forged signature, trusting to the bitterness of the betrayed.¹

With others the prison spy, as in the days of the Inquisition, was left to deal. Mock conspirators were imprisoned with them, in order to take advantage of any moment of sympathy or confidence.²

For such individuals new tortures were invented: all equally base, equally fiendish. Here a crier near the window of a cell shouted: "Your friends have just been shot; your turn to-morrow." There two friends were placed in the same corridor, and the one informed of the other's condemnation; then the "condemned" was suddenly taken away, and shots fired to give impression of his death.³

¹ So Mazzini's signature was held before the eyes of his dearest friend, Jacob Ruffini, whose answer was suicide in his cell.

² This was done with a sergeant of the Guards named Miglio. His fellow-prisoner "had means of communicating with friends outside." Miglio trusted him, writing a few lines with his blood. This was the chief evidence against him.

³ "After the shooting of the sergeants," says Giovanni Re, a prisoner then, "they sought to make me believe in that of Pianavia. His cell was in my corridor. He had a habit of singing. But one Saturday he stopped suddenly. All Sunday there was continual going and coming in his prison. The Governor came and stayed a long time with him. At three in the afternoon the General Commandant of the citadel [of Alessandria] came into my cell with some of the officials and a chaplain, who had more the face of an assassin than of a priest. All seemed troubled and as if in tears. The General asked me if I felt calm. I answered Yes. He then went away, having made the chaplain address a few words to me. All that night the noises continued. At daybreak I heard some one whom I believed to be Pianavia hurried along the corridor, and a few minutes after, three discharges announced an execution." Pianavia was an informer.

In some places the prisoners were deafened by continual noises, and prevented from sleeping. Then after one or two restless and agitated nights, they were assailed with the moral torture of minute interrogations, the extent and effect of which cannot be conceived except by those who have passed through the prisons of Italy.[1]

It was when his moral energy thus harassed was utterly exhausted that the prisoner was tempted to make revelations for the sake of pardon. Some gray-headed father or mother would be brought forward to mingle tears and intreaties with the threats or more villainous promises of the judges.

Those who perished in this unhappy year 1833

[1] The Narrative of Giovanni Re, one of the prisoners at Alessandria, was this: "The following day my books were taken from me, that is to say, a Bible, a book of prayers, and a history of the illustrious captains of Piedmont. My cell was changed, and a chain was fastened to my leg. The cell was dark, bare, with double-grated window, and a door with two bars. The chain, fastened to a ring in the wall, permitted me to approach the window. Opposite to my cell was that of poor Vochieri. There were cracks at the bottom of my door, which had been imperfectly closed; and, as the door of Vochieri's cell was kept open, the light from the window rendered me curious to know whence it came. I looked through the door, and saw Vochieri seated on a chair, with a heavy chain fastened to his foot, and two guards with their sabres drawn, one on each side of him. He was allowed to change his position every hour; not a word was spoken either by him or by his guards. A third sentinel with a musket was stationed before his door. During the day two Capuchins came to speak to him. He remained thus before my eyes, in a sort of agony, for the space of a week; then he was taken away and killed."

This was in Alessandria.

were, at Chambery, Giuseppe Tamburelli, corporal; Alessandro de Gubernatis, sergeant; Effisio Tola, aged 30, lieutenant;—at Genoa, Antonio Gavotti, fencing-master, aged 47; Giuseppe Biglia, sergeant, aged 29; Francisco Miglio, sergeant, aged 47;—at Alessandria, Domenico Ferrari, sergeant, aged 25; Giuseppe Menardi, sergeant, aged 25; Giuseppe Rigasso, sergeant, aged 30; Amande Costa, sergeant, aged 21; Andrea Vochieri, legist. In the beginning of 1834 Volonteri and Borel were executed at Chambery.

Many others sentenced to death, men of property, advocates, physicians, officers in the army, &c., escaped. Many already in banishment were condemned to death. Minor punishments were not wanting. It was a reign of terror, the terror of the ex-Carbonarist Charles Albert, whose military commissions condemned soldiers and civilians, without pretence of justice or legality; those who most outraged both being most rewarded by their brutal master.[1]

[1] One instance may suffice. General Galateri, the Governor of Alessandria, after Vochieri (before named) had been sentenced, went again to him urging him to confess, telling him he was doing the best he could for him. "The best you can do for me," said the fettered prisoner, "is to rid me of your presence." Galateri kicked him. The only favour Vochieri would ask was that in going to the scaffold he might not pass his own house, in which were his children and his wife then pregnant. The favour was refused him. Charles Albert conferred upon Galateri the order of the Holy Annunciation, which entitled him to call the king his cousin. He deserved it.

Disappointed of their first hope, the Association did not give way. Still the great majority of the elements they had prepared was undiscovered, and amidst the rage and horror excited by the savagery of the Government, the simple announcement of determination to seek new opportunity for action was sufficient to rally the momentarily dispersed party in Genoa, and to resuscitate endeavour. Before the year was out another movement was in preparation, failing through the youthful inexperience of the leaders. In this second attempt Garibaldi was concerned. He saved himself by flight. His acquaintance with Mazzini began at that time.

Mazzini's attention was now turned to Switzerland. The Government there too would of course be opposed to any armed action ; but in the face of the public sympathy no very strong opposal was to be feared. Savoy too was discontented and still disposed for insurrection. Circumstances had brought together in Switzerland many German and Polish refugees, scattered through the different Cantons, waiting new occasion for their exertions. Many of the Poles had been expelled from France. "I was pleased," says Mazzini, "at the idea of linking with the cause of Italy that of other oppressed nations, and of planting on our Alps a banner of European brotherhood. Young Europe was in my mind a logical development of the thought which informed Young Italy. And the awakening of Italy ought to be at the same time an act of initiation, a consecration of the high office expected of her in the Past, and, I trust, to be expected of her in the Future. The Federation of the Peoples ought to find its germ in our Legion." The Polish and German exiles accepted the idea with enthusiasm.

Mazzini went to Switzerland. Among the Italians there with him were Agostino and Gianbattista Ruffini, Celeste Menotti, Nicola Fabrizzi, Giuseppe Lamberti, Giacomo Ciani, Gaspare Belcredi, and others, all worthy of Italian remembrance. Committees were formed; money collected, especially through Gaspare Rosales, a Lombard gentleman; arms were got from St. Etienne and Belgium; all things went on well, and the preparations advanced. All that seemed to be wanting was a military leader, not only of capacity but of some name.

There was one Ramorino, a Savoyard, who had been a general during the Polish insurrection, whose conduct in that capacity had not won him the suffrages of the Polish Democrats, but who was supported by the aristocratic party of Prince Czartoryski. Still the mere name of a volunteer in the cause of Poland commanded respect; he was popular too in Savoy. The committees inquired no farther, but insisted upon choosing him for their leader, despite the protest of Mazzini, whose opinion of him was unfavourable.

By the first days of October the expedition was ready. Not so Ramorino, more busy at the gaming-tables than with the duty he had undertaken. Sold secretly to the French Government, he not only spent the funds intrusted to him, but so delayed matters that instead of setting out in October he kept back to the end of January. Meanwhile the exiles' little money was lessened by the cost of living through three months, men became disheartened both in Italy and Switzerland, police agents began to harass them; only Mazzini's tenacity of purpose held the scattering elements together. At last Ramorino came and assumed command, only to alter their plans and to betray them in detail, and when he found his measures sufficient to frustrate any attempt by Mazzini and the Italians alone, to disband the remains of the little army and to return to his employers. Years later he performed a similar act of treachery *for* Charles Albert, who secured his silence by rewarding him with a traitor's death.

No need here to dwell upon Mazzini's personal suffering; the intense and unremitting labour, the agony of disappointment, the certain loss of prestige and power; the doom of Sisyphus which the patriot anticipates in starting; the failure of the Savoy expedition deferred indefinitely the hopes of Young Italy. In Italy was only discouragement. The party shrank. In Switzerland the favour with which the design had been at first received was rapidly turned into irritation as the Swiss were tormented with diplomatic notes, demands for the expulsion of the foreigners who were "endangering the peace of Europe." Their finances exhausted, the exiles were in want of even the necessaries of life. The seeds of disappointment and suffering soon began to show their growth of blame and recrimination, dissension, doubt, and despair. Mazzini remained unbroken. Even at that period of discomfiture, friends falling off and his family pleading for the renouncing of his course, he stood unmoved, unwavering, indomitable by outward circumstances. "My nature," he writes, "was profoundly subjective, and master of its own course. The *I* was even then for me an active force called upon to modify the medium in which it lived, not to passively submit to it. Life radiated from the centre to the circumference, not from the circumference to the centre. Ours was not an undertaking of simple reaction, the movement of a sick man who changes sides to alleviate his pains. We did not reach toward liberty as the end, but as the means for attaining an end yet higher and more positive. Upon our banners we had inscribed Republican Unity. We wished to found a Nation, to create a People. To men who had proposed to themselves an end so vast, what was a defeat? Was it not an appointed part of our educational work, this teaching of imperturbability amid adverse events? Could we teach without setting our example? And would not our abdication have subserved as an argument for those who held Unity to be impossible? The radical spoiler in Italy that condemned her to impotence was evidently not the lack of desire, but a distrust of her own strength, a facile tendency toward discouragement, a defect in that constancy without which no virtue can fructify, a fatal want of harmony between thought and action. The moral teaching which could remedy this evil was not possible in Italy, under the persecuting scourge of the police, in the way of writing or of speech on a large scale, proportionate to the need. A living Apostolate was necessary, a nucleus of Italians strong in their constancy, inaccessible to discouragement,— such as could show themselves, in the name of an Idea, capable of affronting with a smile of faith persecutions and discomfiture, falling one day, rising upon the next, ready always for the combat, and believing always, without calculation of time or circumstance, in the final victory. Ours was not a sect but a religion of patriotism. Sects may die under violence; religions may not. I shook off my doubts, and deliberated how to pursue my way.

"In Italy the work was inevitably slackened. Time was needed for souls to recover, for the masters to believe themselves conquerors, and to betake them again to sleep. But we might make up outside for the loss at home, and labour to rise again one day and fling out a second call to Italy, strong in alliance with foreign elements and with European opinion. We might in the effacing, which I saw was being slowly accomplished, of every regenerative principle initiative of European action, prepare the ground for the only idea which appeared to me called to remake the life of the peoples, that of Nationality, with the initiative influence of Italy in some future movement Nationality and the possibility of the Italian initiative: this was the programme and the dominating idea of all my labours."

Already the publications of Young Italy had attracted foreign attention. Closer relations had been drawn with the exiles in Switzerland, among others with Harro-Haring, a Dane, who had fought for Poland, Germany, and Greece, who was acquainted more or less with almost every European language, a writer of considerable merit, and an enthusiastic believer in Scandinavian Unity as a necessity in the future organization of Europe. Not uninfluenced by him, though perhaps only so far as the seconding of his own thoughts encouraged him, Mazzini passed from his Italian disappointment to combine the first elements of popular into national action by founding the Association of "Young Europe," the first germ of European Republicanism.

Here indeed is the beginning of his Apostolate, and here lies the true meaning of the new Gospel and Revelation of which he was the preacher and the prophet: the Gospel, not plainly preached before, of one associated mission for the whole of Humanity and the need of Nationality for its accomplishment.

Truly the French Revolution of 1789 had proclaimed Liberty for all men, and surely had done much toward clearing the ground in Western Europe for its advent. Also the Carbonari, looking for Italian freedom, admitted men of all countries into their ranks. But the Revolution had asserted only equal *rights*, and the Carbonari, cosmopolitan enough in the philosophic sense, recognized only *the human race* and *individuals*. Country, fatherland, nationality, were words unknown to them or forgotten in the immediate aim. They sought to lift the world without a fulcrum. It was much that they broke down, or sought to break down, the monarchical antagonistic barriers between peoples; but this was not enough. How to bind together the races of the subjugated against the league of kings they did not see; and of organizing a people to accomplish a mission for the world they had no idea. It is the fight of the many scattered, and in some sense antagonistic, against the few closely united and with identical interests, that the cosmopolitan, whether Carbonaro or trade-socialist, takes up as his problem; and it is insoluble except by his defeat. With Mazzini the question had another aspect: he saw the need of the fulcrum. In the organization of peoples into nations, according to their natural tendencies, in the vindication of that word *Nationality* from the odious meaning imposed upon it by kings, in considering a *Nation* but as another word for *a people understanding and united in one solemn duty toward the world*, so finding the sufficient reason for the patriot's duty toward his nation, to act in and with and for it,—in this Mazzini prophesied for the Future, and laid not unknowingly the first stone of the Temple of Universal Freedom, the freedom which provides opportunity for growth and progress and the perfectibility of mankind. In this too he began an era, marked out another step of human advancement, since Christianity itself doctrinally contemplates only the *individual*, however the greater question of *society* may have its germ in the question of *rights* as understood by Christ himself.

In an article written by Mazzini in 1836 these views are more fully elaborated, with the expression of his conviction that the period of *nationalism*, or popular or race prejudice, carrying with it the mere sentimental reaction of cosmopolitanism, was drawing to a close and a new era about to dawn, the era of a true *Nationality*, the organization of a people in its natural sphere as a brotherhood, to work with its fellows for the universal progress of Humanity. "Humanity is the alliance of Nations to accomplish in peace and love their mission upon earth. Nationality is the ordering of the Peoples, free and equal, so that they may move without stumbling, reaching forth reciprocal aid and helping each with the other's labour toward the development of that line in the thought of God which He has inscribed on their cradle, on their past, on their national idiom, on their physiognomy. And in this progress, in this pilgrimage which God directs, will be no room for enmity or conquests, because neither man-king nor people-king will exist, but only associations of brother-peoples with homogeneous aims and interests. The law of Duty accepted and confessed will overrule whatever tendency toward usurpation of another's right has hereto lordlike swayed the relations between people and people, and which is itself only the prevention of fear. The ruling principle of public right will no longer be the weakening of another, but the amelioration of all through the work of all, the progress of each for the benefit of the rest."

"Young Europe" was founded at Berne on the 15th of April, 1834, three days after the failure of the insurrection at Lyons. The pact and profession of faith were signed by seventeen members of the three Associations then in Switzerland: Young Italy, Young Poland, Young Germany. Of the names of the signers I recover only, for the Italians, Mazzini himself, L. A. Melegari, Giacomo Ciani, Gaspare Rosalez, G. Ruffini, and Giglione; and for the Poles Karl Stolzman.

The practical object of the Association was a federal organization of the Democracy of Europe under one single direction, in order that any one people rising against its rulers should find in other countries support, either material or moral, as circumstances might permit. In 1834 the mere promulgation of the idea was all that was possible. "I did not deceive myself," says Mazzini, "with any hope of immediate results. The sphere of the Association was too vast for that." He could but assert the necessity of such combined action, uttering the text on which History even in the few years since then has not spared its solemn comments, proving the wisdom of his prevision. It was also the Republicans' answer to the triumph of the July Monarchy over the people which had foolishly believed in the possibility of a kingly republicanism. Yet more, as a declaration of the right of the Democracy anywhere to act for the whole, it was a protest against the indispensability of a French initiative. This independent view taken by Mazzini he more fully explained in an article *On the Revolutionary Initiative*, published in January 1834, in *La Revue Républicaine*, edited by Godfrey Cavaignac ; and in a remarkable pamphlet entitled *Faith and the Future* (*Foi et Avenir*), published in 1835. Both writings were in French. Toward the end of 1834 he founded the Association of " Young Switzerland," organizing Committees in Berne, Geneva, Vaud, Valais, Neufchatel, and elsewhere; and in July, 1835, began at Bienne in the Canton of Berne, a newspaper in French and German, *La Jeune Suisse*, all the leading articles of which were written by him. Noticeable also here is a pamphlet in French, *They are gone* (*Ils sont partis*), on the expulsion of the Poles and other exiles in that same year by the Swiss Vorort.

So long as Paris, or France, as if by common consent of enslaved Europe, was the one only focus of insurrection (which seemed to be the lesson of 1789), there was need of watching only France. But when the strategic importance of Switzerland became manifest, especially with relation to Italy, the European Governments were forced to turn their attention thither. A "republic" that harboured republican conspirators was in truth an object for monarchic dread. The Swiss Government was therefore ordered to expel the disturbers, and, neither republican nor strong enough to dare to resist, had only to obey. Thiers was at that time the ruling spirit of the French Ministry, and from him and his most worthy master came the orders for expulsion. It mattered nothing that in former days Louis Philippe himself had there found refuge. Mazzini, Harro-Haring, and others, then in the Canton of Soleure, were arrested, but, on the inhabitants threatening to release them, were set at liberty and allowed to pass to Berne. Then, the French Government pretended to connect them with the regicidal attempt of Alibaud. Breaking down in that, nothing was left but the insolent menace of withdrawing diplomatic relations. To this the Vorort succumbed. Writers, printers, all concerned in the publication of *La Jeune Suisse*, were arrested, and the journal stopped. A decree of the Diet condemned Mazzini to expulsion, and forbade his return. Still he remained, repeating the experience of Marseilles. Searched for during that year, not found, he had remained longer but that the life of harassment and seclusion was destroying the health of two friends. In the beginning of 1837 he accompanied them to London.

But the reaction after all he had undergone was telling upon him too. The last months of 1836 had been months of mental and physical suffering: physical, the result of over-exertion and the constant strain upon him; mental, from the reproaches and distrust with which unheroic disappointed men, losing faith, are wont to visit those by whom they were only willing to be led to victory, and whom they could only blame for having led them into danger. This too was aggravated by the doubt weighing upon his own soul (how in times of disaster shall the generous nature escape that doubt?), the fear that he might have exceeded his right in daring to predict a happier future, in urging others on the path of sorrow and sacrifice. Sadly and most pathetically he himself tells the story of his anguish at this time: the old, old story of martyrdom,—that dreariest chapter of it all, when the most heroic must endure his hours and days of loneliest despondency; and when the only alleviation offered him is the cup of mingled vinegar and gall, the sour bitterness of remark: "Let be! leave him! he is conspiring, in his element, and happy."[1]

"It was the tempest-time of doubt" (again quoting his own words), "that time, I believe inevitable once at least in the life of every one who, devoting himself to a great enterprise, can preserve the heart

---

[1] No mere poetic fancy, but a literal fact. "While I was thus agitated and ready to sink beneath my cross, a friend replied to a young girl who, suspecting my condition, was urging him to break in upon my solitude: '*Lasciatelo! ei sta cospirando e in quel suo elemento è felice!*'"

and loving palpitating soul of a man not withered by naked and barren formulas like Robespierre. I had a soul overflowing with and thirsting for the affections of youth, capable of joy as in days comforted by the maternal smile, and fervid with hope for others, if not for myself. But in those fatal months delusions, bitterest awakenings, with a whirlwind of misfortune, darkened all around me, so that I suddenly saw in its naked leanness the old age of my solitary soul and a desert world as my only comfort in the battle before me. It was not only the ruin for an indefinite time of every Italian hope, the dispersion of our best, the persecution which effacing our work in Switzerland took us again from within reach of Italy, the exhaustion of material means, the accumulation of every kind of difficulty, almost insurmountable, between me and the task I had initiated, but the falling asunder of that moral edifice of love and faith from which alone I could draw strength to combat, the scepticism which I saw arising before me wherever I looked, the languishing of belief in those so lately bound as brothers with me on the way that even in the first days we knew to be held by tribulation; and soon, beyond that, the distrust I saw growing around me, in those most dear to me, as to my intentions and the motives which urged me on to a struggle apparently so unequal.

"Little it imported to me even then that the opinion of most ran adverse to me. But to feel myself suspected of ambition, or of any other less than noble impulse, by the two or three beings toward whom I had concentrated all my power of affection, prostrated my soul with a sense of profound despair. And these things were revealed to me in the very months in which, assailed from all sides, I felt more intensely the need of recovering myself in communion with some few sister souls who could understand me though silent; who could divine all that I, in deliberately renouncing every joy of life, was suffering; and who would suffer, smiling with me.

" It was then that they withdrew from me. [*Scritti*, 1862.]

" I came to myself again, without help of others, thanks to the religious idea which I verified in History. I descended from the idea of God to that of Progress; from that of Progress to a conception of Life, to faith in a mission, to the logical consequence of Duty, the supreme rule; and, arrived at that point, I vowed to myself that nothing in the world should thenceforth have power to make me doubt or lead me astray. It was, as Dante says, the way of martyrdom to peace :[1] a forced and desperate peace, I do not deny, for I fraternized with grief and wrapped myself in sorrow as a pilgrim in his mantle : yet peace, for I learned to suffer without rebelling,

[1] . . . . " da martirio
E da esilio venne a questa pace."
Paradiso, X.

and was thereafter in tranquil accord with my own soul. I bade a long most sad adieu to all joys, to all hopes for myself upon earth. I dug with my own hands the grave, not of the affections (God is my witness that I feel them to-day, gray-headed, as in the first days of my youth), but of the desires, the exigencies, the ineffable comforts of the affections; and trampled the earth hard upon that grave so that others should not know the *I* there buried. For reasons, some apparent, others unknown, my life has been, and is lastingly, but that it nears the end, unhappy; but from that day to this I have not for an instant thought that unhappiness may influence our actions. Reverently I bless God, my Father, for what consolations of affection, I know none others, He has vouchsafed to me in later years, which have given me strength to fight against the weariness of existence that then unmade me. But even if these consolations were not, I believe I should be what I am. Whether the azure heaven be serenely splendid as on a fine morning in Italy, or outspread uniformly leaden and death-coloured as in the fogs of the North, I do not see that Duty changes for us. God is over the terrestrial heaven, and the holy stars of Faith and the Future are resplendent in our souls, even when their light consumes itself unreflected, like a lamp in a sepulchre." [*Scritti*, 1862.]

He arrived in London in the winter, in January 1837. To the deep heart-sorrows which weighed him down were added all the pettier cares and annoyances and sufferings of poverty, such poverty as is thoroughly known only in the heart of our modern cities : a crisis of "absolute misery," prolonged through the whole of 1837 and half of 1838. Sparingly supplied during previous years with money from home (sent to him secretly by his mother, in his father's name that he might not know of the father's refusal to help him, not from want of love, but in the hope of so forcing him back to Italy), he had used those funds for the Cause, had incurred obligations also for the sake of others. Now in England the mother's remittances had to provide for four, himself and three companions depending upon him ; and little by little, by the sale of family keepsakes, by pawning his clothes, by all the shifts that poor men friendless and in a foreign land may know, he had to support himself and his friends. "I did not suffer," he says, "for these things more than they were worth, nor for an instant feel myself degraded or cast down. Nor have they left any lasting impression. But for others condemned to endure such things and believing themselves lessened by them, my example may help. I would that mothers would think that no one, in the present condition of Europe, is the arbiter of his own fortune or of that of those dear to him ; and be convinced that by educating their sons austerely and for any manner of life, they would perhaps better provide for their future, for their happiness and souls' good, than by heaping them round with ease and comfort, and enervating the natural inclination which should be trained warrior-like even from the first years to meet privations and sufferings. I have seen young Italians, called by nature to a noble life, turn miserably to wrong, or save themselves by suicide, from trials which I have borne smilingly; and I charged the responsibility to the mothers. My own—blessed be her memory!—had prepared me, with that love which thinks of the possible future, to stand firmly in any happening." [*Scritti*, 1862.]

Literature was the one field open to Mazzini in which to earn a living in England, and at the same time, for he never lost sight of extraneous help, to create sympathy for the Italian question, a question concerning which at that date even the Liberal party was profoundly ignorant; as profoundly ignorant, it may be also said, as of all other European matters.[1] He made literary acquaintances, and began to write for the Reviews. In the *Monthly Chronicle*, in *Tait's Edinburgh Magazine*, in the *Westminster Review*, appeared his first contributions, written at first either in Italian or French, translated for him by friends: articles on the *Condition of Italy*, on *European Democracy*, criticisms of Dante, Goethe, Carlyle, Byron, George Sand, &c., giving new impulses to

[1] The *Westminster Review*, then in the hands of Colonel Peyronnet Thompson, a staunch and devoted Radical, a man of genius, knew nothing of foreign affairs except the French and the glaring wrongs of Poland; and the best London newspaper, the *Spectator*, depended for its foreign news upon the *Journal des Débats*.

English thought, and resuming the broken thread of the old Miltonic story, giving again the clue to a republican future for England as for the rest of Europe. While thus supporting himself, he never remitted his exertions as head of the one revolutionary party in Italy, and found time also to take an active part in the anniversary and other meetings of the Poles, whether in commemoration of their own or of the Russian martyrs for liberty, proving himself not only the active and capable patriot, but also the accomplished scholar, the eloquent orator, the noble of world-wide sympathies.

In 1841 he founded at 5, Greville Street, Hatton Garden, London, a free Elementary School for the poor Italians of London, most of them either organ-grinders or hawkers of plaister casts; giving to it, notwithstanding his other labours, constant and patient attention; the Sunday evening lectures, on morals, history, astronomy, &c., being regularly delivered by him.[1] By these poor fellows, shamefully

[1] The school was under the direction of Luigi Bucalossi, a Tuscan, assisted by Filippo Pistrucci (a well-known improvisatore), his son Scipione (an artist of much promise, who died of consumption after the overthrow at Milan), and Celestino Vai, an old man like the elder Pistrucci. Well I recollect Vai and the two Pistruccis, men whose goodness would have made them remarkable. The school had to be given up when the hopes of 1848 called all Italians back to work upon their own soil. Here I first met Margaret Fuller, at an anniversary festival, when the Directors distributed prizes and served their pupils with supper, songs, and improvisations. It was returning from one such evening with Mazzini that I saw him carrying home one of the

treated by their Italian masters and exploiters, Mazzini was revered almost as a god and loved as a father. One of them going back to Italy, traveled to Genoa expressly to tell Mazzini's mother what her son had done for him.

Simultaneously with the opening of this school he formed an Association of Italian workmen in London, and began an Italian paper, the *Popular Apostolate*, twelve numbers of which appeared between 1841 and 1843, containing a series of his ablest writings, the first four chapters of the *Duties of Man*,[1] Letters to the youth of Italy, articles on Italian Unity, and on the influence of political institutions on the education of the people, &c., &c.

In 1842 he edited the *Divine Comedy* of Dante (*La Comedia di Dante Alleghieri, illustrato da Ugo Foscolo*), published by Rolandi, London, in four volumes, partly from notes by Foscolo, some of which he had found among waste at another London bookseller's, some in a trunk filled with Foscolo's papers, preserved by the Canon Riego (brother of the Spanish

---

children of an Italian workman with whom he lodged. Even in such small things the inherent gentleness of his nature was manifest.

[1] Completed afterwards in the *Pensiero e Azione* in 1858, and published in one volume with *Thoughts upon Democracy in Europe* and a memoir, in London, 1875. A selection of other articles from the *Apostolato*, four chapters of *Duties*, the Letters to *Charles Albert of Savoy* and to *Pio Nono*, the *Records of the Brothers Bandiera*, &c., will be found in a little volume entitled *Prose di Giuseppe Mazzini*, published at Florence in 1848.

patriot), who had nursed Foscolo in his last sickness. He also wrote the preface to the edition.

In 1844 Mazzini's name became known throughout England, and the Italian question was forced upon the mind of the whole country. This first awakening of English thought upon the subject was due to the action of the English Government, when, violating the simplest duty of hospitality, they broke the seals of Mazzini's letters, resealed them to keep him in ignorance of their being opened, and then forwarded information to Austria. The story of the two brothers Bandiera, Italian officers in the Austrian army, not merely betrayed but led to death through the instrumentality of men high in office in England, filled all England with indignation; and the attempt of the principal actors, Sir James Graham and Lord Aberdeen, by reviving the old Gisquet calumny to shift some portion of the obloquy attached to them upon the shoulders of Mazzini, helped, more than perhaps anything else could have done, to make his name famous in the land of his exile. Not only Mr. Duncombe, who took up his case and forced it into parliamentary notice, spoke for the then but little-known Italian; Shiel, and Wakley, and Macaulay, lent their eloquence on the same side; and Carlyle wrote his letter to the *Times*, worth lasting preservation, both for the generosity of its tone and for the evidence it affords of the impression a true man can make even upon those not in unison with his work.

Here is Carlyle's letter—

"To the Editor of the *Times*.

"Sir,

In your observations in yesterday's *Times* on the late disgraceful affair of M. Mazzini's letters and the Secretary of State, you mention that M. Mazzini is entirely unknown to you, entirely indifferent to you ; and add, very justly, that if he were the most contemptible of mankind it would not affect your argument on the subject.

"It may tend to throw further light on this matter if I now certify you, which I in some sort feel called upon to do, that M. Mazzini is not unknown to various competent persons in this country ; and that he is very far indeed from being contemptible —none further, or very few, of living men. I have had the honour to know M. Mazzini for a series of years ; and whatever I may think of his practical insight and skill in worldly affairs, I can with great freedom testify to all men that he, if I have ever seen one such, is a man of genius and virtue, a man of sterling veracity, humanity, and nobleness of mind, one of those rare men, numerable unfortunately but as units in this world, who are worthy to be called martyr souls ; who in silence, piously in their daily life, understand and practise what is meant by that. Of Italian democracies and Young Italy's sorrows, of extraneous Austrian Emperors in Milan, or poor old chimerical Popes in Bologna, I know nothing and desire to know nothing ; but this other thing I do know and can here publicly declare to be a fact, which fact all of us that have occasion to comment on M. Mazzini and his affairs may do well to take along with us, as a thing leading towards new clearness, and not towards new additional darkness, regarding him and them.

"Whether the extraneous Austrian Emperor and miserable old chimera of a Pope shall maintain themselves in Italy or be obliged to decamp from Italy is not a question in the least vital to Englishmen. But it is a question vital to us that sealed letters in an English post-office be, as we all fancied they were, respected as things sacred ; that opening of men's letters, a practice near of kin to picking men's pockets, and to other still viler and far fataler forms of scoundrelism, be not resorted to except in cases of very last extremity. When some new Gunpowder Plot may be in the wind, some double-dyed high treason, or imminent national wreck not avoidable otherwise, then let us open letters :

not till then. To all Austrian Kaisers and such like, in their time of trouble, let us answer, as our fathers from of old have answered :—Not by such means is help here for you. Such means, allied to picking of pockets and viler forms of scoundrelism, are not permitted in this country for your behoof. The right honourable Secretary does himself detest such, and even is afraid to employ them. He dare not : it would be dangerous for him ! All British men that might chance to come in view of such a transaction would incline to spurn it, and trample on it and indiguantly ask him what he meant by it.

"I am, Sir, your obedient servant,
"THOMAS CARLYLE.
"*Chelsea, June* 15, 1844."

Secret committees of the Lords and Commons (Mr. Duncombe was refused an open committee) reported on the transaction, the two reports not in agreement, and both falling short of a full account. Mazzini's comment on the affair was given in his story of the murder of the Bandieras (*Ricordi dei Fratelli Bandiera e dei loro campagni di Martirio*), and in *Italy, Austria, and the Pope*, a letter to Sir James Graham,[1] published in 1845, going fully into the condition of Italy. One extract from this scathing letter may here be noted. The story is complete in itself, and shows to what meannesses monarchical governments are prone, meannesses so unhappily endorsed by our English "Liberal" ministry. It shows also to what Mazzini was exposed his life through.[2]

[1] The weight of public obloquy fell upon Graham, the Home Secretary ; but the worse offender was Lord Aberdeen, Secretary for Foreign Affairs, by whom the stolen information was given to the Austrian Government.

[2] "There was a man among our exiles, since 1833, himself

In 1846 he wrote an address *to the Swiss Confederation* (printed in Italian, French, and German,

proscribed by Austria for having belonged to our national association, Young Italy. He had bravely fought and suffered since 1821 for the Italian cause. On this account he enjoyed our brotherly esteem and the intimate friendship of some among us. But he belonged to those sensual natures, disinherited of religious faith, who fight through reaction and suffer through pride rather than from a profound conviction of duty, and who are capable of exhibiting turn by turn and in jerks the spectacle of all the virtues except constancy. He fell into poverty, had recourse to us and was helped; but the temporary help that his friends, poor and exiled like himself, could give him, was not sufficient to preserve him from the grip of a misery which periodically returned. Without employ, without resources, he began to despair. The Austrian police, in wait for their victim, offered him through their agents abroad a monthly pension if he would decide to play the Judas toward his brothers. He yielded. He thought to reconcile his appetites with an infamous but inoffensive *rôle*, and to gain his pay without compromising a living soul, playing with the Austrian Government. This was in 1842; and all his first depositions, vague, barely indicating the supposed intrigues of exiles who ran no personal risk, corresponded marvelously with the game of mystifier which he had taken up. But the spiral of Crime wound round his soul and showed itself stronger than he. Severe reproaches and at the same time seductive offers of all the money he might need to accomplish his infernal mission, came to him from the director of the Lombard police, Baron Torresani, and from the Austrian ambassador at Paris, where he was living. Degraded in his own thought, lost in the eyes of his compatriots, among whom were rumours of his conduct, he felt himself fascinated; he subscribed to all they wanted. He began to mix truth with falsehood. Then, when the agitation of the States of the Pope toward the end of 1843 became so menacing, he plunged into crime with a sort of drunken fury. He made himself at once informer and instigator. He joined himself to some men who had relations with the interior, but who could make no use of them, wanting money; he told them—' I have money, I will manage for you.' Others, for the several Cantons) in reprobation of the practice of Swiss enlistment in the service of the Pope and other Italian tyrants. Toward the close of the same year, in consequence of the Allied Powers destroying and England allowing the destruction of the little

---

traveling to France, were engaged by him to carry into Italy prohibited writings. With one hand he gave these to them, with the other he wrote their denunciation. They are yet in prison.

"In 1844 Austria required of him that he should avail himself of his old acquaintance with me to spy me more closely. Half by instinct, half by knowledge I had acquired of an immorality committed in his country, I had ceased to have any relations with him. He feared to meet my look, and he did not come. But he shut himself up in a garret in Paris, did not go out of it for some time, and fabricated his report of conversations held with me in London, of revelations which I had made to him, of insurrectional plans that I was directing: a tissue of absurdities with which he mixed enormous ciphers of arms and money furnished to me by unknown Englishmen, and promises from the actual Government of England, in case of an Italian movement, 'transmitted to me,' he wrote, 'by the private secretary of Sir Robert Peel.' His informations were well paid, and he by letter thanked Baron Torresani for the same. But if he mystified the Austrian police with regard to me, he none the less pursued with others his infernal work. He gave notes of introduction to me to Italians traveling through Europe; then he wrote that they came to talk with the director of the revolutionary movements. During his last moments he was occupied in correcting with sulphuric acid the false passports which he intended for the exiles who wished to verify the state of things in Italy: victims whom he sent to perpetual imprisonment or death. His name was *Attilio Partesotti*, of Mantua. I have in my possession the copy of all his correspondence. The miserable wretch, for fear of contradicting himself, had been obliged to keep a book, an exact register of his missives, which he had not time to burn."
—From the French republication of the original English, in *La Revue Independante* of the 10th and 15th of September, 1845.

remains of Polish freedom at Cracow, he suggested, and in the beginning of 1847 set on foot, "The Peoples' International League," the first English Association asserting an interest in "foreign affairs," and taking for its object "to enlighten the British Public as to the political condition and relations of Foreign Countries, to disseminate the principles of national freedom and progress, to embody and manifest an efficient public opinion in favour of the right of every People to self-government and the maintainance of their own nationality; and to promote a good understanding between the Peoples of all countries" (meaning European, of course). To this work Mazzini gave time, zeal, and money. The draft of the first Address of the League was written by him;[1] he also wrote a valuable pamphlet on the *Swiss Question*, issued by the League, explaining the bearings of the Jesuitical Sonderbund; and he furnished the materials for a course of public lectures on the Italian and Swiss questions.[2]

[1] In the English six volume edition of his works the Address is given as his writing. It was written by me from his rough draft, still in my possession. The first six paragraphs and three lines of the seventh, sufficiently pedantic and meaningless, but "wanted as introduction," are from the pen of Mr. Philip Harwood. Their look bewrayeth them. The style is not Mazzinian.

[2] The lectures were given by Richard Hengist Horne (the poet), Thomas Cooper (the Chartist), and myself as honorary secretary of the League. Among the names on the Council of the League were those of P. A. Taylor (one of the founders of the Corn-Law League), P. A. Taylor, junior, M.P., William

In September 1847 he addressed his letter *to Pius the Ninth*, the "Reforming Pope" (as easy Liberals then delighted to call him), surely not with more of hopeful expectation than when he wrote to Charles Albert of Savoy, but unwilling to neglect any possible means for Italy's sake : urging that poor Astyanax of Christendom to become indeed a reformer, truly the servant of all ; to make himself ready either to glorify God in triumph, or, if succumbing, to repeat with resignation the words of Gregory VII.—" I die in exile, because I loved righteousness and hated iniquity." " But to do that, to accomplish the mission which God has intrusted to you, two things are necessary : to be a believer, and to unify Italy. . . . Be a believer ! Abhor being only a king, a politician, a statesman ! Have no covenant with error ; do not contaminate yourself with diplomacy, nor make conditions with fear, with expediency, with the false doctrine of *legality*, which is but a lie invented in the absence of Faith ! Take no counsel but from God, from the inspirations of your own heart, and from the imperious necessity of rebuilding a temple to Truth, Justice, and Faith.

" Unify Italy, your country ! and for that you will not need to work, but only to bless those who will

---

Bridges Adams (the engineer, a man whose whole life was devoted to working for Humanity), James Watson (the most respected of the leaders of the working-class), Richard Taylor (printer and editor of a preface to the *Diversions of Purley*), W. J. Fox (the eloquent Unitarian lecturer), Dr. Bowring, and Douglas Jerrold.

work for you in your name. Surround yourself with the men who best represent the national party! Do not beg alliances with princes! Seek to win the alliance of our People! Say to yourself—*Italian unity ought to be a fact in the nineteenth century.* That will be enough: the rest shall be done for you."

Pearls before swine: there was no response.

MILAN.

1848—the year of European hope. Already at the close of 1847 Ochsenbein had put down the Jesuit Sonderbund in Switzerland. Italy was in a state of ferment. In December fires lighted on the peaks of the Apennines from end to end of Italy commemorated the expulsion of the Austrians from Genoa a century before. As the new year dawned Sicily was in arms. At Palermo, on the 12th of January, the Sicilians proclaimed a Provisional Government. On the 22nd of February the stones arose in the streets of Paris. In March, on the 13th, Metternich was driven out of Vienna; on the 18th, the Austrian Viceroy fled from Milan; and on the 29th, Berlin was in revolt, and the Prussian Monarchy bowed its head to receive sentence. The uprising of Schleswig Holstein followed. Two months later a Provisional Government was formed at Prague. One thunder-burst of Liberty, and then the too swift reaction. The Governments, recovering from their hasty fear, saw how they might exploit the improvised revolutions to their own purposes. On the 23rd of March, Charles Albert of Savoy declared himself the Soldier of Italian Freedom. In

Posen the Germans were pitted against the Poles; desperate conflicts ensued; in spite of all that heroism could do, the Poles were forced to succumb. Then began the bewildering of Germany with royally treacherous promises of a nationality under an Emperor, displacing the active hope of the Republic. In France, though the republic of universal suffrage was proclaimed, the old manipulators were left to manage the elections; home republicanism damaged while the Republic was discredited abroad by the fratricidal non-intervention of M. de Lamartine. In vain the French people, wiser than their leaders, protested against this foreign policy; public opinion was throttled on the first pretext, an accidental tumult on the 15th of May. On that same day Naples was sacked by the Lazzaroni by order of their Bourbon King. On May the 18th, the German Parliament, the elect of universal suffrage, met at Frankfort—to talk. June the 12th, the Austrian General Radetzky, who had been defeated by Charles Albert at Goito and Peschiera on the 29th and 30th May, bombarded Vicenza; June 15th, Padua had to surrender to him; and the whole of the Venetian territory, except Venice itself, was again at the mercy of the Hun. And by the 19th of the same month, Prague had been bombarded by Prince Windischgratz, and the Bohemian insurrection was at an end.

Yet more disastrous was the course of events in France. Cheated by the *bourgeoisie*, hurrying blindly forward after vague hopes excited by competing schools of socialism, played with by political intriguers, and urged at last by want and despair, 40,000 of the proletarians of Paris in June took up arms against the Provisional Government. The enemies of freedom laughed to see Republican fighting against Republican. Eight thousand prisoners and twice that number of killed and wounded evidenced the deadly character of the conflict; and in the bloody dust of the leveled barricades of St. Antoine the shop-keeping republicans, the respectables, only republicans in name and for the time, sowed the dragons' teeth for the bloodier communal harvest of Thiers.

So, in brief, will History write of that hopeful and unhappy time, that swift-passing Spring of so much of promise, so many daring deeds, so many errors, so much of disappointment. Our Italian story is involved in it.

Toward the end of 1847 Mazzini had been for a short time in France. He was again in London when the news arrived of the Revolution of the Three Days; and on the 29th of February left England for Paris. There, taking counsel with the Italians and Poles, aiding Lamennais and the clear-sighted French Republicans, he struggled as he best could in opposition to Lamartine's fatal policy of peace at any price, which isolated France, separating her from the European revolution, not only imminent but actually begun.

On the 5th of March he founded at Paris the "Italian National Association," and immediately upon the breaking out of the Milanese insurrection (March 18th) proceeded to Italy, re-entering his native land after an exile of seventeen years. As he crossed the frontier the custom-house officers knew him; he heard his own words quoted, his name lovingly pronounced. When he reached Milan the people crowded to see him, kissing him, snatching at his hands, welcoming him with tears of joy. The Provisional Government sent for him; he was obliged to harangue the people from the palace windows. The King had to send for him—for him the outlaw, yet under sentence of death as a conspirator. Strange must have been the meeting of the murderer with the comrade of Jacobo Ruffini. For the sake of Italy Mazzini nobly set aside his own feelings. The first public words he uttered in Milan were an encouragement to the royal undertaking; his next, not before May, at the King's request, to allay some disagreement arising between Brescia and Milan. Already he had written, in September 1847, to Filippo Boni—"For all my aversion to Charles Albert, the executioner of my best friends, for all the contempt I feel for his effete and cowardly nature, for all the popular tendencies fermenting in me, if I could suppose him to be so much as ambitious of unifying Italy for his own account, I would say Amen!"

Charles Albert of Savoy was a man without faith. For a moment in his youth ambitious, even then mistrustful, easily scared, vacillating between desire of adding to his little monarchy and fear of losing even that, letting "I dare not wait upon I would," a despot by instinct, liberal only from self-love or presentiment of possible danger, suffering alternately the influence of the Jesuits and of those who would have spurred him to never so gentle an amble on the road of progress, he was the Hamlet of Monarchy, Hamlet-like not unsuspected, among his familiars, of a tendency to insanity. Metternich saw his unfitness as a leader. In a dispatch to Count Dietrichstein (August 2, 1847), foreseeing events, he wrote—" One positive fact should turn them from any idea of a monarchical Italy : the possible king of that monarchy does not exist either beyond or within the Alps."

Notwithstanding, the war begun by Charles Albert, Mazzini was ready to serve: certainly not without *asking* conditions. He was willing to defer his republicanism to the morrow of Italian independence. He was willing to bring his republicans (who but they were on the barricades during the five days of Milan ?) under the royal banner, would the king but promise to be true and proclaim the fight for all Italy, not merely for a larger Savoy. Even without that assurance he would help so far as he might be allowed. Before his arrival in Milan the young men of the barricades had formed a republican association. The rules of the same being communicated to the Government, it was within their right, all parties being called upon to freely prepare for the vote (to be taken later) as to the permanent form of Government. But, their republican views once asserted, they devoted their energies only to the war. Mazzini's only part in the Association was in support of the Government. The *Voce del Popolo*, the republican journal, was equally self-restrained; it occupied itself with the war, and avoided even the word Republic. That in those days Mazzini divided the national party, that he made division among Italians, is an impudent calumny in the face of all historical evidence.

But the Savoyard Cæsar even as he crossed his Rubicon had prepared for a safe retreat. In a manifesto addressed to all the Courts of Europe, the royal patriot declared that "in invading Venetian Lombardy he had no other object than to prevent the proclamation of the Republic,"[1] acting only in defence of his own endangered royalty.

On the 18th of March, the Milanese arose. Pending the five days' contest Charles Albert refused help. Milanese success and popular feeling in Piedmont changed his mind, leaving him no choice, abdication excepted, but to announce through the constitutional mouthpiece, a new ministry *ad hoc*, how much he regretted having to bring the "Sword of Italy" into play. The real position of said supposed patriotic Sword is well explained in the Despatches to Lord Palmerston of the British Resident at the Court of

[1] Dell' Insurrezione di Milano nel 1848 e della successiva guerra: Memoirs of Carlo Cattaneo, Lugano, 1849.

Turin, who was really disturbed on account of the Sword.

Long ago—writes British Resident Abercromby on the 25th of March—I expressed my fears that the Austrian Government would have trouble, and the Piedmontese Government, however unwilling, be obliged to take a hand in the game of Italian liberties. Unhappily the Vienna Cabinet has lost opportunities, "unhappily let slip an interval precious for the interests of Austria," during which timely concessions might have lulled patriotism to sleep (the British Resident having no sort of leaning toward patriotism in Italy), for unhappily "when the news of concessions made at Vienna reached Milan by telegraph, they learned at the same time that a popular movement in the Austrian capital had preceded these resolutions of the Imperial Cabinet." Quite unhappy for Austria: and the British Resident (Residents were much disturbed and in many ways uncomfortable in those hours) is bound to apologize for any unseemly haste—not too hasty in regard to Milan—of the Piedmontese royalty in taking advantage thereof for Piedmont.

It was thus, continues the disturbed British Resident, that the Piedmontese, Savoyard, or Sardinian Cabinet "was forced to adopt a line of policy which, if events had been less favourable for it," or less unhappy for Austria, "had not been chosen." And the Disturbed has the honour to add, " to extenuate the conduct of Sardinia," that " perhaps the general uprising in Parma and Modena, and the movement of Tuscan troops toward the frontier, rendered the position of the King, Charles Albert, very embarrassing, in so much as it became extremely difficult for him to oppose a movement which had a national character."[1]

A later dispatch from Vice-Consul Robert Campbell to Lord Palmerston, dated Milan, March 31, informs us that "there had been a thorough union of all classes, but that since the entry into Lombardy of his Sardinian Majesty two parties had shown themselves: one, the party of the high aristocracy, desiring to unite Lombardy and Piedmont under the sovereignty of H. M. Charles Albert; the other, that of the middle classes, among which must be remarked business men and men of letters, as well as all the educated and enlightened youth of the country, desiring a republic."

In the same dispatch Vice-Consul Campbell speaks also of the enthusiasm and energy displayed by the Milanese themselves in their military preparations. And from another it appears that the unaided Milanese had so effectively repulsed the Austrian General Radetzky that he sought to escape through the Tyrol, but finding his way blocked was compelled to turn at bay and defeat H. M. of Sardinia:—the last chance of Austria, for even his own troops were deserting him.[2]

[1] *Official Correspondence* of the British Embassy with the British Government, printed and laid before Parliament.

[2] Extract from Report of Marshal Radetzky, Cremona, April 2, published in the *Vienna Gazette*.

Consul Dawkins writes also from Venice, that the whole country between Venice and Ferrara had risen. Even Austrian war-brigs, cruising in the Adriatic, had put into Venice and declared for the Republic. In Civita-Vecchia and Florence also were anti-Austrian manifestations. From all of which, and there is abundance of corroborative evidence equally guiltless of sympathy with republicans or insurgents, it is plain that things went well with the Republican party, and as well for the nationality of Italy, until Charles Albert interfered, marking the beginning of his interference by hastening to assure, &c., that the royal marine "had orders to commit no act of hostility against the Austrians unless provoked by them."[1]

Had Mazzini and Young Italy refused all community of action with a power so bent on aiding them only to pick out its own advantage, and with ground of action known to be so opposed to them, who honestly could have blamed them? Nevertheless Mazzini, controling his just suspicions, consented to march beneath the royal flag, to second the royal adventurer, if only out of his action might be some gain for Italy. And loyally he kept his word.

The Piedmontese troops entered Milan on the 26th of March, three days after Pareto had written to the British Resident—

"M. Abercromby knows as well as the undersigned the grave events that have just taken place

[1] Official Letter of the Marquis Pareto, the new Piedmontese Minister, to Abercromby, March 29.

in Lombardy: Milan in full revolution and soon in the power of the inhabitants, who by their courage and firmness have known how to resist the disciplined troops of his Imperial Majesty; insurrection in the neighbouring towns and rural districts; in fine all the country bordering on the frontiers of his Sardinian Majesty on fire." The situation such .. " that it is to be feared it can only result at any moment in one of those revolutions which place the throne in serious danger: for one cannot dissemble that after the events in France, the danger of the proclamation of a Republic in Lombardy may be near. Seeing also that the condition of Piedmont is such that from one moment to another on the announcement that the Republic has been proclaimed in Lombardy, a like movement might burst out in the States of H. S. M." Wherefore, &c., &c., " obliged to take measures which by preventing the actual movement in Lombardy from becoming a republican movement, will avoid for Piedmont and the rest of Italy the catastrophes which might take place if such a form of Government were proclaimed "—

"The undersigned, &c.
"L. N. Pareto."

To Vienna the same Undersigned also wrote that Charles Albert moved for the safety of other Monarchical States (*pour le salut des autres Etats monarchiques*).[1]

[1] Pareto to the Piedmontese Ambassador at Vienna, March 24.

The "Sword of Italy" was indeed the Dagger of the Monarchy. Under such auspices and with such intentions the Piedmontese Traitor, backed by the "Moderate Party," marched to the conquest of Italian independence. The ignorant, hoodwinked, applauded them,—*them*, Charles Albert of 1831, the Austrian Grand Duke of Tuscany, the Lazzarone King of Naples, the Reforming Pope. Italian constitutional devotees, swelling with royally moderated love, lifted their simple heads above the current to bless their deliverers, in anticipation.

Yes! the treason was not only the Savoyard's. Behind him and hiding in his skirts, was a party, not of principle, but "practical," not loving royalty, but hating republicanism, the party of transactions, of compromises, whose political honesty was well worthy of being called " moderate."

" Between the execution of the Bandieras and the death of Pope Gregory XVI., a sect had arisen, babbling indeed of Christianity and religion, but educated half in the sceptical materialism of the eighteenth century, half in French eclecticism, which under their own chosen name of *Moderates* (as if between being and not being, between the future of nations and governments not caring for its development, there could ever exist a middle way) had set to themselves as a problem to be resolved—the conciliation of the irreconcilable : liberty and princedom, nationality and dismemberment, force and uncertain direction. Perhaps no sect of men could have done that, this one less than any. They were writers, endowed with talent but without a spark of genius,—sufficiently furnished with the sort of erudition acquired from books, wanting the vivifying guide of synthesis in their cabinets and among the dead, but without enlightenment as to the work of unification subterraneously accomplished in the last three centuries, without consciousness of the Italian mission or faculty of placing themselves in communion with the people, whom they believed to be corrupt, but who were worth more than themselves, and from whom they were held aloof by their habits of life, certain traditional distrusts, and uncancelled aristocratic instincts, noble or literary. Owing to this moral and intellectual segregation from *the people,* the only progressive element and henceforth the arbiter of the life of the nation, they were disinherited of all real knowledge and all faith in the future. Their historic conceptions, with some slight transmutations, floated between Guelphism and Ghibellinism. Their political conceptions, however they might try to cloak them in an Italian form, went not beyond the terms of the French school of Montesquieu, &c., reduced to a system by the men who directed opinion in France during the fifteen years following the return of Louis XVIII. They were monarchists with an infusion of liberty, just enough to render the monarchy tolerable and to endow themselves with the right of publishing their opinions and of sitting as a sort of consulting-board, without extending the same liberty to the multitude, for fear of arousing the idea of rights which they abhorred and of duties of which they had not even a suspicion. In substance they had no belief: their faith in the monarchical principle was only a faith in the dogma of divine right inselfed in a few families, reposed in certain persons, the monarch placed between God and the Beloved, 'my God, my King, and my Lady.' It was a passive, inert acquiescence, without reverence and without love, for a fact which they found before their eyes and which they did not attempt to examine ; it was moral cowardice, fear of the people whose occasional movement they desired to intrench with monarchy, fear of the inevitable contrast of the two elements which they did not feel themselves capable of mastering, fear that Italy was too impotent to recover with her own popular forces even that meagre portion of independence which they also, tender for Italian honour (their only dowry) would desire. They wrote, with an affectation of gravity, with all the impressiveness of acute and profound discerners, counsels copied from times of normal development, from men involved in parliamentary warfare and citizens of States already formed, to a people which, on the one hand had nothing, and on the other had everything to conquer—life, unity, independence, liberty. To their eunuch voices the people answered with the roar of a lion : driving out the Jesuits, demanding the institution of civic guards, and publicity of debates, snatching constitutions from the princes whilst they (the Moderates) were recommending silence, legal paths, and abstinence from every manifestation that might afflict the paternal hearts of their masters. They called themselves *positivists, practical men,* and merited the name of Arcadians of politics."[1]

Such were the chiefs of the Moderate faction: no need to name them. How many of them, some hungry for power or pelf, some from wounded vanity or premature decay of all their nobler aspirations, are now harnessed to the wheels of monarchical reaction in Italy! And their following? A heterogeneous host: some unbelievers like their chiefs, some believers tired of the unhappy consequences of their faith (not bad at heart, but weary, and in their weakness disposed to take "the easier way"), the rest made up of that great unleavenable mass which is the surest bulwark of wrong of whatever kind, the greatest hindrance to progress, the inert,

---

[1] From *Indications and Documents concerning the Lombard Insurrection and the Royal War* (Cenni e Documenti interno all' insurrezione Lombard e alla Guerra Regia) of 1848 : written by Mazzini toward the close of 1849, translated into French by Geo. Sand in 1850 under the title of *République et Royauté en Italie,* and from the French in the same year into English for the *Friend of the People,* a Chartist weekly paper, edited by G. Julian Harney; appearing afterwards "revised" in the English six-volume edition of Mazzini's writings. In the double translation much of Mazzini's style is lost, but as a history, written with wonderful temper and moderation, the work retains its value. Only precise words, needed documentarily or to exactly define the thought are lost sometimes in the paraphrase. It should however be noticed that the account of the Moderate Party above given is omitted from the history by the Editor of the *Writings,* appearing elsewhere in detached form.

unenergetic, the careless, the emasculated multitude, preferrers of habitual slavery to the irksomeness of exertion. The following was large.

That treason, premeditated treason, was at their head, is perhaps sufficiently proved.

I devote so much of space and attention to this Milanese campaign and to the causes of its failure, partly as necessary in defence of Mazzini, partly because the same character marks the course of events in Italy wherever the royal element has interfered. Ever the same three parties: the Republicans, deferring their own hopes to the morrow of Italian independence; the "Moderates," many of them perhaps desirous of independence and unity,[1]

[1] Not all. And most, if not all of them in those days held unity to be impossible. The first public manifestation of the party was in 1845 at Rimini, where they unfolded a white flag, a well-chosen emblem. Their manifesto of principles went so far as a preference for small local reforms to any idea of nationality. Fulfilling their intentions, Italy might to-day have been still under a federation of petty sovereigns, banded against the nation or plotting each for his own behoof, hypocrites and traitors. Such was the idea of the thinkers of the Moderate Party, from Balbo to Cavour. Giacomo Durando preached advisability or desirability of three, or four, or five Italian kingdoms to be founded by the voluntary subscription of the reigning princes; Mamiani was the centre of a federal apostolate at Genoa; Gioberti, notwithstanding his old adhesion to Young Italy, proposed in 1847 to remonstrate with Austria, so to obtain a change of policy, in order that Lombardy, pacified by Austrian sugar-plums and other reform sweetmeats, might be led gradually to such farther redemption as might be agreeable to the Powers ("*s'ottenesse dall Austria con remostranze un mutamento di politica in Lombardia tanto che pacificata colla dolcezza e colle riforme potesse poi con agio e tempo ricevere d'accordo coi potentati un assetto*

but all willing to defer both rather than suffer the advent of the Republic; and the Royalists *par excellence*, prompt to use and to betray all, in turn or together, and to sacrifice unity and independence (as in this Lombard war, and later at Villa-franca), for the mere sake of a king's aggrandizement. Yet a farther lesson underlies the period: it is the history, probably to be repeated, of every popular movement in which the people trust to leaders whose faith is not as theirs, and whose interests are against them, instead of relying upon themselves.

Before the entry of Charles Albert the Lombard insurrection was everywhere victorious. The enthusiasm of the revolted was as great as the discouragement of the beaten Austrians. Outside Lombardy was an universal fermentation, the leaven of a crusade. The Milanese uprising had sounded the tocsin for all Italy. At Modena, at Bologna, at Leghorn, at Pisa, at Florence, men were arming, eager for the fight. The Austrian Grand Duke of Tuscany to save himself had to declare war against Austria. Rome was stirred. Over the hotel of the Austrian Embassy in place of the Imperial arms, they wrote "Palace of the Italian Diet" (*Palazzo*

---

definitive."—(Letter of Gioberti to Pietro Santarosa, March 16, 1847.)

And Cavour, but a little while before Garibaldi's descent on Naples, was proposing an alliance between Victor Emanuel and the Bourbon, with a central kingdom of Italy for the cousin of Louis Napoleon, under whose auspicious shadow the worthy Triumvirate might have hope of life.

della Dieta Italiana). Ten thousand Romans and seven thousand Tuscans were promptly enrolled, waiting only to be led to action. Even at Naples the King was dragged into the current, and obliged so early as the 26th of March to open the lists for Neapolitan volunteers.[1] For Italy! Never word nor sign of care for the paternal princely wishes or the interests of their Highnesses. *Abbiamo una Patria! abbiamo una Patria! Potremo operare per essa! Liberi tutti, parleranno tutti.* It was for Italy, for independence first, ridding themselves of the foreigner, and then—*A causa vinta, la nazione deciderà!* After the triumph, when all are free, the Nation will decide.

"If in the midst of the barricades of March the Republican banner had been raised, placed there by the hands of the people; if the men who directed the insurrection, assuming a grand revolutionary initiative, had made themselves the interpreters of the thought that quickened in the heart of the multitude ; the independence of Italy had been won.

."The succours refused by the Federal Government of Switzerland to the King were proffered by the Cantons to the Republican insurrection. The French Government, much mistrusting then the intentions of Charles Albert and uncertain of the way he might go, would not have been able to withhold itself from

[1] Correspondence from Rome, Naples, &c., published by order of the House of Commons.

popular enthusiasm and the necessity of a Republican policy. And in Italy itself, without a thought of foreign help, the unanimity of forces and hate against Austria was such as, under the conduct of men wise and of good-will, to assure an easy and decisive victory. Perhaps the dread of that fatal name, and the impossibility of withstanding the impetus of an Italian crusade, would have driven some of our princes on the road of dissension and provoked then the flight which came afterwards : a new pledge of safety for us, seeing that we should no longer have had traitors in our camp. But perhaps also the times were altogether unripe for Italian unity, as important as independence, since independence without unity could not stand.

". . . However the banner was not raised. The people and the monarchy stood united in face of the foreigner on the Lombard territory : the people had accepted the Governmental programme of political neutrality ; and the Republicans had decided to renounce all political initiative, to wait patiently for the will of the people to manifest itself, the war successful, and to devote all their powers to the conquest of independence.

". . . We had no faith in Charles Albert or his counselors. But Charles Albert was in Lombardy and commanded the enterprise, which before all things we had at heart. We could not hinder that fact : we had then to help in order that the fact might not lose its meaning. Behind the King stood an army, Italian and brave ; and behind the army a people, the Piedmontese, slow-natured perhaps, but virile and tenacious, a people effaced in the capital by a corrupt aristocracy, but alive and virginal in the provinces, and the depositary of a great part of the destinies of Italy. Army and people were our brothers ; and to accuse us, as some have done, of an anti-Piedmontese propaganda, was a foolish and ridiculous calumny.

". . . The conduct of the Republicans was simple and frank."

Their very loyalty played into the royal hands. Their apparent acceptance of the King's promises led the people to repose their trust yet more : trust that was only abused. The army would do all for them : so they left it to the army. The King was careful also that they should not trouble him with their help. While Mazzini was urgent for the Government to avail itself, especially in the Alps, of the services of the Republican volunteers, the Government, under royal instigation, was ridding itself of them. They were left without arms, without clothes, without money, forbidden to provide for themselves, hindered from action, and at last recalled and dissolved. When Mazzini asked for the recall of the exiles, officers in Greece, Spain, and elsewhere, they "did not know where to find them." At length he obtained leave to find them himself, with power to send for them on the authorization of the King's secretary, Correnti. When they arrived, the minister, Collegno, refused to employ them. Garibaldi, then returning from Monte-Video, not without reputation as a daring leader, was received coldly and with scorn, and sent on to Turin to see how and if the Minister of War could make use of him. Meanwhile the royal army, not heeding the Alps, was kept idly within the fortresses, giving the Austrians time to recover, to be revictualed, reinforced. The Treaties of Vienna barred the King's advance into the Tyrol; and the defence of Venice was prevented partly by secret influence of foreign governments for fear the Piedmontese should carry the quarrel too far, partly by the avowed hatred of its Republican flag. The Italian princes made their jealousy of the King's ambition a pretext, not without some reason, for withdrawing from the cause. The Pope forbad the Romans to pass the Po. Cardinal Soglia corresponded in cipher with the Austrians. Monsignor Corboli-Bussi was sent by his Holiness to the camp of Charles Albert to exhort him not to be true to Italy.[1] Sometimes the Provisional Government appeared to open its eyes to the situation and turned toward the Republicans; then a secret message from the King sufficed to destroy its better intentions. One sample, given by Mazzini, may be sufficient proof.

"The news of the fall of Udine had struck men's souls with terror. I was summoned at midnight to the Government, and found also convoked a few

[1] So Sir S. Hamilton, writing from Florence, April 14, informs Lord Palmerston.

other influential Republicans. It was necessary, said the members of the Government, to rouse the country, to put forth supreme efforts, to call upon it to save itself by its own forces; and they asked us to tell them how. I wrote on a scrap of paper a few of the things which I thought calculated to reach the end, but declaring that they would be utterly inefficacious if the Government assumed the direction. 'Your Government,' I told them, 'is discredited, and deservedly. Your Government hitherto has done everything to deaden enthusiasm, and to create a fatal confidence. And *you* cannot all at once rise up as preachers of a crusade, of a war of the people, without spreading among the multitude the fatal cry of treason. For new things, new men. I do not ask from you demissions which to-day would seem desertions. Choose three men, monarchical or republican matters not, who have will and knowledge, and who are if not loved not despised by the people. Commit to them, under pretence of too much business or for any other reason, all care, all authority as regards the war. Let the acts I propose emanate from them to-morrow! We will serry ourselves around them, and go bail for them with the people.' Among the things which we proposed was the levy of the whole of the five classes, while the Government thought the levy of the first three sufficient, and that deferred to the end of August, that the peasants might peaceably get in their harvest. And they replied with the blasphemy that the peasants were

Austrian at heart and in tendency: the poor peasants of the first two classes tumultuously indignant against the surgeons whenever they pronounced any of them unfit for service. I insisted that at least they should make a call for volunteers, and I guaranteed, sure that the example would be followed in every city, to form a legion of a thousand in Milan, provided I was allowed to put up a placard and subscribe my own name as the first. I parted from them applauded and with the promise of assent.

"Two days later the permission for the enrolment of volunteers was revoked. And as for the War Committee, it was transformed into a committee for the defence of Venice, then into a commission for aid to Venice, composed of members of the Government; and finally came to nought. The acting secretary of Charles Albert, Castagnetto, had said— 'It did not please the King to find himself with an army of enemies on his back.'"

So passed the first period of the war. In the second the Moderates, foreseeing defeat and now only looking for the gain of a precedent for future opportunities, broke the pact of political neutrality which they accused the Republicans of breaking, and hastened by decree of the 12th of May the vote for fusion with Piedmont. Then, then only, Mazzini publicly protested, for the sake, not of Republicanism, but of Italian unity, against a scheme which tended only to the aggrandisement of Piedmont at the expense of the rest of the Peninsula. The Moderates, enraged at his protest, very moderate as in truth it was, burned it in Genoa as if it had been a public outrage. Then he began the publication of his *Italy of the People:* still not for Republicanism, but only for the Italian war. Nevertheless he and his have been and are to this day accused of having sown dissension to the hindrance of the war, and of contenting themselves with words instead of deeds. The truth is absolutely contrary. The Republicans were the first in the fight, the last to discuss. It was the Republicans who fought on the barricades at Milan while the Moderates were conspiring at Turin. Republicans were the most of those who pursued the Austrians from Milan and drove them to the Tyrol while the Provisional Government was considering how to capitulate; Republicans the men who fought at Treviso, who on the 23rd of May at Vicenza for eighteen hours withstood the shock of 18,000 Austrians and forty cannon; Republicans the students who, forming themselves into a corps, begged to be led against the enemy; Republicans the flower of the Tuscan youth who perished in the redoubts of Montanara and Courtatone, 5000 opposed to 16,000 Austrians, the "Sword of Italy" not stirring to their aid; Republicans who at the end of May formed the "Lombard Battalion," and marched to the defence of Venice betrayed and abandoned by the King. Impartial history will say this, nor forget the then Republican founder of the "Democratic Society," Joseph Sirtori, of later military renown during the war of Venice. It will tell also of Maestri of the Committee of Defence in Milan at the end of the war; of Garibaldi and Medici, the last to abandon the field, careless of royal armistices or treaties. History will say also that every proposition emanating from the Republican, the Mazzinian party, had the one single object of the maintenance of the war; that every demonstration even after the 12th of May was but to encourage the timid and inert Provisional Government. But one demonstration had a party character, that of May 29th, the work of one Urbino, a man outside the Republican party and unconnected with Mazzini. History, caring only for the truth, will vindicate the Republican character of those days. Then such accusations served as excuses for political manœuvres meant to blind the eyes of the uninformed and bring about the cession of Lombardy to the Sardinian State. The aim was reached. On the 8th of June the vote was published; on the 13th, two days after the fall of Vicenza, a deputation, with Casati the President of the Provisional Government at its head, took its way to the camp of Charles Albert to present him with the wishes of his Lombard people. The object of his war was obtained, the fear of the Republic removed; now might the "Sword of Italy" be sheathed in peace, however infamous. Nothing remained but the fulfilment of his arrangements with "the enemy." On the 6th of August, two royal commissioners, Colli and Cibrario, entered Venice to take possession in the name of Charles Albert: the bases of the cession to Austria being already signed.

So soon as the decree of the 12th of May showed the mind of Charles Albert, the King of Naples recalled his troops. No longer need to fear either the Republic or a king of Italy. The Pope was equally reassured. After all it was only a Savoyard game; neither the rest of Italy nor the Powers of Europe need be troubled. The French army (the Minister Pareto had haughtily said on the 12th of May in the Parliament of Turin) "will not enter Italy unless called in by us, and as we shall not call it in, it will not enter." French sympathies in those days were with the Republicans : therefore any possible help was to be opposed. At the same time they sought to bribe the French Government so that when the time came it might agree to a Kingdom of the North. The bribe held out by the royal and moderate patriots was the cession of Savoy. "I have the certainty of this," says Mazzini, then (1849), holding in his hands a map of the future kingdom, made at the time in Turin for the secret use of the Sardinian agents, from which Savoy had been left out. "Thanks to this conditional bargain, Lamartine gave the lie to his earlier Republican aspirations; and while the Secretary for Foreign Affairs, Bastide, was declaring to me, and to whoever cared to listen, that France was inexorably hostile to the ambitious measures of Charles Albert, the French envoy at Turin, M. Bixio, perorated incessantly for the fusion; and sent his secretary to me at Milan to attempt to convince me."

The King had made the same attempt. While yet uneasy as to the result of the Lombard voting, Castagneto, the King's secretary, approached Mazzini through a friend with the proposal that he, Mazzini, should make himself the patron of the monarchical plan of fusion, allow himself to be made use of to draw the Republicans into the royal party; and that in exchange he should have whatever democratic influence he might wish in the articles of the Constitution to be given, speech with the King, &c. Mazzini's answer stood on the old basis, independence of the foreigner, and unity, without which "independence" would be a worthless lie. As to the Republic, "indifferent to what concerned ourselves individually and sure of the future of our country, we had no need to be intolerant. To whoever then would have assured me of the independence and a willing action toward the unity of Italy I would have sacrificed, not my faith, that was impossible, but all active labour for the speedier triumph of that faith. For me solitude, and the faculty, of which none could deprive me, of writing and printing when I might whatever ideas I believed useful to my country was enough; and for the sake of independence the Republican party had not waited for the invitations of a king to keep silence concerning the Republic. But the question then was altogether of war." The policy of federation, of a divided Kingdom of the North, was fatal; it had already extinguished popular enthusiasm, and the chances of the war had become menacing. Nothing but a really national war could regain the lost ground: and for this who was to be the leader? Could the Savoyard lay aside his poorer ambition, forget his petty principality, and dare to be truly the Sword of his country? For that he must break with all the Governments, and trust to the revolutionary elements in Italy. For that he must so devote himself that the Republicans might give to his influence all the hold they had upon the nation without fear of his turning upon them whenever he chose to draw back, with the reproach that they too could compromise upon occasion. In such a spirit Mazzini met the royal proposal. Asked what guarantees he required, he replied—" Let him only sign some lines declaring his intentions." In the *Italia del Popolo* he afterwards stated the purport if not the precise text of the terms he wrote for the King's subscription.

"I feel that the times are ripe for the unity of the country. I understand, Italians! the trouble that oppresses your soul. Up; arise! I go before you. I give as pledge of my faith the spectacle yet unknown to the world of a king the priest of a new epoch, the armed apostle of the people's idea, the builder of the temple of the nation. I rend in the name of God and of Italy the old treaties which kept you dismembered and which have been washed out with your blood. I call upon you to overthrow the barriers which until now have divided you, and to gather yourselves together in legions as freemen and brothers around me, your leader, ready to conquer or fall with you."

Castagneto answered: there was nothing to be done in that direction. Of course not.

What remained? The defeat of the royal army; the surrender of Milan; the return of the defeated King with all his booty, a promise (could it be called so) of some day adding Lombardy to his kingdom. As long as possible false bulletins kept the Milanese in ignorance of the reverses to the Sardinian troops; then came the reaction, Milan prepared for its own defence from the advancing Austrians. Even that was not allowed. The King would make a stand there. A king at bay, and the heroes of the five days! and then—— That came not in the royal programme. Through Mazzini's efforts a Committee of Defence was formed on the 28th of July; on the 3rd of August a royal commissioner, General Olivieri, appeared in the King's name to supersede the Committee. On the 4th, Charles Albert entered, made solemn oath to defend, etc.; and on the 5th announced that the capitulation of the city was an accomplished fact. He had returned only to surrender it to the Austrians.[1]

---

[1] How at this news the people were seized with fury, and the King threatened, the scenes at the Greppi palace, the new words of promise spoken and written by Charles Albert for the moment moved at the spectacle of a people ready to combat to the death, his secret flight, accompanied by details which render the monarchy for ever infamous: all this can be found in the narrative of the Committee of Defence, and in a terrible chapter of Cattaneo's Memoirs, entitled *La Consegna.*

Prepared to defend the city to the last, when the royal interference nullified even that last hope, Mazzini left Milan. He left for Bergamo, where Medici and Garibaldi still held some force. And here we may note an incident throwing other light on the character of the man who, his calumniators were fond of saying, sent others into danger, and always hid himself. It may be given in General Medici's own words.[1]

[1] Jacobo Medici served first in Spain. Going afterwards to South America, he fought in Monte-Video with Garibaldi till recalled with him to Italy by the prospects of the Italian war. He was one of the few brave Republicans who with Garibaldi after the capitulation of Milan and the armistice of Salasco prolonged the war for a month, maintaining an unequal struggle against the Austrian army. We shall hear of him again at Rome and in Sicily.

"After the defeat at Custoza, in consequence of which Charles Albert had to fall back upon Milan, General Garibaldi, then at Bergamo with a division of about 4000 Lombard Republican volunteers, believing that the King of Piedmont, who was yet at the head of an army of 40,000 men, would defend to the utmost, as he had promised, the capital of Lombardy, conceived the audacious project of pushing on ahead and marching towards Milan. His object was to harass the left flank of the Austrians in pursuit of the Piedmontese army, and so to come in aid of any future operations that the resistance of the King in Milan might bring about.

"So, on the morning of the 3rd of August, 1848, Garibaldi with his division about to quit Bergamo to reach Monza by a forced march, we saw appear among us, his musket on his shoulder, Mazzini, who asked to join us simply as a private in the legion I commanded, and which was to form the vanguard of Garibaldi's division. A general shout saluted the great Italian, and the legion unanimously confided to him its flag, which bore on it the words—God and the People.

The miserable history of the Sardine-Lombard Moderates ended not with the surrender of Milan.

"Hardly was Mazzini's arrival known in Bergamo, when the population hurried to see him. They crowded round him begging him to speak. His speech must remain in the memory of those who heard him. He recommended them to raise barricades, and in case of attack defend the town while we marched on Milan; and whatever happened always to love Italy, and never to despair of her salvation. His words were received with enthusiasm, and the column set off amidst marks of the liveliest sympathy.

"The march was very fatiguing. The rain fell in torrents; we were drenched to our very bones. Although habituated to a life of study and little fitted for the violent exertion of a forced march, especially in such weather, his serenity and confidence never weakened for an instant, and despite our advice, for we feared for his health, he would neither stop nor quit the column. It even happened that seeing one of our young volunteers dressed only in linen, and consequently with no defence against the rain and the sudden lowering of the temperature, he forced him to accept his own cloak.

"Arrived at Monza we learned the fatal news of the capitulation of Milan, and that a numerous body of Austrian cavalry had been sent against us, and was already at the gates of Monza on the other side.

"Garibaldi, much inferior in force, not willing to expose his little corps to complete and useless destruction, gave order to turn back upon Como, and placed me with my column as rearguard to cover the retreat.

"For the young volunteers who only asked to fight, the order for retreat was a signal of discouragement; so in the beginning it was made in some disorder. Happily it did not happen so with my column. From Monza to Como that column, always pursued by the enemy, threatened every instant to be crushed by very superior forces, never wavered, remained united and compact, showing itself always ready to repulse attacks, and by its bold front and its good order taught the enemy to respect it during the whole passage.

"In this march, full of danger and of difficulty, in the midst of continual alarms, the strength of soul, the intrepidity, the

Useless, they could be mischievous; unable to do, they strove to undo, labouring everywhere for dissolution of all that was conscientious and enthusiastic in the nation. Turn we from them, and from the disasters of the royal war, to the brief triumph and lasting glory of heroic Rome!

decision, which Mazzini possesses in so high a degree, and of which he later gave such proofs at Rome, were never belied, and called forth the admiration of our bravest. His presence, his words, the example of his courage, animated our young soldiers with such enthusiasm, who else were proud to share danger with him, that they were ready to perish to the last man, in defence of the faith of which he had been the apostle and was so ready to become the martyr; and contributed much to maintain that order and resolute bearing which saved the rest of the division.

"These few details are too honourable to the character of Mazzini to be allowed to remain unknown. His conduct has been, for us who witnessed it, a proof that to the grand qualities of the citizen, Mazzini joins the courage and intrepidity of the soldier."

ROME.

From Como, Mazzini crossed the Alps to Lugano, in the Italian Canton of Tessin, walking forty miles in one night, accompanied by only two or three friends, one of them the young artist Scipione Pistrucci, before spoken of. In Lugano he rested, still seeking to influence, and watching the course of events until the hope of new action in Tuscany called him to Florence. Passing through France (Lombardy of course closed to him), he reached Leghorn on the 8th of February, 1849, at the moment when the Government received news of the flight of the Grand Duke on the previous day. The *Livornese Courier* of the 9th describes the welcome he received. "This morning the *Hellespont* brought us Joseph Mazzini, the man hated by all the Governments of Italy because he has ever remained pure and uncontaminated, and has never bent before the Liberals of mere profession and opportunity. The church-bells rang the announcement of his arrival, and the people hastened out upon the road on which he would have to pass; banners waved; the windows were hung with tapestry; a guard of honour with the minister

Guerazzi waited him in front of the house where he was expected."

He had already been elected a deputy to the Constituent Assembly in Rome deprived of its Papal Government by the flight of the "Reforming Pope," Pio Nono; and thither, after words of counsel to the Tuscans to join their efforts to those of the Romans, he proceeded. On the 9th of February, the downfall of the Pope's temporal power and the inauguration of the Roman Republic was proclaimed by the almost unanimous vote[1] of the Assembly, elected by universal suffrage, freely and spontaneously, without agitation, without corruption, without threats or influence of any kind, without false counting. And not in haste. Throughout the Roman States was not a single protestation in favour of the Pope. The old municipalities elected during the papal rule sent in their adhesion on the 11th of March; and later, on the eve of the French invasion, when all the Roman power was concentred in Rome, when only moral influence upheld the Government in the provinces, the newly-elected municipalities of Bologna, Ancona, Perugia, Civita-Vecchia, Ferrara, Ascoli, Casena, Fano, Faenza, Forli, Foligno, Macerata, Narni, Orvieto, Pesaro, Ravenna, Rieti, Spoleto, Terni, Urbino, Viterbo, &c., two hundred and sixty-three in all,

[1] Of one hundred and forty-four members present (the whole number was one hundred and fifty, and Mazzini and Garibaldi were absent), only eleven opposed the proclamation of the Republic, as inopportune; only five voted against the abolition of the temporal power of the Pope.

H

sent addresses declaring in the name of the populations that the abolition of the temporal power of the Pope and the establishment of the Republic were vital conditions of the State.

And, for once to address those in whose minds the Republic means only anarchy, under what circumstances was the Republic inaugurated in Rome? The Pope had fled from Rome on the 4th of November, 1848,[1] leaving the National Assembly to govern as it best could. The Assembly had sent deputations begging him to return. He refused. Instead he named a Commission to govern for him. The Com-

---

[1] After the assassination of the papal minister Rossi (probably by some pious fanatic, the Jesuits having violently denounced him for his supposed liberalism; but all parties equally disliked him), Pio Nono formed a reactionary Ministry, which caused a popular commotion before the Quirinal. A shot accidentally fired by one of the Swiss Guards was the signal for a fight, during which the Pope's secretary, looking from a window, was killed. Thereupon the Pope appointed a new Liberal Ministry, to control the people for the moment, and disguising himself as a lady's footman fled to the King of Naples at Gaeta, leaving only a brief note to his chamberlain, the Marquis Sacchetti: "I depart. Order the Minister to take charge of the properties in the apostolic palace" (*gli effeti nel palazzo apostolico*).

Two entirely different characters have been drawn of Pio Nono, and both by persons claiming knowledge of him and of the events of those years. On one side it is said that he was a man of liberal intent, only driven from the reforming path he had traced out for himself by the immoderate conduct of his Romans; on the other, it is distinctly said that from the first his assuming the credit of a personal initiative was only a policy, and that he never granted a single reform accept under constraint of fear, and for the superseding of popular action. In one case he would be a reformer; in neither a reformer of any worth.

mission refused. Rome was absolutely without a government. The Assembly appointed a Provisional Government, which for two months managed to exist. Then, yielding to the plainly expressed wishes of the people, it appealed to the suffrages of the States to establish a Constituent Assembly : 343,000 adult males out of a total population of 2,800,000 souls elected that Assembly, which met on the 6th of February, and on the 9th, after an uninterrupted sitting of fifteen hours, decreed the abolition of the Pope's temporal power, and declared the States of the Church a free and independent Republic. On the 10th, the Assembly appointed MM. Armellini and Montecchi (Romans) and Saliceti (Neapolitan) as Executive Committee.

Mazzini took his seat in the Assembly. His influence was immediate. On the 16th, he proposed a Committee of ' War, to organize the army. His friend Pisacane was placed upon it. The army was concentrated upon Rome, and its force raised from 16,000 to 45,000 men. The Republic had not been recognized by Piedmont. Indeed the Piedmontese Minister, Gioberti, had endeavoured to fetch back the Pope under Piedmontese protection.[1] No less the Roman Government prepared to make common cause with Piedmont against the Austrians. But four days sufficed for that second Piedmontese campaign. Begun on the 20th of March, it ended ignominiously

[1] Letter of Gioberti to Muzzarelli, President of Roman Ministry, January 28.

at Novara on the 24th. On the news of Charles Albert's defeat, the Roman Assembly replaced their Executive Committee by a Triumvirate, Mazzini, Aurelio Saffi (Minister of the Interior under the Committee), and Armellini: Armellini, a lawyer, representing the middle classes,—Saffi, a Roman noble, no less true and staunch Republican,—and Mazzini, the representative of the people.

On the 25th of April, the French were at Civita-Vecchia; and, with less than a month to collect an army, to provide funds, arms, and artillery, the Triumvirate was prepared to meet them, the Roman Republic to resist the "Republicans" of France.

Let Mazzini in his own words explain his policy and the real object of all that heroism which the worshipers of success are apt to consider waste, though History sometimes may reverse their judgments.

"To the many evident reasons which bade us fight was added for me another intimately bound up with my whole life—the foundation of national unity. In Rome was the natural centre of that unity, and toward that centre it was necessary to attract the regards and the reverence of Italians. Italians had almost lost their religious feeling for Rome: they were beginning to call it a tomb, and such it seemed. The seat of a form of belief, spent and only kept up by hypocrisy and persecution, inhabited by a shopkeeping class (*borghesia*), living in some measure on the pomps of worship and the corruption of the higher clergy, and by a people, else noble and manly, but perforce ignorant and apparently devoted to the Pope, Rome had come to be regarded by some with aversion, by others with contemptuous indifference. A few individual acts excepted, nothing there had revealed the ferment of liberty which had so often stirred the Romagna and the Marches. There was need to redeem her and place her again on high, so that Italians might learn again to regard her as in the time of a common country; there was need that all should understand the potency of immortality pulsing under the ruins of two world-epochs. And I felt that potency, that palpitation of the immense eternal life of Rome through the artificial surface with which as with a shroud priests and courtiers had covered the mighty sleeper. I had faith in her. I remember that when it was a question whether we should defend ourselves or not, the officers of the National Guard, convoked and interrogated by me, declared, deploring, that nearly all the Guard would in no case aid in the defence. It seemed to me that I understood the people better than they; and I ordered that the battalions should next morning defile before the Palace of the Assembly, that the question might be put to the soldiers. The universal shout of War that rose from their ranks irrevocably overwhelmed the timid doubts of their leaders.

"The defence was then decided upon, by the Assembly and the people of Rome, from a generous impulse and from reverence for the honour of Italy; by me as a logical consequence of a long-matured design. Strategically the war ought to have been conducted outside of Rome, on the flank of the enemy's line of operations. But victory, unless help came to us from elsewhere, was impossible either within or without. Doomed to fall, it was our duty, thinking of the Future, to proffer our *Morituri te salutant* to Italy from Rome.

"Nevertheless, and though foreseeing the inevitable defeat, we could not without betraying our trust be careless of the only possible way of safety, a change in the affairs of France. The invasion was the idea of Louis Napoleon, who, meditating tyranny, desired on the one hand to accustom the soldiery to fight against the Republic elsewhere; on the other hand, to prepare for the suffrages of the Catholic clergy and that portion of the French people, notably in the provinces, which followed their inspirations. The French Assembly, uncertain and divided as it was, dissented from every proposition deliberately adverse to us; had only approved the intervention, deceived as to our condition and the secret end of the expedition. The accomplices of Louis Napoleon asserted that an Austro-Neapolitan invasion for the restoration of papal absolutism was imminent, and declared that the population of the Roman States was inimical to the Republican system, and only kept down by terror exercised by the audacious few. Rome therefore, powerless to resist, would in a few days, the arms of France not interposing, become the prey of Austria. To prove to France the absence in Rome of all terror, the unanimous will of our populations, the possibility of our resisting either Austrian or Neapolitan intervention; to compel Louis Napoleon to unmask his true designs; to fight, separating in our acts the French nation from the President; to achieve at least so much as a proof of our determination, but without abusing our victory, without irritating the pride and susceptible feelings of the French; to supply in such manner an opportunity to the members of the Mountain and our friends in the Assembly for a beginning of resistance to Louis Napoleon: this was our duty, and we were not unfaithful to it. For this orders were sent to Civita-Vecchia, disobeyed by those who gave belief to the lying promises of General Oudinot, to resist, whatever might be his proposals, if only for hours, to prove the unanimous desire of resistance; for this the energy of our declarations to the envoys of the French camp, the urgent preparations and the battle; for this the requests to the municipalities, gathering from all, for renewed expressions of adhesion to the Republican Government; for this the return of the French made prisoners on the day of the 30th of April, the order sent on that day to Garibaldi to desist from pursuing the routed French; and for this generally the attitude assumed and maintained by us during the siege, and which I summed up in saying that Rome was not at war with France, but only in a position of simple defence. That order to Garibaldi was laid to me as an error by those who saw only the isolated fact.

But of what importance in comparison with the idea we sought to impress were some hundred more Frenchmen prisoners or dead?

"And this plan would have succeeded if Louis Napoleon had not violated every tradition of loyalty by entrusting unlimited powers for peace to the envoy Lesseps and nullifying them at the same time by secret instructions to General Oudinot. The 7th of May, moved by our action and our language, the French Assembly solemnly called upon the Executive to adopt without delay such measures as might be necessary to prevent the Roman expedition from being diverted from its true aim, and charged Lesseps to come to an understanding with us. Toward the end of May, between us and the French plenipotentiary an agreement had been reached (*si firmava un patto*) which declared :—' The support of France is secured to the populations of the Roman State: they will regard the French army as a friendly army which has hastened to the defence of their territory. In accord with the Roman Government, and without in the least way (*menomamente*) interfering in the administration of the country, the French army will take such quarters outside (*esteriori*) as may be convenient as much for the defence of the country as for the health of the troops.' By this the war was converted into an alliance; the French army became our reserve against any foreign invasion; Rome remained sacred and inviolable to friends and enemies : Republican diplomacy obtained a victory as splendid as that of the

Republican army in April;[1] we should have been free to meet the Austrians, and we should have defeated them. Every one knows how Oudinot refused to assent to the treaty and decided to break the truce. He had Louis Napoleon's secret instructions directly contrary to those given by him to Lesseps."

Such was Mazzini's programme. He was faithful to it to the end. The Triumvirate was appointed on the 29th of March, and Oudinot landed on the 25th of April. In this brief period, and with the difficulties in the way of prompt action when an Assembly has first to deliberate, he provided for everything. His work, in the words of an eye-witness, was wonderful; "arousing the popular spirit, provisioning the city, tracing (himself) the lines of defence, concentrating the troops scattered through the provinces in two camps, at Bologna and Terni, that he might hold them ready for either Austria or Naples;" every- where present, everywhere active and obeyed, fore- casting everything. The "dreamer," as he has been called, the "conspirator who always hid himself and left the difficulties and the dangers to others," became at once not only the man of action, but the states- man and wise as brave ruler amidst difficulties and dangers which appalled the statesmen and the warriors since credited with the salvation of Italy.

On the 30th of April, Oudinot, who had crept unmolested into Civita-Vecchia under cover of a lie,

[1] On the 30th, when the French were repulsed from the walls of Rome, and routed by Garibaldi.

was under the walls of Rome, not looking for any serious resistance against a veteran army of 10,000 men well supplied with artillery. In Rome they mustered but 8,100 all told, the most citizens who had never been under fire. So assured were the French that they had only to show themselves to be admitted, that the officers were all in full dress, and the rendezvous for the three columns diverging from the high road from Civita-Vecchia, and advancing on three roads, was appointed within the city. They reckoned without their host. Finding Rome fortified, they brought up cannon to make a breach, and for a moment drove in the Roman outposts. Then with less than 2000 men,[1] Garibaldi came out and charged them, drove them back, and threatening them in the rear, broke up the invading force, which retreated in disorder. This was the prompt answer to the calumnies against Rome and her Triumvir, this defeat of picked troops in the open field, with a loss to the French of nearly a thousand men, killed, wounded, and prisoners, Oudinot having to ask for a suspension of hostilities. He immediately retired to Castel-di-Guido; but, in pursuance of Mazzini's policy, was allowed to return and encamp within two miles of Rome pending the negotiations with Lesseps: the French prisoners sent back, both sides meanwhile running parallels and planting batteries.

In the provinces a Spanish expedition of 4000

[1] Eight hundred of his legion, 400 students, 400 other Romans, and the rest foreigners.

men had come to support the Head of Catholicism; the Austrians brought up 28,000 men; Bomba was advancing from Naples with 25,000. The Romans had their hands full. On the 16th of May, at midnight, Garibaldi and Galletti under command of Roselli, now chief, leaving scarcely 1000 men in Rome, sallied forth to attack the Neapolitan. Reinforced by the Bolognese garrison, with 10,000 infantry, three squadrons of cavalry, and twelve guns, they struck the enemy between Palestrina and Velletri, defeated, and pursued him across the frontier, returning to Rome on the 2nd of June. Meanwhile Bologna with only 2,200 men and four poor cannon had to surrender to the Austrians, but not till after a fierce bombardment during eight days. Ancona surrendered after a yet more protracted struggle. By the 1st of June Rome was invested by a French army, 35,000 strong, with 36 field guns, and a siege train of 40 pieces, with skilful artillery officers and engineers. To meet this force the Romans counted less than 16,000 men, of whom about 350 were foreigners, Poles, Swiss, English; perhaps not more than 13,000 effective men, their artillery also as numerically inferior to the French. The old walls of Rome, about fifteen miles in circuit, built partly of volcanic material, partly more modern and more easily penetrable, would have needed 200 guns and some 50,000 men to hold them with certainty of success. Under these circumstances an armistice was demanded, mainly however that meanwhile they might have time to deal with the advancing Austrians. On Saturday the 2nd of June Oudinot wrote—" To afford French residents the opportunity of leaving the city and on demand of the French Minister I agree not to attack Rome before Monday morning, June 4th." Without notice, in the night of that same day (at two a.m. of Sunday, June 3rd) he made his dastardly attack, carrying the weakest and most undefended places.

The treacherous surprise was so great that it was only known in Rome at daybreak. Garibaldi's force had just returned from the pursuit of the Neapolitans by a forced march, and, wearied and hungry, at once assailed Oudinot. The Villa Corsini was retaken four times by the Romans, who had to climb a glacis exposed to a murderous enfilading fire from the Villa and walls on either flank. In one of these assaults, Masina, who commanded the Lancers, actually entered the Villa on horseback. Disabled in one arm he grasped his sword with the other and rode up to the second floor, where he was killed, his men however clearing out the French, throwing them from the windows. Henry Dandolo, who led an attack with only twenty men, was killed; Paolo Ramorino also; Nino Bixio was wounded. Medici with his Lombards (not one hundred men), retreating step by step to the Vascello (a little villa some four hundred yards from the Villa Corsini and eight hundred from the Villa Pamphili, which last was held by the French), kept possession till the French were in the breaches. Even to this day stand the ruins of the Vascello, battered and crumbled by the French cannon. On that day the Roman loss was 600 men.

Oudinot withdrew, not caring further to risk the taking of Rome by assault; and sat down to a regular siege, tracing his first parallels between his head-quarters in the Villa Pamphili and the Porta San Pancrazio, on the very threshold of Rome. Meanwhile Mazzini redoubled his efforts, "performing prodigies surely never yet outdone, considering the little means available" (so writes to me an engineer and military officer). Church-bells had to be cast into cannon, every old musket was in requisition, their short supply of powder had to be husbanded. Recollect that the Roman walls were of little use "even against 9-pound field guns." Oudinot gradually sapped up to within three hundred yards of the San Pancrazio gate, keeping up a continuous breaching fire. But the Romans hindered his work by repeated sorties, of so desperate a character that they were generally hand-to-hand. Time after time the trenching batteries were dismounted. By the 20th, however, they were able to open fire, and under their cover the French stormed the walls and entered Rome.

Yet Rome was not taken. Mazzini, retreating, took his last stand behind the foundations of the old Aurelian wall, which inside the walls proper extended angularly for a mile or more in a line from the San Pancrazio gate to the Portese. Over these foundations a horseman could easily have ridden; they were but a poor defence against siege guns. From here the Romans attacked the French so furiously that after eleven hours of unintermitted fighting the French had to intrench themselves with earthworks *inside the captured bastions*, almost without parallel in the history of war. This inner line of defence resisted for eight days longer, and was at last only carried by the bayonet by the overwhelming numbers of the French, in the morning of the 30th, when the Swiss artillery-men to a man were killed at their guns. It was here that the heroic Luciano Manara was killed, leading on, though wounded, his nineteen men against a position held by 300 French.

Only a few hours before this last assault on the inner line of the Romans, Medici with the remains of his 100 men abandoned the Villa Pamphili, disputing the ground foot by foot. So after two months' resistance, after twenty-seven days of open trenching against it, when but 100 pounds of grape-shot and a few charges for 18-pounders were left in the Roman arsenals, the French invaders overcame, and, yet not entering, called themselves masters of Rome. The loss of the Romans was between 3000 and 4000 men, with 200 officers, Garibaldi's legion losing 460 and the Artillery one-third of their number.

Inside Rome and throughout the Roman States under the Triumvirate, what was the state of things which might excuse the interference of the modern Brennus and his civilized and Catholic barbarians? For the good order maintained one brief sentence may suffice. When Garibaldi had taken the army against the Neapolitans, the city remained almost without defence, and during one whole day, May 16th, there was not a guard at the Government Palace, nor a single soldier to keep order anywhere, the city intrusted absolutely to the good-will of the people. In Rome during the Republic no act of violence was committed beyond in the first days the burning of some state carriages and the destruction of instruments of torture in a convent belonging to the Inquisition. Two priests in the time of the siege, caught making signals to the French, were tried by court-martial and shot; and as the French were entering the city three others who went to meet them with white flags were killed by the enraged people. In the provinces, only in Ancona was there any disorder. There some sanfedisti (brigands hired by the priestly party) were assassinated or assassinated others; and the Triumvirate promptly declared the city in a state of siege, and dispatched a special commissioner (Felice Orsini) to disarm the population, and take such extraordinary measures as might be necessary to restore order. The action was as successful as prompt. This was after the landing of Oudinot.

For the rest, the Official Acts[1] of the Triumvi-

[1] *Actes Officiels de la République Romaine depuis le* 9 *Fevrier jusqu'au* 2 *Juillet,* 1849 : collected from the Roman *Monitor,* and reprinted at Paris in 1849. Containing also the whole corre-

rate tell their own story: the very headings may suffice.

Requisition of arms from private citizens for those soldiers already organized who may be without. The National Guard placed at the disposal of the Minister of War. The Palace of the Holy Office (the Inquisition) appropriated as a lodging for the poor, and a commission appointed to regulate the same. The Canons of the Vatican fined for refusing to take part in the usual religious services. Decrees for a public loan and for the issue of money. Reduction of taxes on salt and tobacco, and abolition of the State monopoly in both. Organization of the army. Requisition of horses. Abolition of forced conventual vows. Dotation of the clergy. Church lands for the use of the poor. Protection for the French in Rome. Administration of ambulances. Decree for public prayers during the siege. Decree of indemnity for appropriations necessary in erecting barricades or for other siege operations, &c., &c., &c.

There is no going back from these authentic reports, the enduring records of a time in which ruler and people were worthy of each other: records which tell at once of a Government alive and responsive to all the hopes and wishes and wants of the governed, and of a people placing its full trust in the power which it had elected. Mazzini as Triumvir was everywhere

---

spondence with M. Lesseps, and with the two scoundrels, Oudinot and Courcelles (the successor of Lesseps). Lesseps may possibly have acted in good faith.

and everything: strategist, tactician, diplomat, engineer, commissary: living in the simplest fashion, dining at an ordinary restaurant for two francs a day (for the last days of the siege his food little more than bread and radishes with coffee); working by day and by night; sleeping at such intervals as he could snatch from almost incessant occupation, and from the continual thronging around him of the citizens and foreigners asking for advice or encouragement. Where can I speak with you? "Here," in the street, where he was to be found as often as in his cabinet. He had no thought of taking rest, accessible to all and at all times, exposing himself fearlessly wherever his presence was needed. One (perhaps more than one) English family will recollect how, to soothe their fears, he spared some moments to show them from the palace-top the city defences. His generous, generous as politic, forbearance toward the enemy, his calm decision with troublesome friends, were equally remarkable. When the French officers were released he moved them to tears: they were ready to throw themselves on his neck or at his feet, swearing eternal gratitude, which did not prevent them from re-entering Rome as "conquerors." Once a popular deputation had an audience of him to demand the removal of the Military Staff. He patiently heard them. From whom did they come? he asked. From the People. Well, he was the servant of the People. While they trusted him, well and good; when they ceased to trust him, they

I

could withdraw the authority with which they had invested him. But when they said the People, by how many were they deputed? Some hundreds. Some hundreds were not the People; but he was ready to hear even a few. Which of the members of the Staff would they have removed, and their reasons? The complainants did not know exactly which, were not clear as to the why; he reasoned with them, and they retired satisfied.

To return to the narrative of the siege. The outer lines forced, what was to be done? Garibaldi was for breaking down the bridges and behind the Tiber fighting on, disputing street by street. Mazzini also for resisting to the last. But he was the elect of the Assembly. It was for the Assembly to decide.

"When it was under discussion in the Assembly whether to welcome the French then moving on Rome or to combat them, I abstained from attending the sitting, that I might not exercise any influence on a decision which ought to be a collective and spontaneous expression. But the enemy's gauntlet once taken up by a people, and by a Republican people in the name of Right, the duel ought not to cease but from absolute exhaustion or with victory. Monarchies may capitulate, republics die: the first represent dynastic interests, wherefore they may help themselves with concessions and resort to cowardice for their safety; the second represent a faith, and ought to bear witness even to martyrdom. For this we had in advance filled Rome with barricades,

intending to the war on the walls to add the war of
the streets, and in the streets of Rome the fight
would have been tremendous. This was rendered
impossible by the French, who visibly were contenting themselves with mastering the city from the
heights they occupied and reducing it by famine.
But the idea of prolonging the struggle so long as
a man or a musket remained was so elementary an
idea in my mind that, despairing of further defence
in Rome, I proposed another action : to go out of the
city, to go forth with our little army and so many of
the armed population as would follow us, the Triumvirs
accompanied by the Ministers, and, if not by all, by a
numerous delegation of the Assembly, enough to give
to the movements of the army a legal authority and
prestige; to rapidly leave Rome far behind us, to
provision ourselves in the Aretino, to throw ourselves
between Bologna and Ancona on the Austrian line of
operations and seek by a victory to raise the Romagna.
This was my design. The French would then have
occupied Rome without vanquishing the Republic,
and under a perennial menace. They would not
have been able to follow us on the new ground without fighting for the benefit of Austria and unmasking
the infamy of their invasion before their own country
and Europe. It was the plan afterward attempted by
Garibaldi; but with only a few thousand men collected
from different corps, without artillery, without support
from the authority of Government, and under conditions which precluded every possibility of success.

"The 20th of June, the French now masters of the bastions and all the heights, I called a council of the military chiefs. Garibaldi replying that he could not quit the defence for a single instant, we therefore went to him. There I declared that the supreme hour of Rome having arrived, as it was urgent to decide what course should be adopted, the Government desired to gather the counsels of the heads of the army before communicating with the Assembly. I said there were three courses open to us : to capitulate, to resist until the city was in ruins, to go out from Rome transporting the war elsewhere. The first was unworthy of the Republic; the second useless, as the attitude of the French announced that they would not come down to fight against barricades and the people, but would look on, tormenting us from the hills with bombs and artillery until we were conquered by famine; the third was what I as an individual proposed. Opinions were diverse. Avezzana and the Roman officers were for remaining in Rome, obstinate in the defence. Roselli, Pisacane, Garibaldi, and some few others, accepted my proposal. Not one, and I record it to the honour of our little Republican army, put his name in the column on which I had written *Capitulation*. I dissolved the Council, and hastened to the Assembly.

"To that, sitting in Committee, the people not admitted, I repeated what I had said to the Council of War, and proposed the part which alone seemed to me worthy of Rome and of ourselves. The Assembly would not accept it. I shall not relate the particulars of that to me most sorrowful sitting. But I found the best friends I had among the members most averse to the plan. Some of them blamed me afterward, and with reason, for not having prepared their minds beforehand for such a decision; but the singularly tranquil and truly Roman energy shown until that moment in the Assembly had deluded me into believing that the proposition would have been hailed with applause.

"A plan proposed by Enrico Cernuschi prevailed, and it was decreed that Rome should cease from the defence.

"I had left the Assembly before this proposition was put to the vote. The decree was transmitted to the Triumvirate, with instructions for us to communicate it to the French General, and to treat with him as to the measures necessary for the protection of order and of persons in the conquered city. I refused to do it. I wrote to the Assembly that I had been elected Triumvir to defend, not to surrender, the Republic, and accompanied the same with some words in which I gave in my resignation. My two colleagues joined me in this.

"The 3rd of July, I placed in the hands of the Secretaries of the Assembly the following protest:— Citizens! you have by your decrees of 30th of June and 2nd of July, you, commissioned by the people to protect it and to defend it to the last extremity, ratified involuntarily the sacrifice of the Republic;

and I feel, with immense sorrow in my soul, the necessity of declaring this, that I may not stand before my conscience keeping silence, and that some document may tell our contemporaries that when you so decreed we did not all despair of the safety of the country and the might of our flag.

"You had from God and the People the double mandate, to resist so long as you had strength the overpoweringness of the foreigner, and to sanctify the principle visibly incarnate in the Assembly, proving to the world that no pact is possible between the just and the unjust, between eternal right and brute force, and that, though monarchies, founded upon the egoism of covetousness, may and ought to yield or capitulate, republics, founded on duty and on faith, do not yield, do not capitulate, but die protesting.

"You had yet strength: in the brave troops who were fighting even whilst you were signing that fatal decree; in the people trembling with the hope of battle; in the barricades of the citizens; in the influence of your assembled authority over the provinces. Neither the people nor the army asked you to yield. The city everywhere bristled with barricades ordered by you as a solemn promise that, ordinary modes of warfare exhausted, Rome would be defended by the people. And none the less you decreed that defence was *impossible*, and rendered it so by pronouncing that baleful word. You have declared that *the Assembly remains at its post*. But the post of the Assembly was the last corner of Italian land on which, even for one day more, it could hold aloft the banner of the Republic; and you, confining the execution of your mandate within the walls of the Capitol, with the dead letter of the mandate have slain its spirit.

"You knew, from the teaching of history and of logic, that no Assembly can remain free for a single moment with hostile bayonets at its door; and that the Republic would fall on the day in which a French soldier should be able to set his foot within the walls of Rome. You then in decreeing that the Republican Assembly would remain in Rome, decreed at the same time and inevitably the death of the Assembly and the Republic. And, decreeing that the Republican army should go forth from Rome without you, without the Government, without the legal representative of the Republic, you, without perceiving it, decreed the first manifestation of dissension among those who were standing strongly in their union, and—but God will not have it so!—the loosening of that nucleus on which are rested the dearest hopes of Italy.

"You ought to have decreed the impossibility of any contact, except that of war, between men called to represent the Republic and men come to destroy it; to have remembered that Rome was not a city, but Italy, the symbol of the Italian thought, and great from the moment in which, while all were falling into despair, she had said, 'I do not despair, but arise'; to have remembered that Rome was not in Rome, but everywhere in which Roman souls sanctified by that Italian thought were gathered together to fight and suffer for the honour of Italy; to have remembered that the Italian soil extends around you, and to have transported the Government, the Assembly, all elements representing that thought and all the well-disposed of the armed people, in the midst of the army, bearing from spot to spot until all ways were closed to you the Palladium of the faith and of the mission of Rome. To encourage you in the hope that this action would have borne fruit, you had both olden records and the modern record of Hungary. But, were there no such examples to encourage you, you, made Apostles of the third life of Italy, ought to have been the first to give the spectacle of a new indomitable constancy to Europe. These things were said to you; you did not accept them; and I, representative of the people, protest solemnly in the face of you, to the people, to God, against the refusal and its immediate consequences.

"Rome is destined by Providence to accomplish great things for the salvation of Italy and the world. The defence of Rome has initiated these great things, and written the first line of an immense poem to be completed, whatever happens. History will keep register of this initiative, and of the part which you all, generous in intention, have had in it. But it will also say, and I groan with freshly-wounded affection in writing, that in the supreme moments in which you should have grown yet more gigantic than your fates, you failed in your mission and betrayed, not wilfully, the Italian idea of Rome.

"May the future find us united to redeem the fault!

"*3rd July*, 1849."

After the Decree declaring that the defence had ceased, and after the resignation of the Triumvirate, the Constituent Assembly appointed MM. Saliceti, Calandrelli, and Mariani, as Executive, to make arrangements with the French and to preserve order; and, voting that the Triumvirs had deserved well of the country, remained to discuss the articles of the Roman Constitution, not yet completed. The French troops entered Rome on the 2nd, and at noon on the following day, in their presence, the Assembly, its last act, proclaimed from the Capitol, amid the shouts of the people, the new Constitution of the Roman Republic.[1]

[1] The "fundamental principles," as below—

1.—The Sovereignty exists of eternal right in the people. The people of the Roman States are constituted into a democratic Republic.

2.—The Democratic Government has for rule equality, liberty, fraternity. It recognizes neither titles of nobility, nor privileges of birth or caste.

3.—The Republic by its laws and by its institutions ameliorates the moral and material conditions of all the citizens.

4.—The Republic regards all peoples as brothers, respects each nationality, and defends that of Italy.

5.—The municipalities have all equal rights : their independence is limited only by the laws of general utility of the State.

Before the entry of the French, the Republic had needed no safeguards but the affection of the people. Cheerful alike under the privations and the dangers of the siege, not a single attempt at revolt had been made, never a murmur of discontent; nor had there been any suppression of public opinion. Mamiani and the old members of the Papal Government, liberal or illiberal, remained unmolested and free. The first decree of the Imperial and Papal "deliverers" was to establish a Council of War for political (*i.e.* patriotic) offences. On the 5th of July, the popular clubs were abolished and meetings prohibited. On the 6th, the Civic Guard was dissolved. On the 7th, the complete disarming of the citizens ordered. On the 14th, they suppressed the journals. On the 18th, any meeting of more than five persons seemed dangerous to the "deliverers." So they freed the Romans from the "Reign of Terror" under Mazzini. Meanwhile he, giving the lie to their accusations, walked unarmed through the streets, watching the saddened faces of his Romans, till his friends told him he was mad. But no man dared to touch him. Even the French officers were

---

6.—The most equitable distribution possible of local interests in harmony with the political interest of the State is the rule of the territorial division of the Republic.

7.—The exercise of civil and political rights does not depend upon religious belief.

8.—The Chief of the Catholic Church will receive from the Republic all the guarantees necessary for the independent exercise of the spiritual power.

awed by the sublime spectacle of that pale, worn, gray man (his black hair turned gray with the two months' toil and anxiety and sorrow) passing among them like the ghost of the Republic, severe and silent, his very patience, the martyr's restraint, rebuking the assassins.

"The French entered, and entering with them the cohort of hostile priests, the centre of conspiracy at Gaeta, I remained for a week publicly in Rome. The talk of the French and Catholic newspapers of the terror exercised by me during the siege made me wish to prove to all men the falsity of the accusation, by offering myself an easy victim to any one who would revenge an offence or obtain a reward from the dominating sect. Besides, I had not the heart to detach myself from Rome. I saw, with the feeling of one who assists at the obsequies of the best-beloved, the members of the Assembly, the Government, the Ministers, all go into exile; the hospitals invaded, where lay our wounded, grieving more for the fate of the city than for their own; the fresh graves of our bravest profaned and trampled underfoot by the foreign conqueror. I was wandering through the streets at sundown with Scipione Pistrucci and Gustavo Modena, both now dead, at the very time when the French, with fixed bayonets moving slowly among the people, gloomy and irritated, ordered the dispersion of the crowd quivering with indignation and boiling over with thoughts of further struggle. It appeared to me that the troops occupying the city had been quartered so incautiously as to afford opportunity for a series of surprises, and I hastened to inquire of General Roselli and of his staff whether, if there were a *rising* of the people headed by me, who had no chain of compacts on my free soul, they would help. They agreed. But it was too late. The popular leaders were in flight, and every attempt failed. I suggested to Roselli to ask of General Oudinot, under cover of avoiding probable collisions, the distribution of the little Roman army in cantonments outside the city. There our soldiers might have recovered from the exhaustion of the long struggle; we should have been able to re-equip them; I would have kept myself concealed and near them; then perhaps we might have been able to seize a propitious moment to throw ourselves into Rome and surprise the enemy. But that plan also, though at first accepted, proved useless. Garibaldi's departure in arms[1] had made Oudinot suspicious, and the

[1] When the defence was over, Garibaldi invited all who were disposed to follow him, promising them only "long marches, dangers, hunger, and death." Three thousand gathered to his standard, and as they dashed through the Porta Pia, Garibaldi, the last to leave the Eternal City, stuck a lance into the ground with a challenge to Oudinot to follow him. At Terni he was joined by Colonel Hugh Forbes, an Englishman, with about 500 volunteers. Beset on all sides by the Austrians, they reached the little moth-eaten "Republic" of San Marino, a sort of nominally free State of some 8000 inhabitants, allowed to exist as if in mockery of Republicanism. Here they were surrounded and terms offered; but these involving the surrender of some twenty-five French soldiers who had deserted to join them, Garibaldi, dividing his force into three bodies, endeavoured desperately to

Roman artillery was ordered to remain in the city. Our soldiers, convinced that the enemy was capable of proceeding to any iniquity, suspected in their turn that they wanted to place them without means of defence between the French and the Austrians and have them slaughtered; the little army fell to pieces, and shortly after was dissolved. Foolish and ruinous designs! But in those days all the powers of my mind were alive with but one idea—rebellion on any terms against the brute force that in the name of a Republic, unprovoked, annihilated another republic.

"Why the priests and the French did not avail themselves of the opportunity I offered to have me dead or in prison is altogether a mystery to me. I remember how poor Margaret Fuller and my dear and venerated friend Giulia Modena entreated me to leave, and preserve myself, as they said, for better times. But had I been able to foresee the new

---

break through. One party was cut to pieces; the other two, under Garibaldi and Forbes, succeeded, though with severe loss, in gaining the open country. There they disbanded: only a few with Garibaldi reaching Cesenatico, a small port on the Adriatic, for the chance of passing through the Austrian fleet then blockading Venice, and so throwing themselves into the city still holding out heroically with Manin. Their boats, however, were nearly all sunk or captured; and Garibaldi himself, with his wife Anita (a Brazilian), who never quitted him, narrowly escaped to shore. Scarcely landed, she, broken down with fatigue and anxiety, died in his arms. Disguised, he crossed the country to Genoa, whence he obtained a passage to Gibraltar. Forbes escaped to Switzerland.

disillusions and ingratitudes and the falling away of old friends which awaited me, and thought only of my individual self, I had said to them—'If you love me, let me die with Rome.'

"However, I left, and left without a passport, and took myself to Civita-Vecchia. There I sent to ask for one from the American ambassador, and got it, but not being countersigned by the French authorities, as required for departure, it was useless. In port was a little steamer, the *Corriere Corso*, ready to weigh anchor. The captain, I think one de Cristofori, himself perhaps a Corsican, was unknown to me; I ventured none the less to ask him if he would at his own risk take me on board without my papers, and unexpectedly he agreed to it. I embarked. The steamer was bound for Marseilles, touching at Leghorn, then held by the Austrians. I found on board an unwelcome spectacle, a deputation of Romans from among those adverse to us, who had to go to the latter port to re-embark for Gaeta, to petition for the return of the Pope. I did not look at them; but they knew me, and the captain feared that on landing at Leghorn they might denounce my presence to the Austrians. They did not; and I reached Marseilles.[1] It matters not that my readers should know how, unprovided with a passport, I entered the enemy's

---

[1] When the Custom-house officers came on board, Mazzini, his coat off, was washing glasses in the steward's cabin. They passed him without notice. After they left he hailed a boat and went ashore.

country, and how I managed to travel across it to Geneva. I have only noticed these personal things because the historians and the newspaper writers of the Moderate Party, liars by calculation, circulated then, and would all now, had they occasion, circulate again their accounts of my *three* passports, of the English protection I had secured beforehand, and of the prudence with which I had provided for my own safety."

From Geneva to Lausanne, where Saffi and other exiles joined him, and where he wrote an indignant and crushing *Letter to MM. de Tocqueville and de Falloux*, Ministers of France, in vindication of the Roman Republic from the accusations against it in the French Chamber, and exposing in all its rascally details the infamy of the French Government. Some brief extracts from this Letter may sufficiently indicate the position. Concerning the condition of Rome before and after the French entry, I have already testified; of the conduct of these French Papal Republicans toward their own country Mazzini writes :

" Faithless servants (as Ministers of a Republic) of an idea which is not your own, in secret opposed to the flag to which your oaths have been publicly given, conspirators rather than ministers, you are condemned to revolve for ever hypocritically and premeditatedly round a lie. Your fundamental assertions are false ; the details false also ; falsehood in yourselves ; falsehood in your agents ; falsehood (I blush in saying this of France, which you have stripped so bare, taking from her at last even her traditional honour) in the generals of your army. You have conquered through falsehood, and attempt to justify yourselves with falsehood. General Oudinot lied when, to delude the populations, and, trafficking in our love for France, to smoothe his way to Rome, he kept to the 15th of July in Civita-Vecchia the French flag unfurled beside our tricolour, which he knew he came to pull down. He lied impudently, affirming in his proclamation that the greater part of the Roman army had fraternized with the French, when all the staff protested and gave in their resignation, when only 800 men (they perhaps now disbanded) accepted the offered conditions of service.[1] He lied vilely when, after having solemnly promised in writing not to assault the city before Monday the 4th of June, he assaulted it in the night of Saturday and Sunday. The envoy Lesseps lied to us when, perhaps with some hope of remedying the evil, he reassured us with continual promises of agreement, and conjured us to attribute no importance to the French movements, undertaken, he said, only from the need of finding an outlet for the soldiers' uneasiness in repose, meanwhile taking advantage of our good faith to study the ground unmolested, to bring up troops, to fortify, and to occupy by surprise, during an armistice, the strategical point of Monte Mario. M. de Courcelles lied when, against the declarations of the Roman municipality, of the foreign

[1] Supposing they were to go against the Austrians.

consuls, and the testimony of the whole city, he affirmed that Rome was not bombarded. . . . You too lied, M. de Tocqueville, when, trusting to the ignorance of your majority, you boasted as a fact unique in history of the choice of the ground before the gate of San Pancrazio from which to assault for the sake of the greater safety of the inhabitants and the buildings.[1] . . . You have all lied, gentlemen! from him who is first among you even to the last of your agents, to us, to the Assembly, to France, and to Europe, giving repeatedly, from the first day of your nefarious enterprise unto yesterday, promises of protection, of brotherhood, of liberty, when you had made up your minds to betray."

Rome was entered by the Gauls: Oudinot, after two months' resistance, with a well-appointed army of 35,000 men, overcoming the Roman force, which never counted half that number. Owlish statesmen and journalists could easily point the moral: of what use these futile struggles for the realization of dreams? For answer, the Defeated had two words—Heroic Rome! Behind that Aurelian Wall was sown the certain harvest of an Italian Nation.

[1] The ground was chosen for the sake of readier means of retreat towards Civita-Vecchia, and because, the heights overlooking the city, they could from them bombard it with safety. They were afraid of the barricades.

THE PARTY OF ACTION.

Velle est agere.

AGAIN in exile—an exile for the rest of life—the noblest Italian of them all, the man who had dared and who could not despair, for his action was based on faith. He might visit his Italy again; he could pass through Europe; but his journeys and his visits must be in secret. Even Switzerland was afraid to harbour the Dread of Kings.

He had to be hidden even in Lausanne, where for a time he took up his abode in order to carry on the *Italia del Popolo*, a paper which he had issued during the last days at Milan; and which he now resumed as a monthly publication for the continuance of the Italian propaganda: hidden because of the fears and ill-will of the Swiss Federal Government (no longer Republican, but moderate *à la mode*), and not without reason else, when emissaries of the Piedmontese Government endeavoured to kidnap him, and were only foiled by the acuteness of trusty friends among whom he lived.

At Lausanne, before the close of 1849, he wrote

his History of the Lombard War (*Cenni e Documenti,* &c., already referred to), and in the beginning of 1850 put out a pamphlet, *From the Pope to the Council* (*Dal Papa al Concilio*), in part a reprint of earlier writing, reasserting the necessity of religious reform, declaring the impotence of the Papacy, and the need of a religious Council.

"Where now," he writes, "is Pio Nono? . . . The Louis XVI. of the Papacy, he has destroyed it for ever. The cannon-balls which his allies discharged against the Vatican gave the death-blow to the institution. . . . Nor Pope, nor King! God and the people only shall open to us the fields of the Future.

"The Spirit of God descends to-day upon the multitudes: individuals, the privileged of intellect and heart, harvest, winnow, and shake out the grain, drawing thence their potent initiative: they do not create nor cancel it. For the dogma of absolute authority, immutable, concentrated in an individual or a determinate power, is substituted the dogma of progressive authority, of the people, the collective, continuous interpreter of the Law of God.

"And this principle, which the People has hailed as supreme regulator in the sphere of political life under the name of CONSTITUENT ASSEMBLY, will inevitably have its application to the sphere of religious life; and the name of that application will be COUNCIL."

During 1850 he returned to England, thenceforward making that his abode; but going abroad, despite all prohibitions and hindrances, whenever and wherever there was action, as he saw occasion for the Italian work from which he never rested. In 1850, in conjunction with Ledru Rollin,[1] Dr. Arnold Ruge, and his friends of the Polish Democratic Centralization in London, he formed the CENTRAL EUROPEAN DEMOCRATIC COMMITTEE, so far as circumstances might give opportunity to practically carry out the object of "Young Europe," the Association of 1834. The proclamations of the Committee,[2] signed by himself, Ruge, Ledru Rollin, Darasz (for the Poles), and afterwards by Bratiano (for the Roumanians), were from his pen.

Before leaving Rome he had organized a secret society to keep the flame of liberty alive. His work for Italy, and through that for Europe, was never intermitted; though in later events, because he would rather be lost in the work than be the cause of jealousy or hindrance to others, his influence was less openly apparent. But in 1852 his teachings again bore fruit, in a conspiracy against the Austrians. It failed, and was followed immediately by another,

[1] Exiled from France since the 13th of June, 1847, for the part he took in the popular manifestation of that date at Paris against the expedition against Rome.

Dr. Ruge was the friend and coadjutor of Simon of Treves, Struve, Hecker, and others of the Extreme Left in the Frankfort Parliament; that is to say, of the really Republican party in Germany. He was also one of those who attempted to rally the remains of the party at Stuttgardt.

[2] See Appendix for the first of these.

planned by the working-men of Milan. They wrote to Mazzini for arms and money. He sent them money, bade them take the arms of the enemy as they had done in 1848, and prepared to assist the movement by aid of Kossuth's influence among the Hungarian soldiers in the Austrian army in Italy.[1] The plan of the insurrection was a series of surprises carefully organized. A mistake in carrying out the programme overthrew all. Thirteen Milanese workmen were hanged by the Austrians; and it was only Mazzini's promptitude in giving warning which saved the mass of those implicated, not only in Milan but in the smaller cities.

By 1854 another attempt was ready, this time in Naples and Central Italy, again prevented by untoward circumstances and the treachery of some Piedmontese Monarchists who had pretended to join the patriots. Again in 1857, Pisacane's attempt on Naples and simultaneous risings in Leghorn and in Genoa (Mazzini there) answered to his persistently reiterated appeal for insurrectionary action as the only education for Italy, the only opportunity for freedom.[2] These attempts, planned by himself, were

[1] Kossuth, then in the height of his popularity in England, having so promised. Not really a Republican, however, only the patriotic Hungarian, he drew back when news came of the failure of the enterprise, and, though but the day before ready to leave London to join Mazzini in Italy, denied that he had authorized the use of his name. Politic for Hungary.

[2] Pisacane seized the *Cagliari* steamer, freed the political prisoners in the island of Ponza, and with a small force effected a landing on the Neapolitan coast at Sapri, hoping to join others

of course misrepresented by the Moderates, who renewed their old exclamations of the unhappy importunity of his Republicanism, and the fatal character of his influence with the people. *The Genoese Insurrection defended* was his reply, in which he exposed the anti-national parties in Italy.[1]

"For twenty-six years," he tells his traducers, "if I am to believe you, I have been fatal to the Italian Cause; for twenty-six years, if I am to believe lukewarm and not-lukewarm gazetteers, I have committed nothing but errors; nay! many times have I been declared utterly extinguished, null, unworthy of mention; yet, nevertheless, grown gray in years and care, my means exhausted, opposed by all the governments, gensd'armes, and spies of Europe, so that, England only excepted, there is not therein an inch of ground I can tread legally or without danger, from time to time I reappear, an agitator followed, you can no longer say by a few, and feared by the Powers, who are strong in public and secret organization, strong in their armies, in their gold, and some of them even (if their press speak truth) in opinion. Why is this?

"I will tell you, all you who stand lukewarm and

---

of the Republican party who awaited his action. Met by overwhelming numbers, he fell at the head of his men, most of them falling with him. The Genoese movement was put down by Victor Emmanuel; that of Leghorn by the Austrian Grand-Duke of Tuscany.

[1] Republished in England by his friend, Joseph Cowen, the popular member of Parliament for Newcastle-on-Tyne.

irresolute in the presence of this state of things. I will tell you why it is, and at the same time teach you how you may destroy my *fatal* influence. I am but a voice crying Action : but the state of Italy cries for action, and the best men of Italy, the people of her cities, and her youth yet uncorrupted by cowardly ease or the sophisms of the semi-intellectual, demand action ; and the men of the Government by their terrors, and in the illusions they seek to spread, betray their presentiment of action ; and the scourge and the cap of silence[1] at Naples point to action ; and the glorious memories of '48, and the unspeakable shame of the people, to whom these memories belong (and whose teachers lead it, the Belisarius of Liberty, to beg, from the protocols of every conference, from the memoranda of all semi-liberal ministers, a deceitful hope of amelioration), call for action as a solemn duty : this is the secret of my influence.

". . . Do you wish to destroy it ? Act! Act better and more efficaciously than I ! Where I, left alone by you the lukewarm and by too many others, act on what you call a small scale, unite and act upon a larger ! It matters not whether, as you ought, you unite with me, with us; it does matter that you yourselves form a Party of Action. The Party of Action should be without limits, and have a nucleus everywhere. Preach unanimously to Italy that there is but one path of honour and salvation

[1] A special method of torture in the Neapolitan prisons.

before her, that of preparing herself to rise with her own forces, and of rising. You also are Italians: prepare yourselves! Agitate Piedmont till she awakens to a sense of her duty! . . . Aid us if we succeed in acting, as we will aid you should you attempt. You will then have no cause to fear the tyranny of either patriots or masters. Our masters must succumb to an unanimous effort; and the patriots whom you fear will, believe me, bless the hour when, abdicating their grave and deeply-felt responsibility, they can withdraw as simple soldiers within the ranks of the uprisen majority."

To which the royal rejoinder of Victor Emmanuel was the sentencing Mazzini to death, clinching the old sentence of Charles Albert, Cavour making it the occasion to declare in the Sardinian Parliament that the Monarchy of Piedmont existed "in virtue of the treaties" it respected.[1]

Yet the challenge was met after a fashion, the fashion of the dishonest politician, "statesman" if you will, who plots to prevent action that may not turn to his own account, and plots also to steal the reward of the action he cannot prevent. Cavour's account was altogether Piedmontese. So, if he could not stay Mazzini's work for Italy, he could thrust in his hand to take the spoil. Lo, at his word, a new "national" party sprang up, above all things anti-

---

[1] Treaties guaranteeing Lombardy to Austria, Tuscany to an Austrian Grand-Duke, Rome to the Pope, and the Two Sicilies to the Bombarder.

republican, but liberators and unifiers of Italy, at the same time truckling for French help at the price of Italian territory. The price, if not offered, accepted by Cavour, for Napoleon's help in liberating and unifying, that is to say in extending the Piedmontese kingdom and deferring the Republic, was Nice and Savoy to Napoleon, a kingdom of Central Italy for his cousin, and the throne of Naples for Murat. Thereupon Napoleon moved to emulate his uncle. Still it was war against Austria, and, forgetting past betrayals, the people were ready to prove Mazzini's words of their hungry desire for action. In vain the Moderate Party preached moderation lest too great patriotic willingness should embarrass the new Sword of Italy, needing room for sufficient sweep. Sixty thousand volunteers would never do; of the 60,000 they accepted 4000, giving the nominal leadership to Garibaldi, careful that he should not do too much. Magenta and Solferino were won, and the Emperor, having his meal of glory, kicked the King of Piedmont aside, and concluded peace with Austria, leaving Venice and Venetian Lombardy in Austrian hands; for the rest dictating some sort of confederation of Italian States: which Mazzini's teaching of unity brought to nought. He had been aware of the secret treaty, and had denounced it some months before the war. At his instigation Bologna and Tuscany refused to obey French orders to take back their old masters; at his instigation they annexed themselves to Piedmont. So possibly Victor Emmanuel might be encouraged to do more. Liberator Cavour was bidden by Napoleon to decline the gift; but the popular will prevailed. Again Mazzini wrote urging the King to pursue the war, promising the loyal support of the Republicans. All parties would then be at an end : none left in Italy "but the people and yourself." The peace had made Cavour unpopular; hated also for personal reasons by the King, who only succumbed to the influence of the stronger mind, he had to resign. Brofferio, the historian, carried Mazzini's letter to the King, who said that he had already read it, that he was determined that Italy should exist at any cost, and desired Brofferio to offer Mazzini an interview.[1] Mazzini, the rebel under sentence of death, proposed his terms: no mere union of present princes or progressive piece-meal unification (a pet idea of the more honest of the Moderates), but war for the immediate unity of the whole of Italy; and he exposed his own plans, answering for a revolution in the South, and promising to keep secret and in the background. While the King was hesitating Cavour returned to power; the King repented of his heroic mood; the old intrigue was resumed, this time for an Italy in three—Victor Emmanuel, our Cousin, and the Bombarder as presiding Trinity; and any further thought of concert with Mazzini was dismissed.

[1] In fairness toward Victor Emmanuel, let it be said that he always held Mazzini in personal respect, hesitated not to avow the same; but political necessities—his Ministers—the position of a constitutional king, &c. &c. Nevertheless, "Je déteste mon métier!" was his own comment.

Thenceforth the Cavourian royal policy was clear enough : Mazzini's influence was to be hindered at all hazards. Could his action be altogether prevented, well ; if not, Cavour was ready according to circumstances to meddle and thwart or take advantage of his success.[1] Mazzini proceeded on his way alone.

[1] As samples of the Cavourian tactics, take the following extracts from the *private diary* of Admiral Persano, he being at anchor in the Cagliari roads at the time Garibaldi sailed from Genoa to Sicily.

"May 9—By order of the Governor of Sardinia sail for Maddalena with orders to arrest Garibaldi, who left Genoa with two steamers, if he should put into any part of the Island of Sardinia" (so compromising the King); "but to allow him to proceed if I should meet the expedition in the open sea. Not finding these orders clear, I put into Tortoli to dispatch a letter to Count Cavour, in which I said that inasmuch as Garibaldi could not have sailed without knowledge of his Majesty's Government, it could hardly be that he would put into Sardinia save from stress of weather : so that I should return to Cagliari, where the Count could telegraph me.

"May 31—Garibaldi writes me that his expedition was in full success.

" June 3—La Farina, Deputy in Parliament, brought me a letter from Cavour saying Farina had his full confidence, and ordering me to send him to Palermo *secretly*.

"June 5—Cavour writes me that certain officers of the Navy of the King of Naples having shown symptoms of friendship for the cause of Italy, they were to be promised promotion, &c., if they would effect a rising in their King's Navy in favour of Victor Emmanuel. . . . I leave with my squadron for Palermo, informing Count Cavour of the fact, and that I was resolved to support Garibaldi" (then in the full tide of victory).

"June 11—Cavour approves of my sending the *Governolo* " (sloop of war) "to Messina" [with secret instructions to favour a rising there, proposed to Cavour by Persano on the 8th, after hearing of the surrender of Palermo to Garibaldi].

Sure of his ground in Sicily, he urged Garibaldi, whose little force of volunteers, not disbanded at the close of the war, was devoted to him, to head an expedition to the Island. Garibaldi at first consented, but drawing back out of deference to the King's orders, not without some jealous objection to being second to Mazzini, Mazzini therefore sent Rosalino Pilo, a young Sicilian nobleman, to head the movement. Detained by stress of weather, Pilo, arriving in Palermo on the 11th of April, 1860, found the work already begun. Taking command, he worsted

---

"June 12 — *Washington*, *Franklin*, and *Oregon* arrive at Cagliari." [These three ships were the second Sicilian expedition under the command of an Englishman, Capt. De Rohan, who chartered them at his own expense. They were afterwards drafted into the Italian Navy, De Rohan never receiving any payment for them.]

"June 13—Receive dispatch from Cavour, saying Mazzini and friends were on board steamship *Washington*, and asking me to have them arrested by Garibaldi, as Mazzini's presence in these waters would force the King to recall his Navy from Sicily, and so ruin the cause of Italy; if Garibaldi refuse, I am at once to leave these seas. Went immediately ashore and saw Garibaldi, who promised to arrest Mazzini if he acted in opposition to the King, but declined to arrest him merely for being on board the *Washington*: whereupon I resolved in the interests of Italy to arrest him myself.

"June 19—The *Carlo-Alberto* and *Gulnare* return from seeing the second expedition land safely in the Bay of Castelamare, according as I had ordered. Find that Mazzini was not aboard any of the ships of that expedition.

"June 21—Medici and Garibaldi came on board my ship, and I then informed the latter of the orders I had from Count Cavour to escort every expedition destined to reinforce the Dictator." [Garibaldi had assumed the title on the 8th.]

the royal troops in every encounter, and maintained the insurrection until Garibaldi, no longer able to hold back, landed at Marsala on the 11th of May to replace him. In the moment of victory Pilo received a gun-shot wound and died with a smile on his face as he heard of Garibaldi's arrival.

Garibaldi's wonderful successes need not to be here related in detail. To his own daring heroism much was due, but Rosalino Pilo deserves to share his renown. The plan, the preparations, and the first impetus, were the work of Mazzini. Cavour certainly helped too in his own manner, bribing the Neapolitan naval officers (as Persano informs us) and Neapolitan generals also, so perhaps somewhat smoothing the road for Garibaldi. Did he not also, when the game was covered, point the royal rifle over Garibaldi's shoulder? For which most gracious service the grateful Dictator, wavering in his Republicanism, presented to his royal master as a free gift the Island of Sicily with its inhabitants, and a little later the realm of Naples, the magnificence of which action has already been sufficiently lauded by the polite Muse of History.

Meanwhile Mazzini, compelled to act in secret, had been preparing, his Sicilian project succeeding, to take advantage of the popular enthusiasm and of Garibaldi's power to extend the war to Rome and Venice: true to his faith in the unity and common interests of Italy. Three expeditions, successively raised by him, had gone to the South; a fourth he destined for the Papal States: his plan being, after driving out the Pope's heterogeneous army (then under command of General Lamoricière), an achievement which promised little difficulty, to leave the Romans to defend themselves, and to push on, joined by Garibaldi, to Venice. Garibaldi agreed. The King approved. But again the shadow of the Republic scared him. Scarcely was his consent given, when he wrote with his own hand a letter, *to be only shown*, forbidding the project. Ricasoli, then Governor of Sardinia, under this last order stopped the volunteers. The insurrectionary movement in aid of the enterprise had already begun in the Roman States; and while the Two Sicilies were being conquered for the "Sword of Italy" by Garibaldi, the brave "Sword" was sheathed, and Rome abandoned to Lamoricière. The cruelties committed by the French General in Perugia and elsewhere, inconveniently rousing the indignation of all Italy, the Sword had to be unsheathed, Cavour apologetically writing to Napoleon of the kingly necessity. "If we are not in the Cattolica before Garibaldi we are lost." *Ego et rex meus!* "The revolution will invade Central Italy. We are constrained to act."[1]

[1] Dispatch from Cavour to Talleyrand, Sept. 10, 1860. The French Minister Thouvenel wrote also (Oct. 18):—

"Signor Farini has explained the extremely dangerous and embarrassing position in which the triumph of the Revolution personified to some extent by Garibaldi threatened to place the Government of his Sardinian Majesty." [Victor Emmanuel *vice* Charles Albert.] . . . "Garibaldi was about to pass freely across

Thus the great statesman (if it be statesmanship to baulk the hopes of patriotism, to demoralize a people by a policy of dirty tricks and dishonest manœuvring, to lie and steal and corrupt), thus Cavour in 1860 prevented the unity of Italy, and won the crown of the South for the unwetted brows of his warrior master: trembling as they went about their work, the dread of Mazzini ever on them. He was not in the *Washington*, but he was in Naples; not hidden, but in danger: the Moderates pointing him out as a divider of the national party (Pallavicini, from whom better things were due, writing publicly to ask him to leave, so, intentionally or not, asking for him to be driven out), and the more violent Monarchists, Bourbon, priestly, or other, seeking his life. On the walls they placarded—"Death to Mazzini!" One night a few Italian friends (I am proud to say, among them an Englishman, from whose lips I had my story) had to watch armed lest the lazzaroni (or sanfedesti?) should break in to assassinate him. The next morning Garibaldi spoke to the people—"Who harms Mazzini harms the friend of Garibaldi." He was there to prevent if possible the foolish abnegation (I would not call it worse) of Garibaldi, and to make the war Italian. In vain: the melodramatic interview

---

the Roman States raising the populations, and having passed that frontier it would have been impossible to prevent an attack upon Venice. There was but one course left to the Cabinet of Turin . . . to give battle to the Revolution on the Neapolitan territory, and immediately call together a Congress" [of Napoleon, &c., to decide what next].

between the Dictator and his Sovereign, when the Dictator handed over the Two Sicilies, with their nine millions of souls, and the Sovereign replied—" I thank you!" closed the Sicilian chapter.

Mazzini persisted, for the sake of Venice, of Rome, of Italy. In 1861 he writes from London (I extract from a private letter in his own handwriting now before me)—"I am sorry that G. did not sign the receipts. I shall not come to Italy unless (1) Garib : himself should tell me—'I wish you to come'; (2) or sufficient funds in the hands of the Central Committee or mine should make it possible to organize action. My coming now would only give rise to talk, suspicions, jealousies, conjectures, which would do harm without any practical results.

"Garibaldi spoke the truth; but both he and our friends Crispi, Bixio, &c., have been weak in the end of discussion. *Concordia* is a sacred word, and for its sake I have myself sacrificed my dearest thoughts and my individuality during these last two years; but it is only possible when there is unity of aim and conscience. There is neither for the man who sold Nice, who wrote and spoke the words that are in your Blue-books, which I quoted in my pamphlet, *La questione Italiana e i republicani*, and which ought to have been quoted to Cavour in the House; there is neither in the man whose policy is a Bonapartist one for a nation possessing now twenty-two millions of inhabitants. Between him and the patriots *Concordia* is a lie and an absurdity. Either we believe Cavour useful to our cause, and ought not to attack him at all; or we believe him pernicious to it, and ought to proclaim boldly and conscientiously the dualism which we reproach.

"As for Garib: I have not the least influence over him; but those who have it, and to whom he is a friend, ought to persuade him that he has duties to perform toward the Nation, derived from his genius, his immense popularity, and his solemn promises, these duties summed up in one word— action, on Venice.

"Action on Venice is the signal of insurrection in Hungary, Poland, and the East: it is the glorious initiative of nationalities given to Italy.

"Action on Venice will compel the Government to step in.

"L. N. cannot come down to Italy to support Garibaldi or to support Austria. Our policy therefore would emancipate itself at once from Bonapartism.

"Action on Venice is possible; I told Gar: and you *how*.

"We only require money for the operations: half a million of francs.

"Gar: ought to help in collecting them, either by one of the means proposed or by a short appeal to the country, organizing the movement—' *Un franco per Venezia*,' and meanwhile privately asking people who can give more to give more.

"The money partly collected, I would, if he wished, go to him and communicate the *how* in all its details,

L

taking his instructions. *We* would initiate the movement, if he chose, and then hand it over to him, or he would initiate it himself: in fact he would be the arbiter of the practical decisive work.

"Should he accept this, he ought now to state to Italy that he has tried to do good in Parliament with the Government—that he has not succeeded—that the Government having declared that they will not take the initiative of the emancipating war, the country must help herself—that universal manifestation of opinion for Rome and an universal offering for Venice ought to take place.

"We shall all work for him.

"Tell him these things!"

(*April* 22, 1861.)

A more private letter is written in 1862: it may help to show the man.

"Cernuschi has been my friend at both Milan and Rome: there he left me. He has many qualities, both moral and intellectual, but he is crotchety to a degree, vain, a federalist, and convinced, at least until very recently, that France is the initiating power, and that we must follow her inspirations and fates. There is nothing to be got from him, I fear, except witty epigrams and dissolving remarks.

"I am better, only working does me harm. I cannot take up now a course of gymnastics, but I try to take exercise and behave generally better than I did hitherto toward myself.

"Do not react within yourself against ungratefulness or any other fault in our men : the actual generation comes out of slavery and slavish education. Trust the next!—and as for you, conscience and the esteem of the few are the only things to be aimed at."
(*March* 15, 1862.)

Again, two years later, the same to the same:—
" . . . Why do we not act? I am at it since one year. Foreseeing the crisis, and mainly for the sake of Poland, then up, I was during six months last year on the Continent, for the purpose of organizing the Venetian movement. I succeeded. At a later period, when they saw the thing going on well, Garib: and his friends established a Central Committee; and I was, for peace' sake, compelled to put my work in their hands. Since then more than 1000 muskets going to the Venet: territory were seized by our Government. Now a certain amount of arming is required there as a condition for a rising. We, or rather they, are trying to replace the seized arms. The money is in their hands, not in mine. Gar: is theoretically with me, but besides writing short notes like 'Act! I am ready,' he does nothing. Shall we succeed? It may be, but I cannot say. If we do, we shall be followed in Hungary, and other provinces. I have a vast deal of work ready, but wanting an initiative, very. I ought to have the thing entirely in my hands; and I have it not.

"The King? I have been in contact with him the last five months; and men of mine are still. He is *morally* a coward. He asked me to have a Galician movement before. I promised it. Then he asked for a Hungarian rising before our own action. Evidently he wants to have Austria destroyed: then to declare war against her. I remonstrated against the seizure of arms. But he does not want Venice to be armed, for fear *we* should act there. All that I could write through you I have written ten times. I shall not write any more. It is yours to write, to tell him the same things you tell me about the opportunity—to urge him to have a moment of energy—to prevent his horrid Cabinet, Perazzi and Spaventa, watching and seizing again our arms—to accept our declarations about our action having nothing to do with political questions, but only with the national one—and not to drive me through despair to resort to republican agitation. It is a true shame if we miss the opportunity.

"*Voilà tout!* If spite of all we succeed and can act next month..."

(*June* 3, 1864.)

Yet once more he sees an opportunity through impending war.

"In all probability war is decided by the three powers, Prussia, Austria, and Italy. A proposal supported by England, Russia, and France—the latter two hypocritically, for they wish and work for war—is the cause of the delay; but it will most likely be rejected, and war will ensue. You will do what mind and heart suggest. Within two or three days you will most probably have from Italy new elements for your decision.

"No! I am not well. Pains and cramps are now my companions almost every day. Talking and writing do harm. I regret it, not for the sake of my *individual*, but of the little I might still do for Italy."

(*May* 1866.)

These letters (a few out of the very many in my possession) may be sufficient to show his resolute persistency through all adverse circumstances, the falling off of friends and the treachery of inimical allies. They refute, though refuting may not silence, the falsehoods (not mistaken accusations, but falsehoods, for those who were loudest against him knew better) of those who have habitually reproached him with dividing the Italians. They also give clear insight into the character of *the man*, telling of his foresight, his thorough unselfishness, his absolute integrity, and his never-failing readiness to devote all powers and hopes and ideas to the realization of that one first practical step, his country's nationality ; not stooping to win it by the baseness of intrigue, but seeking it through only honourable endeavour. Herein lies the real difference between him and his great opponent. Cavour may have thought, have wished for Italian nationality; but he was content to get it by instalments, and by any means however vile, at the cost of debasing and demoralizing the Italian character. Mazzini's whole action was educative; his unwavering aim not merely to tie together with regal or other fasces so many millions of men, and call that caravanserai-host a nation, but to lift up into the unity and bond of nationhood a people dignified by the struggle, and conscious of duty toward the world. Grant that both sought, each in accordance with his nature and position, to make an Italy: but the one cared not if it were enslaved or lamed: the other would have it in all the strength and integrity of an intelligent and noble freedom.

Again, even in 1864, Victor Emmanuel faltered; nor only faltered: for in that year the shameful convention was signed by which Italy bought the streets of Rome of Louis Napoleon, on condition that Florence should be the Italian capital, and for price (stated only in a secret protocol) ceding Piedmont from Savona to France, in case Austria should by any action lose her Venetian territory.

Mazzini was aware of the protocol, and publicly denounced it. Then, after years of stedfast forbearance, not to divide the nation (let who will gainsay it), he raised again his Republican flag and openly declared that, where one side had been so flagrantly and continually faithless, there was no longer a contract. "We Republicans," he said, "swore to create Italy, with, without, or against the Monarchy;

we bowed to the popular will and attempted *with*. If this convention become an accomplished fact, not only *with* but *without* the Monarchy, they mean to shut us out. We will act then *against* them, and in their despite. One only path being left, the path of revolution, the people must follow that; must attack Austria in Venice, win Rome without conditions, and, proclaiming liberty of conscience in the centre of religious despotism, proclaim also a National Constitution, establishing independently, and in spite of kingly interference, the will of a freed Italy.

"Do this at any cost, and by the overthrowal of every obstacle in your path! If among the obstacles you find Monarchy, then, in the name of God and of Italy, let us not draw back before a phantom, but rise up a Republic!"

In 1865 the citizens of Messina, in protest against his banishment and unannulled death-sentence, elected him as their representative to the Italian Parliament. He thanked them: but under no circumstances could the Republican take oath of allegiance to a King. In 1866 Palermo spoke for the Republican.

On the 19th of March, St. Joseph's Day, the name day of Mazzini and Garibaldi, 80,000 Italians took part in a festival in honour of the Liberators of Sicily, and in answer to a proclamation of the "Association of the Future" calling upon the people of Palermo to keep the 19th as a holy day, so "to proclaim again before the world that Italy marches irresistibly to the conquest of her proper rights."

The day began with a service in the Church of San Crispino, attended by the National Guards, the university students, and delegates of different societies from all parts of Italy. Thence they proceeded amid shouts of *Viva Mazzini! Viva Garibaldi!* with banners, flowers, and hymns, followed by crowds from the neighbouring country, Messina, Catania, &c., to a large public garden outside the walls, to crown a marble bust of Garibaldi in the centre. After crowning the bust with flowers and reciting some verses ("Venice and Rome sent this garland"), the procession moved to the Theatre S. Cecilia, where songs, speeches, and improvisations were sung and said in honour of the day, and declaratory of the popular craving for Rome and Venice, and letters read from Mazzini, Garibaldi, Victor Hugo, Ledru Rollin, and others. The day's programme was completed by a resolution, drawn up by the Committee conducting the festival, that the next anniversary should be kept in the Forum at Rome. Eighty thousand Italians, with the whole of the National Guard of Palermo, testified by their presence the high esteem in which Mazzini is held by his countrymen.[1]

Nor did the men of Palermo testify only by flowers and songs and acclamations. Before the year was out Palermo was in insurrection for the Republic; bombarded by Victor Emmanuel, the insurrection suppressed, submitted to a military government. And while these things were going on in emancipated and annexed Sicily, the King, following at the heels of Louis Napoleon in a new war against Austria, when Louis was again tired of glory, had Venice flung to him as one flings a bone before a hound.

Well might Mazzini write, resuming the course of happenings through which at last the unity of Italy

[1] Condensed from an Italian newspaper report of the proceedings at length.

was reached :—"They, who to serve royalty persist in regarding consequences and not causes of events, may say what pleases them to-day. History and the conscience of Italy will declare that it was the popular element which willed our unity when Monarchy was still plotting for confederations, with Austria, with the Bourbon, with the Pope; History will declare that the French design of a Bonapartist kingdom accepted by the Monarchists was only overthrown by us; that the emancipation of the South was the work of our volunteers and of the people; that the monarchical invasion of the Papal States was a necessity created by the preparations for a similar expedition made by us in Tuscany and Genoa; that Venice was not a victory won, but an alms bestowed; and that, without the alarm excited by the guerilla bands in Calabria and the Centre, the attempts at Piacenza and Pavia, the imminence of like movements in other cities, and the sudden proclamation of the Republic in Paris, our Monarchy would not even now (1871) be in Rome."

In 1870 he was on his way to Sicily. Little by little, yet faster even than the steps of Italy to freedom—from the foreigner, he had seen the sluggishness which follows enthusiasm, and the contentment with mere material gain which it had been the business of the monarchical party to teach, creeping over his Italians. This man was now a royal general; this other sat in Parliament; another had made some market of his principles; old friends, how many, alas! had fallen in the fight, and some had outlived their hope and faith: but in Sicily under the iron rule of Medici (the old twice hero of Lombardy and Rome become royal governor) the people were not contented; and even the late bombardment of Palermo had perhaps helped to keep up what was not exactly love of Piedmontese supremacy. Frequent offers come to Mazzini of revolutionary uprising for a Sicilian Republic, and separation from the rest of Italy. His influence against this for a time prevailed: opposed as he ever was to any dismemberment of the Nation. But when he found them determined to act, with or without him, he went; not believing in the success of the attempt, but to turn it if possible from Sicilian separation to a beginning of Republicanism for all Italy. Betrayed, for the first time in his life, by one trusted with a knowledge of his movements, he was arrested at sea, and imprisoned in the fortress of Gaeta,—Gaeta where in 1848 the fugitive Pope had found a refuge. The insurrectionists, finding Medici prepared, were unable to proceed. So, that danger tided over, as it might be inconvenient to keep Mazzini a prisoner, advantage was taken of a birth in the Palace, some weeks later, to grant him an amnesty and release him. He returned to England; soon after going again to Lugano, to publish there his *Roma del Popolo*, resuming his old apostolate, to devote to that the remainder of his life.

"The delusions and errors of the past ten years,

the false route upon which our new-born Italy has been seduced by leaders incompetent and corrupt, have convinced me, to my sorrow, that the political education of my countrymen is less advanced than I once hoped. The Italian question, which I believed might ere this have become a question of action, is still a question of education."

Old, yet more in sorrow than in years, outworn and weary, sick, and seldom free from pain, he set himself down to the task begun forty years before, to teach his people the true road of progress, through freedom on the path of duteous work and aspiration. One year more, then the end. The sword had destroyed the scabbard. Frail, enfeebled by long disregard of his own health, he had not strength to meet a sudden attack of pleurisy. He died on the 10th of March, 1872, under an assumed name, at the house of a friend in Pisa.

Mazzini's views, religious and political (the two not independent of each other, for he looked on politics as only the practical methods of realizing a religious faith), in great part, I trust, explained in the story of his life, may be briefly summed up:—Belief in God and in the continual progress and perfectibility of the human race, whence he deduced the need of perfect harmony of faith and action, the worship of a continual search for the Divine Law regarding Man, the right of unimpeded action, and the duty of unresting endeavour to fulfil that law, not only in each individual, but through the mutually helpful organization of individuals as nations. Wherefore he insisted upon the importance of nationality, to take advantage of the identity of nature and similarity of habits and tendencies in peoples, binding them together in closer brotherhood. So his "freedom for Italy" was not merely because of her material sufferings under a foreign yoke, but for the sake of that unity without which her work as a nation could not be accomplished, that special work which he believed to be reserved for her,—to give for the third time a new law to Europe, teaching the nations how to live. As a logical consequence, he believed in freedom and nationality for the other politically divided kingdoms of Europe, in furtherance of which he sought to establish his "young Europe" and the later "European Committee," as pledge of common aims and promise of brotherly assistance from one to other of the oppressed peoples, and as the germ of a real European Confederation, the Confederation of free Nations, in place of the "Holy Alliance" of Monarchs.

He believed that the Papacy was dead, and had left only an enormous soulless body, whose galvanic motions are without power to lead the world beyond the merest individualism, the "salvation" of so many isolated souls; that France also, the revolutionary teacher of political rights, had completed her mission, and was powerless for any farther initiative. He looked therefore for a new Religious

Council (he hoped to be had in Rome) to revivify
the faith of mankind, to assert and proclaim with
living power the bases of those new aspirations and
new hopes for some better ordering of society, now
moving the few to prophecy and stirring the many,
the continual multitude, to partial revolts which the
scared Ghost of Authority is utterly unable to prevent or to suppress but for a moment; and he knew
that such a Council (using the word in the old religious
sense) could not sit in the shadow of any throne,
temporal or spiritual,—could have being only when the
Voice of the whole People in their Assembly should be
ready to echo its assertion, to acclaim its proclamation,
abled by their free constitution to put the same in
practice through conviction of the worth of nationhood, not merely for the protection of certain of its
constituents from remaining civilized savageries, but
for the religious education of all in the ways of Duty,
duty not only to *their* families and *their* country, but
to the great family of Humanity of which nations are
but members.

For next to his belief in God and human progress
he believed in Association : in the power and in the
necessity of the free banding together of equals as the
only lever, the only leaven, of sure progress. Opposed
to the special schools of Socialism, because of his
perception of the materialism, the selfism of some,
and his resolute denial of the usurping authority of
others,—nevertheless his life through from the first,
with every weapon he could reach, example, exhorta-

tion, indignant sarcasm, he fought against the unhappy individualism of our age. He, Lamennais, "exile, everywhere alone," without home, without family or kindred, with no ties of affection (separated even from the few who bore his name), whose dearest friends were the comrades of the battle-field, tomorrow dead or out of sight never to be met again,—he more than all cared for the free, frank, self-respecting but thoroughly trusting association of men united to accomplish those great ends of life which he believed to be common to all and demanding the consentaneous labour of all, that trustful association which needs no encircling fetters of patriarchal or monarchical or pontifical authority, which needs only faith in human nature and the loving brotherly affection of men confiding because honest. No man ever trusted more in natural probity and goodness. He knew too, no man so well, how trust begets trust; how trust can make men honest. It was hard to make him believe in the dishonesty even of such knaves as Gallenga.

I well remember his telling me of an instance of the general feeling of affection toward him, in a great measure attributable to his trust in others, though also partly to be accounted for by his fearlessness even in the days when he was most hunted and calumniated. He was in Lugano. One night returning to his lodging he entered a wrong house; turning back through the darkness he met and tried to avoid a passing stranger. His hand was taken, and he was told not to be alarmed: he was safe because known.

Another incident may show that this trustfulness, the characteristic of an ingenuous and brave nature which he never lost through all his disappointments and disillusions as regarded the men with whom he had to be in contact, was not because he was incapable of the wariness of a prudent man. He knew everything he cared to know. With a correspondence vaster and more wide than perhaps was ever maintained by any man not in a Government, with hunters ever following on his trail, and spies seeking to overlook him, he had sources of information which kept his unhesitating faith from foolishness. One man came to him in London with an intention of harm. Mazzini saw him, heard his name, his story, heard him patiently through; then, "Your name is not ——, but ——; you came from such a man, from such a place; your purpose is ——." The man confessed, was disarmed. Conspiracy, secret contriving, the doom of his life, was hateful to his nature. Never franker, more ingenuous, more trustful soul than that of this ever-plotting, always hidden conspirator!

That needful and compelled duality in his own life perhaps only caused a greater hatred of the duality of common life. He would not in any way accept it as good. As faithful thought with him was the seed of energetic and persistent action, as he could not divide the political from the religious, recognizing (as before said—surely to bear repeating) politics as only the practical application of the Higher Law, refusing the name of policy to the course of that tribe of shuffling gamesters, time-servers, self-seekers, and the like, who to-day assume the style and title of politicians,—so he was unable to comprehend any exception from the law of religious duty, whether in literature, painting and sculpture, or music. The line of duty ran through all the web of life : he was impatient of the atheistic dogma of " Art for Art's sake," as if apart from the beauty of inspired and aspiring thought and the eloquent expression of that for the sake of creating the more perfect beauty of noble and godly deeds, there could be any need for the incitement of a lower pleasure,—as if the God-given faculties of Genius, in whatever direction, were only tools with which the artist or poet might erect his own monument or dig the grave of his own soul. Throughout his many literary criticisms it is not the pettier critic's task which will content him. Whether he writes of Dante or of Byron, of Goethe, of George Sand, or of Carlyle, it is not the excellence of this or that phrase which arrests his attention ; when he speaks of music or of sculpture, it is not the difficult instrumentation which affects him, nor the make of the shoe for which he cares either in appreciation of its fitness or to criticise the stitching or the cut : keen enough to notice the smaller as the larger parts as mere " works of art," not forgetting the mint and anise in his tithing, it is to the whole and the informing spirit of the whole that his praise or his rebuke is given,—it is with regard to the weightier matter of its accordance with the orderliness of Universal Law that his verdict is pronounced. Not that he confounded the offices of the preacher and the poet, since the divisional use of words if only for the purpose of distinction in our thoughts must be maintained (Dante and Byron, his two favourite poets, are not exactly didactic), but that he allowed of no right whatever to personal gratification out of harmony with the universal good. To him our earth was the Temple of the Holy One; and he believed in no little off-chapels, even for unsaintly Saints of Art.

As a literary man (with this qualification, that he could not have been only a literary man) he must take high rank. His comments on Dante, his criticisms of Goethe, Carlyle, and others, may be read for their purely literary merit as well as for their profound thought and critical perception; and his more careful political writings, all not equal, and of course much of repetition in a series of forty years, may stand beside the most statesmanlike papers of times more statesmanlike than our own. His style, peculiarly his own, is vigorous, of the purest Italian (so Italians tell me, and he wrote with almost equal facility and with the same good taste and manly strength in French and English—better English than his translators'),—passionately earnest, yet ever the words well chosen and well marshaled, reminding the reader in their sustained length of sentence and vehemence of argument, intreaty or invective, of the mighty poetic prose of Milton.

Professor Masson (the author of a Life of Milton),

M

a shrewd, not enthusiastic Scot, scholar and critic, not by any means disposed (I believe) to endorse Mazzini's political conduct, or to accept his Republican ideas, bears testimony to the universality, the other-greatness, of the "Italian Patriot, that preëminently, but more."

"He was a Theosophist, a Philosopher, a Moralist, a Reasoner about everything from a definite system of first principles, a Thinker on all subjects, a Universal Critic of Art and Literature. His general writings, partly collected and republished in conjunction with those appertaining to Italy and his own political life,[1] illustrate sufficiently both the systematizing habit of his mind and the wide range of his reading and culture. He knew something about everything. He had a consecutive scheme of the History of the World in his head; he had an acquaintance with the chief Greek and Latin poets, and the characteristics at least of the chief English, Spanish, German, and even Slavonian authors; in Italian literature, and in contemporary French literature, his knowledge was extensive and minute; he had at least looked into Kant and Hegel, and caught the essence of some of their abstractions; he was

[1] *Scritti editi e inediti di Giuseppe Mazzini;* the earlier volumes published by G. Daelli and afterward by Robecchi Levino at Milan, the later by a committee at Rome, under direction of Mazzini's trustiest friends, MM. Campanella, Quadrio, and Saffi. An English edition in six volumes of *Life and Writings*, autobiographical and political, literary and critical, alternately, not well translated, was published by Smith, Elder & Co., London, 1864 to 1870.

intelligent on subjects of Art, and especially of Music;
and he had no objection to the last novelty in physical
science."

These things, his opinions, the broad outlines of his
character and his capacities, may give some idea of
his greatness, an image however vague of the man
who for forty years defied the constituted powers of
Europe, crying as of old a Voice in the Wilderness,
preparing the way of a new era. Add the personal
description : rather below the average height, slight,
but beautifully formed, until in later years so attenu-
ated that he was almost a skeleton ; of dignified
bearing, with a grand head, handsome in his youth
before his black hair turned white, in his age noble
and severe, his features finely cut, generally calm, but
brightening with a smile as loving as a woman's, with
eyes like coals of fire as if the unwavering flame of
his soul looked ever through them : such was his
outward presentment. When he met you, his hand
had an English grip; his welcome was an expressive
heartiness, a southern warmth withal, that drew you
close. His magnetism was intense and never-failing.
He took hold of every one. No one could turn from
him with indifference. Gentle and gracious to all,
cheerful with his intimates, not without humour and
the appreciation of humour, and sometimes a touch of
good-natured satire ; in his speech impressive, vehement only when speaking of some great wrong, or at
times mock-vehement at some argument which too
rudely opposed his cherished ideas; a good talker,

tenderly courteous toward women, fond of children, kind and compassionate, simple and self-denying in all his habits, firm in his friendships, companionable, none more so in the days when I had most frequent intercourse with him; in every act and word and look, a man whom man or woman once meeting could not but love and reverence for ever. I linger over these details; they tell of my own recollections of the friend; but what description can fully present the man himself, one to be "ever honoured for his worthiness," the noblest man that ever lived in the tide of time?

RUFFINI—THE BANDIERAS.

RUFFINI—THE BANDIERAS.

Et si religio jusserit signemus fidem sanguine.
Saint Catherine.

[NOT from any paucity of names equally worthy of honour to be found in the long line of Italian martyrdom I have chosen Ruffini and the brothers Bandiera, but because they were of the first, and also because, in Mazzini's own words, so closely as the weakness of translation may permit, I can present their story, which is a part of his. He had intended to write a series of such records for a London publication, the *People's Journal*, at the time when the " People's International League" was calling public attention in England to the cause of Italy ; but he wrote only the two I here give. I add some words, his also, from the *Italia del Popolo* of a later date.]

JACOBO RUFFINI.

THE man of whom I am about to speak had not a life of renown. Doubtless he would have had, but without seeking it, if he had lived longer. He was young, endowed with great faculties, but born for the joys, the sorrows, the duties of private life; feeling an intense need of love and none of celebrity. And if I choose him from among the many who suffered in 1833 for the Italian national cause, it is not only because he was my friend, but because he proves, better than any other, the condition of a country in which the tenderest, the most loving souls find themselves dragged by a sentiment of duty into the struggle, the revolt against that which is.

Jacobo Ruffini was my friend, my first and best. From our first years at the University to the year 1831, when a prison and then exile separated me from him, we lived as brothers, our souls interpenetrating each other freely. He was studying medicine, I law; but botanical rambles at first, then the common ground of literature, and, above all, the sympathetic instincts of the heart, drew us together little by little until an intimacy succeeded, the like of which I have never found, and never shall find again. I do not believe I have ever known a soul more completely, more profoundly; and I affirm, with grief and consolation, that I never found a blemish in it. His image ever comes to my mind when I see one of those lilies of the valley, which we so often admired together, with their perfectly white corolla, without calyx, and with their delicate sweet perfume. Like them he was pure and modest. Even the slight bending of his neck toward his shoulder is recalled to my mind by the curvature of the lily's trembling stalk.

Through the loss of his elder brothers, through the frequent and dangerous sicknesses of his mother, whom he adored and who well deserved it, and through domestic complications of every kind, he knew life only as sorrow. Endowed with an exquisite, almost feverish sensibility, he had early contracted an habitual melancholy, tending to fits of sadness amounting almost to frenzy. And yet there was in him no trace of that misanthropical tendency so natural to remarkable natures in enslaved countries. He had little joy in men, but he loved them; he had but little esteem for his contemporaries, but he reverenced Man, man as he shall be, as he can and ought to be. A strong religious disposition combated in him the despair with which everything seemed to contribute to inoculate him. That holy idea of *Progress*, which substitutes Providence for the Fatality of the ancients and the Chance of the " middle ages," had been revealed to him, first by the intuition of his heart, and afterwards by a deep study of History. He worshiped the Ideal as the end of Life, God as its source, Genius as God's interpreter, almost always misunderstood. He was sad because he was in advance of others, and because he felt that, like Moses, he should never live to reach the Promised Land. But he was habitually calm, because he knew that the end of our terrestrial existence is not *happiness*, but the accomplishment of *duty*, the exercise of a mission even when it presents no hope of any immediate result. His smile was the smile of a victim; but it was a smile. His love for mankind was, like the ideal love of Schiller, a love without individual hope; but it was love. His own sufferings in no wise influenced his actions.

In 1827 and '28 his attention was forcibly attracted by the literary question. It was the time of the great quarrel between those who were called the *romantic* and the *classic;* and who should rather have been called the supporters of *liberty* and *authority*. The one party maintained that, the human mind being progressive, every epoch ought to find a different literary manifestation of it; and that we should seek the precepts and inspirations of art in the heart of the living and actual nation. The others pretended that in art we had long ago reached the Pillars of Hercules; that the Greeks and Romans had furnished models which we should be content to copy, and that all innovation, whether in form or spirit, was dangerous. The unity of the human mind, which renders us unable to conquer a principle without seeking to apply it to every mode of our action, and the condition of Italy, naturally drew those who studied the question on to political ground; and the Governments, by their fears, precipitated them upon it. The young men who made their first campaigns in favour of romanticism became suspected; journals purely literary were suppressed, solely because they maintained independence in art. To this brutal negation given by force we replied by transporting the question to the national ground, and by preparing to try, hand-to-hand, the principle of blind and immovable authority. Jacobo Ruffini was one of the first to climb to the source. In 1829, a year before the French insurrection, he had given his name to the men who followed, between exile and the scaffold, the holy route which leads to the national organization.

In 1830, when the movements in France awakened the alarms of the Italian Governments, that of Piedmont was the first which proceeded to arrests. I was then thrown into the fortress of Savona, and I never more saw my friend. When, some months later, I quitted Italy, he had, on some vague suspicion, been sent away to Taggia, a little provincial town of the Riviera of Genoa.

These petty persecutions served only to strengthen in his soul the thought of devoting himself entirely to the national cause. Among some letters written from the place of his banishment to his mother— letters full of a child-like love mingled with the sad presentiments of age—I find a fragment of an eloquent and impassioned address to the Piedmontese King, to engage him to put himself at the head of an Italian Crusade. It was then (1831) the first year of the reign of Charles Albert, who as prince had conspired like us, and who as king forgot his promises, his friendships, and his duties.

At the beginning of 1832, all hope in the King

having been destroyed, Jacobo Ruffini gave his name and his activity to "Young Italy," and became one of the directors of the labours of the Association in Genoa, his native town.[1]

Ruffini had felt from the first that his fate was decided; he awaited it firmly. They warned him of the immediately impending arrest, they advised him to flee. He replied that those whose example had led others into danger ought to be the first to die.

Arrested, questioned, pressed, he was content to smile. One day he was called before the Auditor of War, Kati Opizzoni. "You are a brave young man," said Opizzoni to him: "you have worked for good, and you bear to-day the appearance of a man of conviction. But see! you have believed yourself leagued with a band of heroes, and it is only a troop of cowards who have betrayed you. You think to bury with you the secret of a holy cause; and you are sacrificing your youth, your family, your aged mother, in order not to confess that which your most intimate friends have declared against you. Look, however!" And he passed a document before his eyes. It was a complete denunciation signed with the name of a friend possessing all his confidence.[2]

---

[1] Here in the memoir as written by Mazzini follows an account of the conspiracy of 1833, and the arrests and persecutions of the patriots by the Piedmontese Government, as already recounted, and not needing repetition.

[2] Signed with the name of Mazzini. Opizzoni's address was the formula, with occasional variations, in vogue to obtain confessions from prisoners.

The signature was forged. But for a man with a nervous sensibility like that of Ruffini it was not the moment for a cool and clever verification. There was a resemblance. He believed it.

"Send me back to my prison!" he said. "I am too much agitated at this moment. To-morrow you shall have my answer."

Returned to his cell, he tore a nail from the door and opened a vein in his throat. In the morning they found his dead body, and on the wall these words written in his blood: "This is my answer; I leave my vengeance to my brothers."

THE BANDIERAS.

THE name of the brothers Bandiera has often been pronounced, but very few know anything of them beyond the simple fact of their adventurous enterprise and tragical end. What they were, what a life of virtues and of noble thoughts they could have devoted to their country, and through their country to Humanity, if a country had not been denied them, is not known. And yet this is most important to the Cause for which they are dead; it is this which elevates their enterprise to the importance of a symptom of the state of things and of minds in Italy.

ATTILIO and EMILIO BANDIERA, sprung from one of the old patrician families of Venice and sons of the Baron Bandiera, rear-admiral in the Austrian navy, had followed the paternal career, and held high rank in the fleet when they began to be known in the ranks of those secretly devoted to the success of the Italian National cause. "I am an Italian," wrote Attilio, the elder of the two brothers, in the first letter I received from him, dated August 15, 1842,— "I am an Italian, a soldier, and not proscribed. I am rather feeble in body, ardent at heart, very often cold in appearance. I seek to temper my soul in the practice of stoical maxims. I believe in God, in a future life, in human progress; from Humanity, taken as a point of departure, I descend in my thoughts to country, to one's family, to the individual. I hold as certain that justice is the basis of all right: I have long concluded that the Italian Cause is but a dependence upon that of mankind; and I console myself for all the difficulties of the present by thinking that to serve Italy is to serve Humanity altogether. I have therefore decided to devote all my being to the practical development of these principles."

And in a later letter Emilio in his turn said to me—"We wish for a country, free, united, and republican; we propose to ourselves to have no faith but in the national means, not to count upon foreign succour, and to throw down the gauntlet of defiance so soon as we shall be sufficiently strong."

How did they arrive at this?—they, soldiers, bound

by all the exigencies of discipline, deprived of all
contact with the patriots of the Peninsula, living on
shipboard, now at Smyrna, now at Constantinople,
another time off Syria (where they distinguished
themselves in the action of the combined English
and Austrian forces), scarcely greeting with their
eyes the vanishing shores of their country. " I have
never until the other day," wrote Attilio in the
letter I have quoted, "been able to read a single
writing of 'Young Italy.'" And yet at this period
they had already organized an important work on
identical bases. The Italian spirit fermented in them
in virtue of their origin. The Austrian uniform
weighed upon their breasts; the Austrian flag,
flying over vessels manned almost exclusively by
Italians, appeared to them an outrage. And the
name they bore, devoted to the universal reprobation
of Italy in consequence of the arrest by their father,
at sea, in 1831, of the patriots who were leaving for
France, gave to their desire of action an additional
impulse. In their most private talk they avoided
all allusion to their father; but one saw in the fire
of their sad and sombre regards that they felt the
want of rehabilitating their tarnished name. For
the rest, they fulfilled all their domestic duties. They
passionately loved their mother. Attilio was both
husband and father; but the duty of raising a young
soul to the worship of the Just and the True reinforced his duties toward his country; and his wife,
since dead of grief, was worthy of him.

I am not able to state here either what the brothers wished to do, or the causes which nullified the results of the Italian agitation of 1844. But, as in all prolonged preparations, treason was already in the beginning of that year creeping into our ranks. Denounced, first to their father, then to the Austrian Government, by a man who had feigned to join them, they were, toward the end of February (1844), compelled to flee, during the night, in an open boat, to different points: Emilio alone, Attilio with an old soldier, Mariano, who desired to follow him, and who now expiates his fidelity in the dungeons of Santo Stefano, in the Kingdom of Naples. "How will they support this ruin?" wrote Attilio at the end of the letter which announced to me the treason and their flight—"my poor mother and my wife, frail creatures, perhaps incapable of resisting such great griefs. Ah! to serve Humanity and one's Country has been and will be always, I hope, my first desire; but I must confess that it costs me much." His wife had been informed by the brother, at Venice, of their projected flight; she had kept the secret from the family, without letting them for an instant divine what she suffered. But when she knew *him* out of reach, grief got the better. She died a short time after. She was fair, good, and brave. And if I had not very long firmly believed that the woman and the man who, loving each other, die of suffering, must one day be reunited as angels in some holy mystery of eternal love, the sole thought of this woman dying of a broken heart, without unjust irritation and without complaint, for the man who was himself after some months to die in his turn in bearing witness for his faith and doubtless thinking of her, this sole thought would be sufficient to give me such belief.

Emilio had repaired directly to Corfu. The Austrian Government, afraid of the moral effect which the flight of the two officers must produce in Italy by revealing to all how the Italian spirit was at work even in their army, endeavoured to make them appear as mutinous children, and to prevail on them to accept a pardon. "The Archduke Rainieri," wrote Emilio to me on the 23rd of April, "Viceroy of the Lombardo-Venetian Kingdom, sent one of his people to my mother, to tell her that if she could succeed in bringing me back to Venice he would engage his *sacred* word of honour that I should be not only acquitted but restored to my rank, to my nobility, to my honours. He added that my brother, older than I, had not the same right to hope; but that, the clemency of the Emperor Ferdinand was so great, he would very probably end in obtaining the same conditions. My mother believes, hopes, departs on the instant, arrives here. I leave you to imagine what I suffer at the moment I am writing to you. It is in vain that I endeavour to make her comprehend that *duty* orders me to remain here, that I should be happy to see my country again; but that when I shall direct my steps thither it will not be to live an ignominious life, but to die there a glorious death; that my safe-conduct in Italy henceforth rests on the point of my sword; that no affection ought to be able to detach me from the flag I have embraced; that the flag of a king may be abandoned, that of a country never. My mother, agitated, blinded by passion, cannot understand me, calls me impious, unnatural, assassin; and her tears rend my heart; her reproaches, though I feel not to merit them, are to me as so many strokes of a poignard; but the desolation does not deprive me of mind; I know that these tears and this anger fall upon our tyrants, whose ambition condemns families to such struggles. Write me a word of consolation!"

I know not what others will think of the refusal of Emilio, but to me he appears yet greater at this moment than when, calm and cool, he fell under the fire at Cosenza. Many men think that they *love* when they aspire to happiness and follow a shadow here below, even in betraying their duty; many women, alas! educated in the slavish habits of despotism, preach, without knowing it, in the name of *love*, to their children or their husbands, the abandonment of that Law of God, the eternal worship of the Just and True. And *love*, the purification of two souls, the one through the other, loses itself in the personal or sensual instinct of the brute. But when Faith, to-day extinct in men's souls, shall have rebuilt its temple of Love, the saintliness of Emilio's affection for his mother and his refusal will, I repeat, in the eyes of all be the fairest flower in his martyr-crown.

Attilio rejoined his brother at Corfu. They were no more separated. They received a citation to appear before an Austrian court-martial, to which they together replied by a refusal expressed in some lines which were published in the Maltese journals. War was thus declared; and another young officer, their friend from infancy, handsome as an angel, pure as a child, brave as a lion, DOMENICO MORO, quitted the *Adria*, which happened then to touch at Malta, and went to say to them—" We have lived, loved, and suffered together; together we will die."

For to die was their clear purpose. The two Bandieras, open as they were to all great thoughts, were above all men of action. They respired it at every pore. Impatient to bear witness, they searched on all sides to find the arena into which to fling themselves. Ignorant of details, they instinctively comprehended Italy such as she is to-day: full of national aspirations, but backward and uncertain in her knowledge of the means which compass great things; rich in individual devotedness, weak in anything like collective action: fretted by the common evil, the difference between theory and practice. The Italians, they said, need to learn that life is but the realization, the incarnation of thought; that *only they believe* who feel the necessity, come what may, of translating into acts that which they think to be the True. Italy will live when Italians shall have learned to die. And for that there is no teaching but by example.

Thus they resolved to die. The severe bearing of Attilio, the serene piety of Emilio, betrayed the reflection of the same thought: the first had the air of meditating the accomplishment of the mission he had imposed upon himself; the second had bidden adieu to the things of earth and waited tranquilly until his brother should strike the hour. They were consecrated victims, hearts devoted to death.

We all knew that. And jealous to preserve for better combined efforts two such precious lives, we strove desperately against the fatality of the idea which dragged them on. But they were too strong for us. During a short time, while we had only to contend against the sombre rapture of their sacrifice, we hoped to conquer. Later, the Italian Governments, alarmed by informations to which I will not return, but which Englishmen will do well not to forget,[1] began to throw the weight of all their scoundrelism into the scale; and we were lost. In June the agents of the Neapolitan Government poured into their ears the most encouraging reports; Calabria was in flames; bands of insurgents overran the mountains; they only waited for chiefs to organize their action, and these chiefs were expected from among the Italian exiles. The Bandieras

---

[1] Referring to the informations given by Lord Aberdeen to the Austrian Government when he had Mazzini's letters opened at the English Post-office.

believed this; sold all they had, of jewels, of souvenirs of value; converted all into arms, and set forth.

"In a few hours," said the last letter I received from Attilio, written on the 11th of June, "we set out for Calabria. If we arrive safe and sound, we shall do our best, militarily and politically. Seventeen other Italians follow us, exiles for the most part; we have a Calabrian guide. Remember us, and believe that if we are able to set foot in Italy we shall be firm in sustaining the principles we have preached together. If we fall, tell our countrymen to imitate our example. Life has been given to us only to employ it usefully and nobly; and the cause for which we shall combat, and die, is the purest, the holiest, that ever warmed human breasts."

A traitor had been placed among them. He quitted them on the 16th, as soon as they disembarked; and went by Cotrone to declare to the Government the direction they had taken, their plan, their force. They wandered three days in the mountains, till at last, reaching the village of San Giovanni in Fiore, usually ungarrisoned, they found themselves surrounded by forces twenty times superior. They fought, however; one of them, Miller, fell dead; another, Moro, riddled with wounds; two contrived to save themselves in the mountains; the rest were made prisoners.

On the 25th of July, at five in the morning, Attilio and Emilio Bandiera, with seven of their companions,—Nicola Ricciotti, Domenico Moro, Anacarsi

Nardi, Giovanni Venerucci, Giacomo Rocca, Francesco Berti, Domenico Lupatelli,—were shot to death at Cosenza.[1] Their last moments (described by an eye-witness) were worthy of them. Awakened from a tranquil sleep, they dressed themselves with care, with even a sort of elegance, as if they were preparing for a religious solemnity. A priest, who came to confess them, was mildly repulsed. "We have sought," they said, "to practise the law of the Gospel, and to make it triumph even at the price of our blood. We hope that our works will recommend us to God better than your words. Go and preach to our oppressed brothers the religion of Liberty and Equality!" Arrived at the place of execution, they asked the soldiers to spare the face "made in the image of God." One cry of "Viva l'Italia!" and all was said.

Some months after, a letter reached one of our friends in Corfu, written by one of the condemned, twelve hours before the fatal moment. The calm solemn tone in which it is written reminds me of the heroes of Plutarch; and I bring it forward here because it must be enough to prove what

---

[1] Nardi, exiled in 1831, was an advocate, and son of the Nardi for a few days Dictator of Modena in the movement of 1831. Rocca and Venerucci were workmen; Miller, from Forli, exiled in 1831, a workman also: all three remarkable for natural shrewdness, of kindly bearing, and exemplary in conduct. Rocca had been in the service of the Greek poet Salamos, who treated him as a friend. Venerucci was a clever mechanic. Berti was an old soldier of the wars of the first Napoleon.

men accompanied the two brothers in their enterprise.

"To Signor Tito Savelli, Exoria, Corfu.

"Dear Friend,—I write to you for the last time: within twelve hours I shall be no more. My companions in misfortune are the two brothers Bandiera, Ricciotti, Moro, Venerucci, Rocca, Lupatelli, and Berti. Your brother-in-law is exempted from this fate, but I know not to how many years he will be sentenced. Remind your family and all friends of me as often as possible. If it be granted me, I will, before ascending to the Eternal, revisit the Exoria.[1] Kiss for me my Dante and all your children. When you think well, you may make my fate known at Modena and to my brother. Receive the affectionate remembrances of all my companions. I embrace you.

"Your Nardi.

"*From the condemned cell at Cosenza:*
24th of the 7th month, 1844.

"P.S.—I write with handcuffs, and therefore my writing will appear as if written with a trembling hand; but I am tranquil because I die in my own country, and for a sacred cause. The friend who used to come on horseback was our ruin. Once more, farewell!"

[1] Exoria (exile) was the name given by the exiled Dr. Savelli to his house in Corfu, where Nardi had been living. Dante, Savelli's eldest son, was Nardi's god-son.

[The following funeral oration was to have been spoken before the National Association in one of the churches in Milan on the anniversary in 1848 of the martyrs' death. Not being delivered as intended, it was published by Mazzini as a supplement to the *Italia del Popolo* of the 4th of August, the day before Charles Albert's capitulation.]

To the Memory of the Martyrs of Cosenza.
July 25, 1844.

When I received from you, O young men! the charge to pronounce in this temple a few words sacred to the memory of the brothers Bandiera and their martyr companions at Cosenza, I thought that perhaps some one of those who would hear me might exclaim with noble indignation—"To what end are these laments for the Dead? The martyrs for Liberty can only be worthily honoured by winning the battle they have begun. Cosenza, the land where they died, is a slave; Venice, the city which gave them birth, hemmed in by foreigners. Let us emancipate them, and from this moment no sound be on our lips but that of war!" But another thought arose, and said to me—Why are we not victorious? Why is it that, while the North of Italy combats for Liberty, Liberty perishes in the South? Why is it that a war, which ought to have leaped with a lion's bound to the Alps, drags along for four months slowly and uncertainly as the crawl of a scorpion girt by a circle of fire? Why is it that the rapid, powerful intuition of the genius of a People risen again to life has sunk into the weary and incapable fancy of a sick man turning in his bed? Ah! if we all had risen in the holiness of that *idea* for which our martyrs died,—if the banner of their faith had gone before our young men in their battles,— if with that collective unity of life which was so powerful in them we had made of every thought an action, of every action a thought,—if their last words devoutly garnered in our minds had taught us that liberty and independence are one and the same thing, that God and the People, that Country and Humanity, are inseparable terms in any undertaking of a people that wishes to become a Nation, that Italy can not be unless she be One, holy through the equality and love of all her sons and great through her worship of the Eternal Truth, by her consecration to a high mission, to a moral priesthood among the peoples of Europe,—we should to-day have victory, not war; Cosenza would not be condemned to venerate in secret the memory of the martyrs; the dread of seeing it profaned by the insults of the foreigner would not withhold Venice from honouring them with a monument; and we assembled here might, without uncertainty as to our fate, without any cloud of sadness on our brows, gladly invoke their sacred names and say to those forerunning souls—"Rejoice, for your brothers have incarnated your idea and are worthy of you!"

Not yet, O young men! is their adored conception resplendent, pure and perfect, upon your banners. The sublime programme which they dying bequeathed to the nascent Italian generation is not yours so mutilated and torn to fragments by false doctrines which, elsewhere overthrown, have taken refuge amongst us. I look, and see an agitation of separate populations, an alternation of generous rage and unworthy quiet, of free cries and formulas of servitude, in all parts of the Peninsula: but where is the heart of the Peninsula? Where is the unity of this unequal manifold movement? Where the dominating Word of these hundred voices of ministers of diverse counsels ever crossing each other, misleading and seducing the multitude? I hear talk, usurping the national omnipotence, of a Northern Italy, of a League of States, of a Federal Pact among the Princes; but where is ITALY? Where is the common country which the Bandieras saluted as Initiator, for the third time, of an era of European civilization? Intoxicated by the first victories, improvident for the future, we bore not in mind the idea revealed by God to those who suffered; and God punishes that forgetfulness by deferring our triumph. The movement of Italy, brothers! is by the decree of Providence the movement of Europe. We rising become sureties of moral progress for the European world. But neither political fictions nor dynastic aggrandisements, nor theories of opportunity, can transform and renew the life of a people. Humanity lives and moves only in one faith. Only great principles are the stars which guide Europe to the Future. Let us, O young men! turn to the sepulchres of our martyrs, to ask from the inspirations of those who died for us all, the secret of victory, the adoration of a Principle, even Faith. The Angel of Martyrdom and the Angel of Victory are brothers; but the one looks toward the heavens, the other toward the earth; and only when, from epoch to epoch, their regards encounter each other between earth and heaven, creation beautifies itself with new life, and a People arises from the cradle or the tomb—Evangelist or Prophet.

I will in few words tell you, young men! what was the faith of the martyrs. As to the externals of their lives, they are to-day a part of history well known to you; I need not remind you of it. The faith of the brothers Bandiera, which was and is ever ours, rests upon a few simple and incontestable truths, which scarcely any one ventures to declare false, but which yet are betrayed or forgotten by almost every one.

God and *the People:* God at the pinnacle of the social edifice; the People, the universality of our brethren, at the base: God the Father and Educator, the People the progressive Interpreter of His Law.

There is no real society without a common faith and a common purpose. Religion declares the faith and the purpose; polity (the political) orders society toward a practical interpretation of this faith, and prepares the means for attaining this purpose. Religion represents the *principle;* politics should be the *application.*

There is only one sun in heaven for the whole earth; there is only one law for all who people earth. It is the law of the human being, the law of the life of Humanity. We are here, not to exercise our individual faculties according to our caprices (faculties and freedom are means, not ends), not merely to labour for our own happiness on earth (happiness can only be obtained elsewhere, and there God works for us), but for this, to consecrate ourselves to the discovering of as much as possible of the Divine Law, in order to practise it so far as our individual faculties and the times allow—so to shed forth knowledge and love among our brethren. We are here to labour to found fraternally *the unity of the human family*, so that it may one day present but one fold and one shepherd, the Spirit of God, His Law. To attain the True, God has given us *tradition*—the voices of the preceding generations of mankind, and the voice of our own *conscience*. Where these are in accord with one another, there is the True; where they stand in opposition, there is Error. To conquer this harmony, this accord between the conscience of the individual and the conscience of the human race, no sacrifice can be too great. The Family, the City, the Country, Humanity—these are but different spheres in which our activity and power of sacrifice should be exercised for the attainment of that supreme purpose. God watches from on high to ordain the inevitability of human progress, and to sustain those priests of His truth and guides of the many in their pilgrimage, the Powers of Genius and of Love, of Thought and of Action.

From these principles, pointed to in their letters, in their proclamations, in their discourse, from the conscience they so deeply felt of a mission confided by God to the Individual and to Humanity, the brothers Attilio and Emilio Bandiera and their fellow-martyrs at Cosenza derived the rule of their labours, the consolation which gave serenity to their lives, a religious cheerfulness in death, and, even when men and circumstances betrayed them, an undying hope in the future of Italy. The immense energy of their souls gushed forth through the immense and intensest love with which their faith informed them. And could they now arise from their graves and speak to you, they would address to you, O young men! with that high power which has not been given to me, counsels not unlike to those I now utter.

Love! Love is the soul's wing toward God, and toward the Great, the Beautiful, the Sublime, which are God's shadows upon the earth. Love your family, the companion of your life, the men ready to share with you your sorrows and your joys, the departed who were so dear to you and who will be ever dear! But let your love be the love which Dante taught you, and which we have taught you: the love of souls advancing, and not raking the soil in search of a peace not given to the creature on earth, a delusion that inevitably sinks into egotism. To love is to promise and to receive promises for the future. God has given love here as a sign of heaven, that the wearied soul may have on whom to lean and whom to lift on the road of life; as a flower sown in the path of Duty, which does not alter Duty. Purify, fortify yourselves by better loving! Do, albeit under bond of increase of earthly sorrows, so that the sister soul may never here or elsewhere blush either for you or through you. The time will come when, from the height of the new life, embracing the past and understanding its secret, you shall smile together upon past griefs and trials well endured.

Love your Country! your Country is the land where sleep the ashes of your parents, where also is spoken the language in which the Lady of your heart murmured, blushing, her first words of love. It is the dwelling-place which God has given you, wherein, working toward perfection, you may prepare to ascend to Him; it is your name, your glory, your sign among the peoples. Give it your thought, your counsel, and your blood! Build it up beautiful and grand as our heights present it to you. But beware of leaving on it the trace of a lie, or the slavery which would contaminate it; be careful not to profane it by dismembering it. Let it be one, even as the thought of God! You are twenty-four millions of men, endowed with active, splendid faculties; you have traditions of glory which the nations of Europe envy; before you stands an immense future; your eyes behold the fairest skies which are known to Europe; around you smiles the loveliest nature that Europe can admire; and you are encircled by the Alps and the sea, those outlines drawn by the finger of God for a giant people. And such you ought to be, or else not be at all. Not one man of these twenty-four millions should remain excluded from the fraternal pact you have to frame, not one single glance not free should be raised to contemplate this heaven. Be Rome the sacred Ark of your redemption, the Temple of the Nation. Has it not already twice been the Temple of the destinies of Europe? In Rome two extinct worlds, the Pagan and the world of the Popes, lie superposed one on the other, like a double jewel on a diadem. Create a third world vaster than the two! From Rome, from the Holy City, from the City of Love (Amor—Roma), the purest, the wisest among you, strengthened by the inspiration of a whole people, shall dictate the Pact by which you shall be bound as one and represented in the future alliance of Peoples. Until then you have no Country, or you have it contaminated.

Love Humanity! You cannot separate your mission from the end proposed by God for Humanity. God has given you your Country for your cradle and Humanity for your mother; and you cannot love your cradle-brothers if you do not love your common Country. Beyond the Alps, beyond the seas, stand other peoples fighting, or making ready to fight with you the sacred battles of Independence, Nationality, Liberty: other peoples who tend by different ways to the self-same end, perfectibility, association, the foundation of an Authority which shall put an end to moral anarchy, which shall reknit earth to heaven, and which men may love and follow un-blushingly and without remorse. League yourselves with them as they would unite with you! Invoke them not if your own arms can-vanquish; but tell them that the hour is about to strike for a terrible conflict between Right and blind Force, and that at that hour you will be with all who advance under the same banner.

Love, O young men! and revere Ideas! Ideas are the words of God. Superior to all of Country, superior to Humanity, is the Country of the Intellectual, the City of the Spirit, in which the believers in the inviolability of Thought, in the dignity of an immortal soul, are brothers. And the baptism of this brotherhood is martyrdom. From this high sphere descend Principles, which alone can redeem the peoples. Let your insurrection stir from them, and not from the mere insupportableness of suffering or the fear of the wicked. Wrath, pride, ambition, lust of material prosperity, are weapons common to both the peoples and their oppressors: and besides, should you conquer by their aid to-day you would fall back again to-morrow. But principles belong to the people alone, and the oppressors will not find arms wherewith to oppose them. Reverence enthusiasm! Adore the dreams of the virgin soul and the visions of the first days of youth!— for these dreams of earliest youth are the fragrance of Paradise which the soul retains in issuing from the hands of its Creator. Respect before all things your own conscience! Have on your lips that truth which God placed in your heart! And harmoniously uniting in all that tends to the emancipation of our soil, even with those who dissent from you, bear ever erect your banner, and boldly promulgate your faith!

These words, O young men! the martyrs of Cosenza would tell you were they still living among you. And here, where perhaps invoked by our love their holy souls are appeased, I summon you to receive them into your bosoms, keeping them as treasures against storms which still await us, but which, with the names of our Martyrs on our lips and their faith in our hearts, we yet shall overcome.

God be with you, and bless our Italy!

JOSEPH MAZZINI.

July 25, 1848.

LAMENNAIS.

LAMENNAIS.

"La foi et la pensée ont brisé les chaines des peuples ; la foi et la pensée ont affranchi la terre."—Paroles d'un Croyant.

IN 1848, in the first days of the French Revolution, I accompanied Mazzini to Paris. I was the bearer to the Provisional Government of the first congratulatory Address from England, from a meeting hastily convened, chiefly of working-men. Then I first saw the Abbé Lamennais, taking to him a copy of the Address, to be published in his journal, *Le Peuple Constituant*, in which he daily put forth his views of the crisis and of the duties of the people and the Government : a journal begun on the morrow of the Revolution, and continued until the unhappy days of June, when Cavaignac (the General) suppressed it. I found Lamennais in the Rue Jacob, in a plain, scantily-furnished room, which served him for editorial office and sleeping-room, a small, frail, worn, most earnest man, giving his days and nights to the service of the young Republic. One evening calling to see him, he was out, and I had to wait. Meanwhile I spoke on the stairs with a lad who went on his errands, did

O

his chores, carried out his paper, &c. How eloquent he was in praise of his master's goodness! The man whom the Papacy, fearing him, deemed worthy of a special anathema, the man whose greatness of soul and intellect commanded the reverence of the foremost minds of Europe, held also the heart-strings of the people.

In 1815, writes Mazzini, in the *Monthly Chronicle* (London 1839), a foreigner of modest aspect and timid bearing presented himself at the town residence of Lady Jerningham, sister-in-law to Lord Stafford. He went, with an introduction from I know not whom, to seek a situation as a teacher. He was poor and poorly dressed. The lady put a few laconic questions to him, and dismissed him; because, as she told a friend, "he looked too stupid." That young man was Lamennais.

Nine years later (1824) a priest, the rapid sale of whose writings, to the extent of 40,000 copies, had made him famous, who, writing against the revolutionary spirit of the time, displayed an eloquence equal to that of Bossuet, and learning and logic superior, was traveling, full of fervid faith and hope, from France to Rome, in order to confer with Leo XII. In the Pontiff's chamber the only ornaments he saw were a painting of the Virgin and his own portrait. Leo XII. received him with friendly confidence and admiration, taking his advice in the appointment of Cardinal Lambruschini as Apostolic Nuncio to France. On every side he was greeted with a chorus of thankful praise, which, though it could not dim his clear and severe judgment, yet filled his heart with joy; he believed it presaged a new epoch of life for the Church, that Rome inspired by his voice would rise to the height of that vast social mission which his own imagination, and the needs of a generation wearied with scepticism and desirous of an aim, called for from her.

That priest was Lamennais.

Yet eight years more, and the same priest, saddened and oppressed with thought, was again wending toward Rome, this time to clear himself from accusations which assailed not only his works but his motives. He went to justify himself in the presence of that Authority whose past was sacred to him, and in whose service he had laboured unceasingly for twenty years. Pure in soul, and led by one of those illusions which only the shock of facts can overthrow (too often destroying the soul also), he was on his way to make one last effort to revive that decayed Authority, to endeavour to infuse one drop of the life-blood of Humanity into its exhausted veins. The then Pope, Gregory XVI., received him coldly, and that only on condition of his keeping silence as to the very question of his journey. Full of sorrow and of bitterness, the priest departed; bowed to his superiors; submitted to the discontinuance of his work; and retired, wounded to the heart, to the solitude of La Chenay, about a league from Dinan. Disheartened, but not broken, instead of giving himself up to despair, he meditated upon the new life to succeed that now proved extinct. His eagle glance explored the heights and depths of the world, searching for and studying every sign of that life to come, while prayerfully waiting the inward inspiration that should reveal to him the site of the future Temple of the Deity.

One day when both Rome and the Monarchy believed him crushed and conquered, he arose as if by an irresistible impulse, his voice with double power as the voice of one of the prophets of old, his speech with all the religious solemnity of one who after long seeking had found at last the truth. And this time the Pope neither welcomed nor received him, but started in his pontifical chair to anathematize (in his Encyclical of the 7th of July, 1834) Lamennais' *Words of a Believer*, that little book of huge depravity (*libellum . . . mole quidem exiguum pravitate tamen ingentem*) which had disturbed his dreamy sleep, and which stirred the hearts of all who were alive in Europe.

FÉLICITÉ ROBERT DE LA MENNAIS was born in 1782, at St. Malo in Brittany. His family, wealthy through commerce, is said to have been ennobled by Louis XV., for generous aid rendered to the poor in a time of famine : a generosity that may have been the archetype of Lamennais' noble life. The family wealth was lost in the Revolution, and at the time of Félicité's birth they were too poor to afford him any regular education. His mother died during his infancy. Restless and vehement as a child, the boy was reared in freedom, untrammeled by school rules or much tutorship of any kind, passing his days between the sea-coast and the family library, where he was often shut in by an old uncle, with Horace and Tacitus as his companions. So he grew, in solitude and silence, reading without order whatever he could get hold of, and communing with the stormy seas that beat against the barren rocks of Brittany, exciting the enthusiasm even of his boyish years.

Like all powerful natures, his youth was troubled with religious doubt and incredulity. What minds that dared to think at all but were submerged for some period, long or short, under the ebbing wave of the negational philosophy of the French Revolution, the sway of which is felt even to this day! Then the tumult had not subsided. But young Lamennais could not long remain in doubt; and, reared a Catholic, at least in form, it was natural that seeking a belief he should incline to the only one within his reach, that too laying claim to his affection as being oppressed by the ruling powers, held in leash if not in connivance with them. Atheistic Force in the person of the Great Napoleon reigned over France; scepticism and materialism were in vogue; the Church was ruled by the State, protected, that is tolerated, made use of, and enslaved. To the ardent and religious soul of Lamennais in this forced impotence or prostitution of the Church the cause of all the evil of the time was to be traced. The hour had not come for him to look farther. Born and bred a Roman Catholic, he believed in the sovereignty of his faith, in its certain moral triumph unrestrained by these external hindrances. So he was led in 1808 (the year after the Spanish insurrection) to publish his first work, *Reflections on the Condition of the Church in France*. It was at once an utterance of true religious feeling and a Voice from the People, and as such a presage of the epoch to come; but of the book itself it must be owned that it was merely a violent and intolerant assault upon the disposition to negation displayed by the eighteenth century, and an appeal to the clergy to rekindle men's faith in things spiritual by worthily representing that faith themselves. There was nothing in his language to offend the existing powers; but it was bold, and as if foreseeing the genius that must one day fraternize with the People, the Imperial Police took fright and suppressed the work.

Four years later, in conjunction with his brother, he brought out a second work, *On the Institution of Bishops*. When Napoleon fell, he went to Paris, remaining there in poverty until the return from Elba. It was then that, already obnoxious to the Empire, he sought an asylum in England, where he lived some seven months, poor and unnoticed. Returning to France after the final overthrow of the Emperor, he retired to Brittany, and in 1817, having then turned thirty-four years of age, entered the priesthood at Rennes. In the same year he published the first volume of his work *On Indifference in Matters of Religion.* This was his first experience and his first illusion.

His first illusion. The Revolution had persecuted Religion; the Empire had degraded it in making it depend upon the State; the new Monarchy promised to restore its honours. Right Divine and the Catholic principle of Authority, starting from the same ground, must of course acknowledge an identity of interests. Outside the governmental corps the one principle of action was reaction, merely opposition. So was it among the masses, representing the instinct of the age, the perception that no real vitality was left in the Church; so was it with speculative thinkers, almost all of whom belonged to the purely rationalistic and experimental school; so too in the ranks of the politicians, the Liberals of that day, followers of the superficial school of Voltaire, mere destroyers or but assertors of rights under compromise, and incapable of comprehending the conception of a progressive epoch.

Trembling at the recollection of the excesses of the Revolution, irritated by an indifference threatening the nation with intellectual torpor more perilous than an active hostility however falsely grounded, convinced that the policy pursued by the dominant schools led only to incredulity and had in it no germs of a future, Lamennais was driven to rest his hopes upon the existing powers. He cherished the idea of a Monarchy so linked with Religion as to be able to put an end to the existing moral anarchy, and to reconstitute a vast and prolific unity. His work (*On Indifference, &c.*) is based on the notion of a chimerical alliance of the two. The volumes (issued successively between 1817 and 1824) were, like his first work, unjust and intolerant, violent in the political portions and imperfect although powerful in the philosophical. The real merit of the work consisted in its undeniable eloquence, and in that it was a forcible expression of a real need, a need already forefelt by poetry, the need of re-establishing Tradition as the source of Authority, of breaking through the circle in which rationalism and materialism had enclosed the human mind, and of going forward under the double guidance of a religious faith and the conscience of Humanity. The author of the work *On Indifference* thus served, though unconsciously, the cause of progress. He restored to Tradition, without which no philosophy can exist, its rights; and he infused new life and gave new consecration to philosophy itself, by bringing it into contact with the social world from which it had gradually been farther and farther withdrawn.

Led astray by his political leanings, Lamennais misconceived the bearing and consequences of his own principles; and his view of Tradition was narrow and arbitrary; but he reopened the true path, and that alone is sufficient to give a philosophical value to his work. The restitution of this one vital element of human intellectual progress is the principal characteristic of the book. For the rest, his belief in Monarchy was rather the prompting of opportunity, to be given up when the Monarchy showed itself as little cognizant as the Empire of its duties whether toward the people or to the faith. He allied himself to it, not so much because of its intrinsic merit as because it presented an appearance of stability from which he anticipated a potency for good. At times he made it evident that he had suspicions; and his frequent reproofs of the Monarchy for its lack of energy already betrayed that Republican severity which afterward inspired the *Words of a Believer*, and which the conduct of the Monarchy was well fitted to foster and to provoke.

Surrounded, if we could believe the scribes of royalty and orthodoxy, by an aureole of religious piety and "most Catholic" fervour, the restored Monarchy, caring only for the Church as its accomplice and supple tool, held it firmly chained to the chair of State, while pretending to revere it, preventing all freedom of action or criticism, and making religion itself hateful when men saw nothing but a mere forced and hypocritical alliance, in which the State Church as it were accepted complicity in every action of the State, however injurious to the country or repugnant to the instincts of Humanity.

While yet unconvinced of the hopelessness of the task he had set himself, Lamennais wrote on the Monarchical side: first in the *Conservateur* (Chateaubriand's paper), then in the *Drapeau Blanc*, then in the *Mémorial Catholique:* always however preserving his independent attitude. Little by little he abandoned the cause of Monarchy, and more and more devoted himself to the Religious Question. His dissatisfaction was still more openly evinced in 1825, when he published his *Religion considered in its relation to civil and political matters*, a book prosecuted by the Government, and for which he was condemned to a fine of thirty-six francs; and expressed again in the *Progress of Revolution and the War against the Church*, published in 1829, in which he maintained the cause of religious independence against the Government.

1830 arrived. The new monarchy, the issue of fifteen years of purely negative and sceptical opposition, could hardly be more religious than the monarchy it displaced. To organize power with firmness and maintain it by corruption, constituting it upon a basis of material interests, so leading men's minds away from the path of ideas and moral progress,—to manage somehow for harmony between the inclinations of the people's representatives in Parliament and the personal objects of the Citizen King,—such was the programme of the monarchy of 1830, the "Monarchy surrounded by Republican institutions" of the respectable Louis Philippe. Without principles, without belief, without care either for the people or for the Church, no wonder that at last the single-minded apostle of religious duty found reason to hold Empire, Legitimacy, and Constitution in equal disesteem.

Out of France was yet worse. In Italy, in Austria, in Russia, where the people were most cruelly oppressed, the Church was but an instrument in the hands of Injustice, hardly worthy to be called an accomplice. Lamennais' experience was complete: that illusion, the dream of Paul with Cain or Judas on his right hand as his minister to reform society (it is easy to note the folly of a departed illusion), was gone for ever. In disdainful anger he burst the bonds that so long had held him. Yet remained one anchor of his hope, one element of Authority to be tested in the service of righteousness, a power great in the majesty of its gigantic Past, the accredited representative of Him who had loved the people: the Papacy. To the Pope, to the head of the Church, to the Church itself, since the magisterial power was faithless, Lamennais turned to depend on that alone: from one illusion proceeding to another.

It was part of his education. He has been accused of inconstancy, of fickleness, of seeking only victory: so changing after defeat. But *progress* and *change* are not identical terms. To progress is to live; and the true life of genius consists precisely in its assimilation of the great manifestations of its age. For popular applause, for victory for his own sake, Lamennais cared not; his was rather the temperament of the martyr; he followed only what he believed to be truth, ever searching as he went. And looking with earnest eyes, even through the most orthodoxly coloured spectacles, he could not but see the passing shadows of the time. Throughout Europe were signs and appearances of the new life of the peoples struggling to escape the grave-yards of the Peace of 1815. In the movements of Poland, Belgium, Switzerland, Italy, were revelations of the new popular principle; the prophetic thrill that then ran through the lands could not but be felt by him, felt and understood. " We live," he wrote, " in one of those epochs in which all things aspire toward renovation. Never was there a presentiment more intense, a conviction more universal. And accordingly as we contemplate the future or the past, life or death, some of us hope, others fear. But we all believe in approaching change, in an inevitable great revolution. It will come, and quickly. In vain they strive to maintain the things that were; in vain they would retrace the course of time or perpetuate the existing anarchy. In the inner nature of things is a supreme and irrevocable fatality stronger than every other power. . . . The people are impelled by an irresistible force. Notwithstanding all efforts, they will go whither they are called; nothing can arrest their course along the path of the ages, for it is upon that path man is gradually prepared for eternity."

Wherefore was it not the duty of the Church, recognizing this pilgrimage of the life of the peoples, recognizing also their natural disposition (well manifested in all the movements between 1815 and 1830) toward justice and order, to lead and regulate their progress, not thwarting but presiding over the providential instincts of the multitudes? From the civil he appealed to the only religious Government he knew, from Louis Philippe to the Pope.

In 1830 he began the daily publication of *The Future* (*L'Avenir*), prefixing as a motto the words "God and Liberty," and defining its object, for the promotion of a doctrine destined to "destroy the reign of force and to substitute for it the reign of justice and charity, so realizing the unity of the human family." At the same time he founded a "General Agency," an association for the protection of ecclesiastics from governmental violations of their liberties, especially as regarded education, and generally to maintain those rights of association for prayer, or study, or deliberation as to remedial measures, whether of religion, civilization, or for the sake of the poor,—rights which he considered to belong more particularly to the Church, and to be unjustly interfered with by the State. Later, looking back on the Polish massacre, and to the conduct of the Liberal party in regard to "foreign questions," he proposed the union of all persons who still "persisted in the hope that the nations would one day be free, and in the determination to labour toward that aim."

These efforts, of the General Agency, and especially the journal, were not without result. Local associations were formed; the provincial papers copied his writings; and several schools were instituted. And, that nought of the earthly portion of the just man, the praises of the good and the persecutions of the wicked, might be withheld from him, the Government seized his journal and summoned him before the Tribunals.

In vain. But now a severer trial was before him: in the proof that his heroic effort to restore life to the Rome of the Popes was without effect, that Rome was but a tomb, and the Papacy a corpse. That corpse, galvanized by diplomacy, rose up to curse the daring priest who believed in the practicability of the Gospel. The old man of the Vatican was only one more bad king among the many; he had committed moral suicide on the day when he refused to listen to the voice of progressive Humanity. Even now, while Lamennais was appealing to him to raise the banner of Christ and Liberty, the king-pope was calling in the Austrians to put down liberty in his own States; while Lamennais was laying the wreaths of his saddest eloquence on the sepulchre of Poland, the Head of Christendom was cursing the Polish patriots and obliging his fellow-pope, the Russo-Greek, by fulminating against the Polish bishops; while Lamennais was collecting money for the Irish, the Papal purse was hiring ruffians to murder the unarmed men and women of Forli and Cesena. Rome persecuted all who sided with Lamennais. In some of the French dioceses ordination was denied to young men suspected of approving the teachings of *The Future;* parish priests and professors were suspended for the same reason. The "religious" press heaped calumny and outrage on the apostles of God and Liberty; and the rumour of a Papal condemnation was already spread when Lamennais, loyal and devoted to the last, for the moment discontinuing his journal, set off for Rome, with two of his co-editors, to dispel the doubts of Gregory XVI. and explain his views to him.

His book, the *Affaires de Rome*, contains an exact and dispassionate account of his journey and reception, of the inefficacy of his arguments, of the Encyclica of the 15th of August, 1832, and of the resignation with which he submitted to the suppression of his journal and the dissolution of the Agency. But submission was not enough; he must declare publicly his acknowledgment of the right of Rome to order or to silence him, whether in things spiritual or things temporal. Persecution went to the extent of interference through his dearest affections, the Bishop of Rennes wringing from his brother a promise to separate from him. In a moment of weakness Lamennais gave way; signed his unqualified adhesion to the Papal Encyclica, and heart-bowed went into retirement at Chenay. This was at the end of 1833.

They thought they had slain the Censor. They had slain his last illusion; and he survived. How many youthful, ardent spirits succumb beneath the first! How many, strong in faith and hope when starting, at the first disillusion stoop to scepticism and halt discouraged: the discouragement of disenchanted egotism ! At the age of fifty-one Lamennais for the second time drained the bitter cup of impotent disappointment to its dregs. And yet (the example stands almost alone) he did not despair. In that small and delicate frame, which seemed sustained only by the force of will, was the soul of a giant, of a hero. God had stamped the seal of a great mission on his Napoleonic brow; and that brow, furrowed by the anathemas of King and Pope, bowed, but for an instant, not before their fury, but beneath the weight of a divine idea, then rose serene, irradiated with new youth and crowned with the presaged glories of the future. Here are some of the thoughts that upheld him as he passed through that valley of the shadow of death.

"Indifference, inertia, a naturally yielding disposition, and more than all the paralysis of fear, these are the causes that deaden or corrupt the weak consciences of the many who wander hither and thither without governing rule of conduct, crying Peace! Peace! when there is no peace possible. They are afraid of fatigue, they dread the struggle, they fear everything but that which is most to be feared. I say to you that there is a glance descends from on high like a curse on these men of little faith. Wherefore, think they, were they born? God has not placed man on this earth as in his final dwelling, or to waste his days in slumbrous indolence. . . . A duty, an absolute duty governs him from his cradle up, growing with his growth, and accompanying him to the tomb: a duty toward his brethren as well as to himself, a duty toward his country, toward humanity. . . . No! our lips shall not be silent while the world is overwhelmed by impending death. We will not stand motionless, like veiled statues, on the shores of that torrent which threatens the foundations. . . . Let all who have at heart the things of eternity arise with us! Let all who with heart and soul love God and Man, counting all else as nought, join their hearts and their voices to ours! Why be troubled, though many refuse to unite in action with us? Shall we waste the energy of our hearts in idle tears for this? Faith demands, not tears, but action; it requires of us the service of sacrifice, sole origin of our salvation; it asks for Christians able to say—We will die for this; yet more for Christians able to say—We will live for this."

No more looking to King or Pope! Only to the God crucified between them, and to the people, among whom henceforward his hopes were sown for the harvest of the Republic. Once again his sight had pierced through to the Infinite, as when a child he contemplated the tempest on his native rocks.[1] Now not the immensity of the elements of material Nature couched his eyes; it was the immensity of power for

---

[1] One who knew him writes that he remembered and would speak of the sense of pride which took possession of him one day when, but nine years old, he saw a terrific tempest on the Breton coast, how, hearing the prosaic remarks of those around him, he drew apart, recognizing within himself the instinctive sense of the Infinite revealed to him by the raging of the elements.

human perfection, the multitudinous elements of human progress through which he beheld the God, whose image, Humanity, he, like Pascal, viewed as a single man, living for ever, for ever increasing in knowledge, the progressive interpreter of the Divine Will,— Humanity, initiator under God of its own advance,— now at the instance of individuals, now through the action of multitudes, according to time and happening, —but ever from experience to experience, from epoch to epoch, intent upon the heights of perfectionment, seeking to comprehend the aim of duty toward the realization in practice of the divine ideal within it. In Humanity, in the universality of citizens, supreme above all temporal powers, in the universality of believers superior to Popes, in the People, steadfast and capable of improvement while all else is doomed to change and death, he saw at last the one willing and capable depositary of the germs of that social and religious future for which his heart had been yearning, for which it could not cease to yearn.

From that day the third period, the Republican period of Lamennais' life, began : the merely Romish priest was now the priest of the Universal. The first expression, one might say effusion, of his new life was the *Words of a Believer (Paroles d'un Croyant)*, that book of power, as if his lips had but that moment touched the coals from the altar, in the lyrical passages of which, says his friend Mazzini, "the three undying sisters, Religion, Charity, and Poetry, are heard together in lovely harmony."

Those words, as sparks thrown on a train of powder, sent fire through Europe. Perhaps since Paine's *Common Sense* rang the knell of kingship on one side at least of the Atlantic, no book has had so rapid and so wide an influence. There was reason in the papal cursing; for the apostle preached even from the papal stairs, and the answering words of condemnation were from the heart of a Believer. Some brief quotations may show the spirit of his preaching.

"In the beginning work was not necessary in order that man should live: the earth of itself provided for all his wants.

" But man did evil; and as he had revolted against God, so the earth revolted against him.

" That happened to him which happens to the child rebelling against its father: the father withdraws his love, and abandons him to himself; the servants of the house refuse to serve him, and he goes forth seeking here and there a poor existence, eating the bread he has earned in the sweat of his brow.

" Since that time God has condemned all men to labour, giving to all their task whether of body or of mind; and those who say—I will not labour! are the most miserable.

" For as worms devour a dead body, so vices devour such men; and if not vices, life-weariness.

" And when God willed that men should labour, he hid in that labour a treasure, because He is our Father, and the love of a father dieth not.

" And for him who makes a good use of this treasure, who does not waste it like a fool, there comes a time of rest, and he is as man was in the beginning.

"And God gave man also this precept: Help each other, because there are among you both strong and weak, able and infirm; and yet all ought to live.

" And if you do thus, all shall live: for I will reward the

pity you have had for your brethren, and I will render your toil productive.

* * * * * * * *

"Now there was in old time a wicked man, one cursed of heaven. And this man was strong, and he hated labour: so that he said to himself, What shall I do? If I labour not I shall die; and labour is unsupportable to me.

"Then a thought of hell entered into his heart. He went out by night and seized some of his brothers while they slept, and loaded them with chains.

"For, he said, I will force them with rods and with the whip to labour for me, and I will eat the fruit of their toil.

"And he did that which he had thought; and others seeing that did the same; and there were no more brothers, there were only masters and slaves.

"That day was a day of mourning over all the earth.

"Long after there was another man yet more wicked than the first, and more accursed of heaven.

"Seeing that men were everywhere multiplied, and that their multitude was innumerable, he said to himself:

"I could perhaps easily enchain some, and force them to labour for me; but they must be fed, and that would lessen my gain. I will do better; they shall work for nothing. Truly, they will die; but as their number is great I shall amass riches before it is much lessened, and there will always remain men enough.

"Now all this multitude lived on what it received in exchange for its labour.

"Having spoken in such a manner, he privately turned to some and said, You work during six hours, and they give you a piece of money for that; work for twelve hours and you will gain two pieces of money, and you will live better, you, your wives, and your children!

"And they believed him.

"Afterwards he said to them, You work only half the days of the year; work every day, and your gain will be double!

"And they believed him again.

"Now it happened that the quantity of work being increased by half, without the need of work becoming more, half of those who before then lived by their labour could find no one to employ them.

"Then the wicked man, when they had believed, said to them, I will give employment to you all on condition that you work the same time, and that I pay you only the half of what I paid before. I am quite willing to do you a service, but I cannot ruin myself.

"And as they starved, they, their wives, and their children, they accepted the proposal of the wicked man, and blessed him, for, said they, he gives us life.

"Continuing to cheat them in like manner, the wicked man augmented always their labour while always lessening their wage, till they died for want of the necessaries of life, and others hastened to replace them: for the indigence of that country had become so great that whole families sold themselves for a morsel of bread.

"And the wicked man, who had lied to his brothers, amassed yet more wealth than the wicked man who had enchained them.

"The name of the one is Tyrant; the other has no name but in Hell."

His words were of and for the France, the Europe, of that date (1833), not yet enlightened by nor reaping much from the lessons of the political economists. Free Trade, the preventive of panics, scarcities, and suffering of the producers, had not then spread wide the healing on its wings over the earth, to suspend the doom of Labour.[1]

[1] Recollect that (so quickly time passes) it was only in 1836 that the Courts of Massachusetts affirmed (not without protest) the right of a slave to be set free on entering the Bay State;

Looking then to the political status, the sham-republican constitutionalism of the days of "king-citizenship," he writes—

"Do not be cheated with vain words! Many are they who seek to persuade you that you are really free because they have written on a page of paper one word of Liberty, and have stuck the same on the corners of every street.

"Liberty is not a placard to be read at a street-corner. It is a living power felt within oneself and around one, the protective genius of the domestic hearth, the guarantee of social rights, and the first of those rights.

"The oppressor who hides himself under her name is the worst of oppressors: he joins falsehood to tyranny and injustice to profanation. For the name of Liberty is holy.

"Beware then of those who cry—Liberty! Liberty! and who destroy Liberty by their works.

"Is it you who choose those who govern you, who command you to do this and not to do that, who tax your goods, your industry, your labour? And if it is not you, how are you free?

"Can you dispose of your children as you wish, trust to whom you prefer the care of instructing them and of forming their morals? If you can not, how are you free?

"The birds of the air and even insects assemble together to do in common what they cannot do alone. Can you assemble together for your interests, to defend your rights, to obtain even some solace of your miseries? If you can not, how are you free?

"Can you without permission go from one place to another, make use of the fruits of the earth, even the product of your own labour, dip your finger in the ocean and let one drop fall

---

that so late as 1854, even in Boston, Theodore Parker had to preach, in words fervent as these of Lamennais, of the "dangers which threaten the Rights of Man in America."

into the poor vessel in which you cook your food, without exposing yourself to a fine or the possibility of a prison?[1]

"Can you lying down at night be sure that none will come during your sleep to search through the secretest places of your house, to drag you from the bosom of your family and throw you into a dungeon, because Power in its fear had doubts of you? If you can not, how are you free?

"Liberty will shine on you when by dint of courage and perseverance you shall be enfranchised from all these servitudes.

"Liberty will shine on you when from the very bottom of your souls you shall have said—We *will* be free; when in order to become so you shall be ready to sacrifice everything and to endure everything."

Yet one more bead from this most prayerful rosary; an echo of the anguish that but too many of the best hearts of Europe have had to suffer since the first whisper of the Republic. Not wanting in tenderness or pathos that stern and vehement rebuke of crowned and triple-mitred Wrong.

THE EXILE.

" He went forth wandering over the earth : God guide the poor Exile!

" I have passed among the peoples and they have looked at me, and I at them, and we have not known each other. The Exile is everywhere alone.

" When, at the decline of day, I have seen rising from the hollow of a valley the smoke of some cottage, I have said to myself—How happy he who in the evening returns to his home and rests in the bosom of his family! The Exile is everywhere alone.

" These trees are grand, these flowers are beautiful; but

---

[1] The France of 1833. Salt was a State monopoly.

they are not the flowers nor the trees of my own country; they say nothing to me. The Exile is everywhere alone.

"This brook flows gently through the plain; but its murmur is not that I heard in my childhood; it brings no remembrance to my soul. The Exile is everywhere alone.

"These songs are sweet; but the sorrows and the joys they awaken are not my sorrows or my joys. The Exile is everywhere alone.

"They have asked me—Wherefore do you weep? And when I have told them, none have wept with me, for they could not understand me. The Exile is everywhere alone.

"I have seen old men surrounded by children, as the olive-tree by its off-shoots, but no one of these old men called me Son, not one of these children called me Brother! The Exile is everywhere alone.

"I have seen the young girls smile, a smile pure as the breath of the morning, on him whom their love had chosen for a husband; but never one smiled on me. The Exile is everywhere alone.

"I have seen young men heart to heart strain as if of their two lives they would make but one; but not one has grasped me by the hand. The Exile is everywhere alone.

"He has no friends, nor lover, nor father, nor brother, but in his country. The Exile is everywhere alone.

"Poor Exile! cease to groan: we are all banished as thou art, seeing pass away fathers, brothers, lovers, and friends.

"Our country is not here below; vainly man seeks it here; that which he mistakes for it is but a shelter for the night.

"He went wandering over the earth. God guide the poor Exile!"

The *Words of a Believer* was followed by the *Book of the People* (*Le Livre du Peuple*), *Modern Slavery* (*L'Esclavage Moderne*),[1] *Politics for the*

[1] The three works have been translated into English, the *Words* into almost every European language. *Modern Slavery,*

People (*Politique à l'usage du Peuple*); various articles in *Le Monde, La Revue des Deux Mondes,* and *La Revue de Progrès; Amschaspands et Darvands* (the Persian Genii of Good and Ill), a series of conversations laying bare the deeper causes of human unhappiness, &c., &c., &c. Among his many writings, the same profound and loving thought pervading all, may be specially mentioned (for the sake also of the book) a preface to the *Voluntary Servitude* (*De la Servitude Volontaire et le Contr' un*) of Etienne de la Boëtie, the friend of Montaigne.

In November, 1840, he was condemned to twelve months' imprisonment for a pamphlet, *The Country and the Government*, exposing the treasons of Louis Philippe and his valet Thiers. Immediately after the Three Days of 1848, on the 27th of February, he began a daily paper, *Le Peuple Constituant*, in which he wrote regularly until it was suppressed by General Cavaignac in the days of June, because he dared to see yet some right on the side of the insurgent people. During those months of wild theories, of hopes ill-expressed, of bitter squabbles and recriminations, and of false teachings on the side of "order" tending to disorder for the sake of monarchical reaction, Lamennais' voice was ever that of a true Tribune of the People,—boldly advocating their rights, as boldly telling them of their faults and errors, ever inculcat-

---

though but a pamphlet, should command the attention of whoever cares to understand the struggle between Capital and Labour. Needless to say on which side is Lamennais.

ing faith and patience while indignantly and perseveringly vindicating them from their traducers. No Communist, but no less a social reformer, a Republican, not for the sake of enthroning the wealthier class, but for the good of the whole Commonwealth, not setting class against class, but earnestly seeking to bind all together on the way of simple righteousness with freedom for all, his wisdom might have saved France if the politicians, the intriguers, or even the honester theorists, would have listened to him; and had his more noble and nobly wise counsel (backed by Mazzini's exhortations and those of Ledru Rollin also) been accepted in the first days, the name of Poland had not been omitted from the manifesto of the foreign policy of the Provisional Government, nor the opportunity been given for Lamartine's successor to perpetrate the outrage upon Rome. France perhaps—unless the logical outcome of corruption in high places during the years of the "Napoleon of Peace" required a corresponding and continuing national corruption and degradation—might have been spared the Second, the Lower Empire.

When the 2nd of December drove out the best and manliest, when Victor Hugo went into exile, Lamennais, enfeebled with his weight of nearly seventy years, remained in France, but not to bow or bend. That proud yet gentle, that severe yet most serene, though pitiful gaze looked past the blood-empurpled Tyrant to the Future of his own prophecy. As they dared not raise a hand against Mazzini in those dark days of Rome, as Charles the Dissolute left Milton to die unprofaned even by a royal pardon, so Lamennais commanded the respect which left him in his last days unmolested. He died at Paris after a brief sickness, in the morning of the 27th of February, 1854. The last work on which he was employed was a translation of Dante's *Paradiso*.

His dying hours were not unworthy of his life. His relations plagued him with endeavours for a recantation. He rejected them, and refused to see a priest. A Wickliffe, a Lamennais, does not recant. Careful only that he should not be misunderstood, that an unpublished work, *Discussions, Criticisms, and Thoughts concerning Religion and Philosophy*, should neither be suppressed nor mutilated, he died in the full possession of his mental faculties, "his independence, his lucidity, his energy, and his firm will, preserved to the end;"[1] died as he had lived,

---

[1] Words of those present, attested by the signatures of Giuseppe Montanelli, Armand Lévy, Henry Martin, and others, in a document produced before the Civil Tribunal of the Seine when the Jesuits contested his Will. It seems that a niece of "the Abbé" (still so called) was most pressing for his conversion. On the Sunday afternoon (he died at 33 minutes past nine on the Monday) his friends had left his bedside (he seemed so strong) that he might have some moments of repose after signing a codicil to his Will. Toward 3 o'clock the doctor thought him sinking. "We went again into the sick room. His breathing was difficult. We had been for some moments kneeling by his bed when suddenly he fixed his eyes upon us, and, looking intently and then pressing the hands of those nearest to him, said : 'These are good moments.' One of us saying that we should ever be united with him, he replied : ' It is well : we shall meet.' David

believing in God, loving the People. At no time had he much of this world's goods; and of his little the poor were sharers. In his Will he disinherited any of his family who had taken part against the insurgents of June. He ordered his body to be laid unmocked by priestly ritual in the paupers' grave (*la fosse commune*), not even the Cross to be planted over him. The preacher of Fraternity, the prophet of the Future, needed not even the most sacred emblem of the Past. A plain staff had hanging from it a scrap of paper with the name of FÉLICITÉ LAMENNAIS when Béranger bowed over his old friend's grave.

The following extract from a letter written by him shortly before his death shows the horror he had of the Jesuit party. Alluding to a refusal of one of his correspondents to let him look over some of his own

---

d'Angers (the sculptor) arrived, and stayed some minutes. Then came Carnot, who had passed the previous night with him, and then the Abbé's niece. Her first words were: 'Fely! do you wish for a priest? You do wish for a priest, don't you?' Lamennais answered: 'No!' 'I beseech you to send for one,' she resumed. In a yet firmer tone he answered again: 'No! no! no! let me be quiet!' Again after a while intreating him, his only reply was: 'I want nothing whatever except to be let alone.' The friends around then compelled her to desist... He went on to talk of his manuscripts, which he had intrusted to his friend Forgues. 'Be firm,' he said to him: 'they will try to circumvent you; publish all, without changing or suppressing anything!' Later, when the niece was regretting that he should die in that way, for, she said, 'it was he who made me a Christian,' and M. Levy assured her that if he desired a priest there would have been no hesitation in sending for one, she acknowledged that it was so, 'his wishes were unfortunately too plain.'" *Signed by* G. Montanelli, and others.

letters, he writes: "I should be silent on a subject of this kind were it not that I entertain but too well-founded fears of what is likely to happen. Madame Y—— has violent political passions, and she has moreover blindly and entirely delivered herself over to the Jesuits. Now, after my experience of them and of people who are guided by them, I cannot doubt that, if their purposes would be in any way served by it, this correspondence which I am not even permitted to read over would be unhesitatingly garbled and mutilated for publication. This was one of the reasons which made me desire to have the letters in my own hands. I can now only protest by anticipation against anything that may one day be attributed to me in the form of extracts from these letters. I even disavow expressly any passage which may be literally correct, but which, separated from the explanatory context in a long correspondence, would easily be twisted, by persons who are utterly without scruples, to a meaning wholly different from the true one."

"For us and for our age," wrote George Sand in earlier days, "he initiated a crusade more glorious and more memorable in the sight of future generations than the crusade preached by St. Bernard: for not the sepulchre but the heritage of Christ is the prize of the conquest to which we are led by the Breton priest. The battle is no longer against Islamism, but against the impiety of social life; we seek, not the ransom of a few Christian slaves, but the redemption of the human race."

And Mazzini in his review of Lamennais' genius (published in the *Monthly Chronicle*, London, 1839, which has supplied the material for much of this memoir) writes thus in summing up his value—

"This man, often accused, by those who either have not read him at all, or who have read him but superficially, of sudden and inexplicable changes, has indeed always pursued one single sacred idea, the good of the people through the medium of a religious faith. He did but change the instruments with which he strove to realize that idea, when those he wielded broke in his grasp through rottenness or the weakness of decay. And the series of these changes resumes the experience of a whole epoch. If we had gained nought else from Lamennais, he would still have deserved our affection and our gratitude. He has, so to speak, sacrificed himself for us; he has explored the path we have to tread, and pointed out to us where lies the abyss beneath the flowers, where the void is hidden by the semblance of life. He compelled the monarchy to unmask and the Papacy to utter its last word in the Encyclica of 1832. And when at length he came among us, crying, *There is neither life nor hope save in the People*, it was not merely the cry of a noble soul athirst for love, he brought with him incontrovertible demonstration."

PESTEL AND RYLÉIEFF.

PESTEL AND RYLÉIEFF.

"For our liberty and yours."

TZAR of all the Russias, Saviour or Pacificator of Western Europe, Alexander, the son of Paul, went home under the shadow of his laurels. His army, instead of laurel, took with it the leaves of Western books, the thoughts of Western minds, enough to trouble the unhappy Emperor almost before he recrossed his Slavonic threshold. All is not gain even in victorious war. Even in 1815, before he was well at home, secret societies began to honeycomb his Russia. Two brothers, Alexander and Nikita Mouravieff, officers in the army, stationed in Lithuania, founded there a political association. Finding that it took root, they went to Petersburg to sound the minds of the army there. They found more than sympathy; they found men already discussing the necessity of association and prepared to join them. Soon afterwards they made acquaintance with Pestel, the son of the Governor of Western Siberia, a colonel in the Line and aide-de-camp of Marshal Prince Wittgenstein. He entered promptly into the conspiracy, and almost immediately became its soul and centre. It spread rapidly. Whatever was distinguished among the youth of Russia became soon affiliated to it; young men of the army, literary men like Ryléieff and Bestoujeff, young men of the most noble families, such as the princes Obolenski, Troubetzkoi, Odoesski, &c., all eagerly enrolled themselves in this first phalanx of Russian emancipation. The time was favourable for a political and secret association. Literary propagandism was active, and the influence of literature among a people without other liberty acquires dimensions not known in freer lands. The revolutionary poems of Pouchkine and Ryléieff were in the hands of all the young folk of the empire, even in the farthest provinces. No well-educated girl but knew them by heart; no officer but had them in his haversack; no priest's son (the peasants' copying clerk and letter-writer) but had made his dozen copies of them. That whole generation, however men may have since cooled down, felt the influence of those first sparks of freedom falling upon their souls.

The conspiracy spread rapidly, to Petersburg, to Moscow, in Little Russia, even among the officers of the Guard. At the beginning its intentions were constitutional, "Liberal" in an English sense. But hardly had this opinion been accepted before the designs of the leaders, Pestel especially, went farther, and the society, sifting out its less radical members, reconstituted itself on a Republican basis, no longer content with a representative monarchy as the term of their endeavours, but thinking, not without reason, that the power which would be needed to limit absolutism might suffice to annihilate it. The chiefs of the Union in the South (the Association being divided into North and South, Petersburg and Moscow the two centres) had in view a Republican federation of the Slaves, and desired a revolutionary dictature which should organize the forms of the Republic.

It went farther. When Pestel visited the Society of the North, he placed the question upon another basis. He thought that the proclamation of the Republic would be worthless if the question of the land was not also brought into the revolution. We are speaking of the time before 1825. Social questions were not then much troubling the thoughts of Europe; Gracchus Babeuf, " the fool, the savage," was already forgotten; St. Simon wrote and no one read him; Fourier philosophized with much the same result. The advanced Liberals of that time, the Benjamin Constants and Paul Courriers, would have exploded with indignation had they heard the propositions of Pestel, propositions made, not in a club of proletarians, but to an association formed in a very large proportion of the rich nobility. Pestel proposed to them to save their lives by the expropriation of their estates. Of course his opinions offended too much the principles of political economy to be accepted. But he was not accused of desiring pillage and massacre; and notwithstanding all objections to these his opinions, he remained the head of the Southern Society; and would more than probably, had they been successful, have been made Dictator,—he, a socialist before socialism was.

For all this Pestel was neither a dreamer nor an Utopian. On the contrary, his genius was eminently practical, and he understood the thought of his people. Leaving the lands to the nobility there would only have been an oligarchy, owners and serfs; the people would not have understood their enfranchisement, the Russian peasant not caring for freedom but with his land. It was Pestel who first thought of making the people take part in the revolution. Agreeing with his friends that the insurrection could not succeed without the support of the army, he wished also to draw into it the aid of the religious sects,[1] a project whose wisdom will be proved in the future. Now all is over, we may see the illusion of Pestel: neither were his associates capable of accomplishing a social revolution, nor were the peasants ready to make common cause with the army. But it was the illusion of a man of prophetic mind, right in theory, but wrongly anticipating the date of realization. Nevertheless the

[1] Numerous throughout Russia. Pougatcheff, himself a sectary, knew how to avail himself of them when, in the reign of Catherine the Second, he raised the Oural Cossacks, and for a time, defying the imperial armies, held Eastern Russia almost to Moscow under his domination.

Association was an immense school for the teaching of later generations.

In the North the reconstructed Association at Petersburg pursued its way with energy, at first with Prince Troubetzkoi at its head, then with Nikita Mouravieff and Prince Obolenski, still later under the leadership of Ryléieff. He, at once poet and man of action, seems to have been, only excepting Pestel, the most remarkable man in the movement. He was co-editor with Bestoujeff of the *Polar Star*, an almanac which circulated in the universities, the lyceums, and even the military schools. His poems, particularly that of Voinanowski (of the time of Mazeppa), his popular legends, have great beauty. Young, poetic, he was the Schiller of the conspiracy, the enthusiastic element, the Girondist element, using the term in its best sense. Not so much hopeful as devoted, he knew that Siberia or death was the likely end, but "when," he asked, "have we seen liberty conquered without victims?" "I know," says the Cossack Naliwaiko to the priest who confesses him, "I know what awaits me, but I joyfully bless my lot." This was Ryléieff. Although the nominal head of the Association was Prince Troubetzkoi, it was Ryléieff who toward the close of 1825 was its real leader.

There are two remarkable features in the history of this conspiracy: the one that for more than nine years it was never betrayed by any fully-initiated member till the treason of the two princes Jablonovski and Oginski in 1825; the other that during its proceedings other similar associations were encountered and drawn into the main union. Russia appeared to be one vast hotbed of conspiracy. Least numerous was the Republican party, mostly young men, acting from the generous disinterestedness and ardour of youthful convictions, working to raise the whole of the Russian people to a position of freedom; among them young men of the highest rank, possessors or heirs of large estates, which they were willing to sacrifice by freeing their serfs, the only source of the Russian nobles' wealth. The larger party of the conspiracy, not prepared to go so far, looked only for the overthrow or curbing of the imperial tyranny which weighed upon themselves; and these were so numerous that, after the explosion, the Government dared not even think of punishing all concerned, the Commission of Inquiry finding no family of any note altogether guiltless of participation. Beside these two parties was a third, in some measure perhaps composed of both, jealous of the supremacy of Pestel, opposing his influence, and by their reliance upon inferior men preparing for failure. The opposition to him was most manifest in the North, even Ryléieff himself not free from it. The younger and more enthusiastic did not understand the mature man who did not believe that a few months could settle all, but who foresaw the necessity of exceptional measures providing for a prolonged term of transition. It was in some sort a repetition of the old dispute between Vane and Cromwell, the strife always occurring in times of revolution, between the men who think honesty and true ideas sufficient, and the men, not necessarily insincere if more worldly wise, who must model out of and with the elements in their hands,—the difference between, not the false statesman, "that character so tainted and equivocal in our day" (to borrow the words of John Bright), but the true statesman, who is prophet and practical man like Cromwell, and the less practical enthusiast like Vane, or Ryléieff. It is the quarrel that splits up most revolutionary attempts (does not the attempt at revolution of itself beget dissidence and revolt?), breaking the point of the arrow never so well directed else against the heart of arbitrary, self-centred, single power.

The fear lest Pestel might become the Napoleon rather than the Washington of the Revolution prevented that thorough understanding and unity of action without which, certainly in rebellions, there is no success. Yet the variously arising societies met with in the course of propagandism during the ten years of the conspiracy, all springing from the same need and all with one common object, anti-imperial if not agreeing upon further questions, had readily merged themselves into the one strong current. Even the Poles were drawn into it (the first ground of understanding between the two peoples), and, though not then prepared to pronounce for a Republic, gave cordial assent to a Slavonic confederation, and united their efforts to those of their Russian compatriots.

The moment for action approached. The Association of the South ramifying everywhere in the southern division of the army, and the Petersburg Association surrounding the throne[1] and daily gaining ground among the aristocracy, the time was propitious. Pestel, who perfectly understood the pressing necessity for action, was not content with the moderation of Petersburg or the want of perfect unity between the two Associations. In 1824 he went to Petersburg. He demanded the fusion of the two societies under one direction, and after long debate they consented to it. But on the other hand they opposed the extreme and decisive measures which he proposed. There was yet a party which held to a constitutional *régime* and would only proclaim the Republic in case the Emperor refused to accept the Charter, in which event they would exile the family.

Pestel did not change his opinion. "We would make a clean sweep," said he; and his plan was by a *coup-de-main* to take possession of the Emperor and the whole Imperial family; to seize also the Senate and the Synod, to force them to proclaim the new Government, and that done to dismiss all superior functionaries, civil and military, and to replace them with members of the Association. He had to leave

---

[1] Through the young Prince Odoeffski, an officer of the Guard, they were daily informed of all that was done in the palace, done or said.

Petersburg without completely succeeding. Then he proposed a general definitive reunion for the beginning of 1826, but requiring that, if they then failed to agree, they should proceed immediately to action.

The position was difficult. The young turbulent enthusiasts of the South were hardly held in by the authority of Pestel; and when suddenly without given reason the Government removed Colonel Schweikowski, an ardent conspirator, from his regiment, the conspiracy was all but breaking out. On the other hand, the Association was too large, too numerous to be kept much longer secret. It was rather a wonder that it had remained so for so long. Suddenly the death of Alexander disconcerted all their plans. Alexander dead, Constantine, the elder brother, refused the crown; Nicholas, the younger, coquetted with it. This moment of anarchy seemed opportune for the conspirators. Already betrayed in the South and at Petersburg, they saw nothing better than to take advantage of this abdicating confusion, of this interregnum with its two emperors, of the alarm on both sides, of those who took part with Constantine, and those who sided with Nicholas. Some regiments had actually taken the oath to Constantine, proclaimed in the first moments after the death of Alexander; and the conspirators resolved to contradict the report of his resignation (he was then at Warsaw), and to persuade the army that Nicholas was usurping. The 26th of December (the 14th in the Russian Old Style), the day appointed for administering the oath of fidelity to the new emperor from the authorities and the army, was fixed for the outbreak of the revolution at Petersburg. The Dictator of the Northern Association, Prince Troubetzkoi, was to take command, and to appear for that purpose with all the influential men of the union, in Isaac's Square, whither the conspirators were to repair with such regiments as they could gain over.

Doubt and indecision had already sapped their strength. Even on the 24th Prince Troubetzkoi was undecided. It needed all the energy of Ryléieff to get him to consent to action. Drawing from his pocket a letter addressed to Nicholas by a young officer (afterwards General Rostofzoff, the Emperor's aide-de-camp, and chief of the military schools) and showing it to the members present, Ryléieff said— "You see we are lost; but it is better to die with arms in our hands."

He was right. The moral effect to be produced by the day of the 26th of December, 1825, will outweigh the loss of all that hopeful time; the cannon of Isaac's Square would awaken the Future. Until then it was not believed possible for a political armed insurrection to attack in the midst of Petersburg the Giant of Tzarism. They might assassinate in the palace a Peter or a Paul, to replace them with their like. But there was nothing in common between these palace-plots and a solemn protest against despotism made in the face of day and sealed with the suffering and blood of heroes. If they might not count upon success, they could comprehend the grand significance of their act. One of their youngest, a poet also, Prince Odoesski, on the eve of their endeavour, embracing his friends, said to them— "We go to death, but to how glorious a death!"

On the morning of the 26th, no sooner were the troops ordered under arms to take the oath, than they were addressed by the conspirators in their ranks. At first the marines of the Guard under the command of their general laid hands on the haranguers, but the eloquence of the brothers Bestoujeff prevailed, and the whole battalion followed them. The Finland regiment also declared for Constantine; the grenadiers of the Guard were gained over; a part of the regiment of Moscow followed. But here a check was given. Their generals had gathered round them the grenadier company with the standard of the regiment, and exhorted the troops to obedience. But the Bestoujeffs and Prince Rostovski pushed aside the bayonets pointed against them and dashed sword in hand into their midst. After a brief fierce conflict they had possession of the standard; the two generals, the colonel, and some soldiers, lay bleeding on the ground; the regiment no longer hesitated, but followed their daring leaders, with loud acclamations, to the place of meeting. On reaching Isaac's Square, the more timid of the aristocratic leaders, the more moderate men to whom the direction of the rebellion had been intrusted, were not to be seen. Through the day they waited for them. At the time which he had appointed for the outbreak, Prince Troubetzkoi was taking the oath to Nicholas.

The revolted regiments formed in front of the Senate House. They stood there passive and irresolute: how act without the acknowledged leaders? Summoned by the Tzar to take the oath of allegiance, they answered only with fierce cries for Constantine and the Constitution. After some parleying and fruitless attempts on the part of the old Metropolitan, Seraphin, whom the soldiers bade depart in peace, and of General Miloradovitch, a veteran and favourite with the army, who fell mortally wounded,[1] Nicholas ordered a charge of cavalry. Orloff charged three times, and three times was repulsed. The regiments that had not revolted were then ordered to fire upon the insurgents. Some refused, some fired over their heads. Then the artillery was ordered to fire grape. At the first order not a cannon was discharged. All-amazed, the commanding officer exclaimed to the cannoneers—"Have you not heard?" "Yes! but these are our brothers." "And if I ordered you to fire upon myself would you dare to disobey me?" Military discipline prevailed. They fired; but not before the doomed regiments had time to bid the crowd disperse. "Get out of the way! This is

---

[1] He was reproached with some former act of treachery, and his harangue cut short by a pistol-bullet fired, it was said, by Kachofski.

becoming dangerous. We do not want you to be killed for us." Then round after round of grape-shot was poured on the patient mass, yet waiting for their chiefs. By night the massacre was over, and Nicholas was lord in Petersburg.

While this was taking place in the North, Pestel, betrayed by an adjutant, was with some of his friends arrested at Toolchin. Others of the Association took up arms and broke open the prison, delivering the brothers Mouravieff[1] and some others; but unfortunately Pestel had already been removed. Sergius Mouravieff, Kouzmin, and Bestoujeff Roumine, then desperately raised the standard of revolt, gained over some troops to their side in the town of Vasilkoff, and proceeded on their march in hope of being joined by others. But it was in vain that they appealed to either their patriotism or their religion. In vain was Bestoujeff's *Republican Catechism* read to them. They answered only to the cry of Constantine and double pay. In the South as in the North the more politic conspirators hung back, waiting the events for which their cowardice provided; and the few bolder spirits were too few for the work. Near Belaya Tzerkoff the insurgents encountered the imperial forces. A battle took place. Conscious of how much depends upon the onset, the Mouravieffs charged right upon the artillery; but the eldest, Sergius, was desperately

---

[1] Not the Mouravieffs who originated the conspiracy. There was also a Southern as well as a Northern Bestoujeff.

wounded and Hyppolite fell dead at his side at the first discharge. Their soldiers fled; in vain the leaders strove to rally them. Mouravieff and Bestoujeff both wounded, Mouravieff's youngest brother Matthew with Kouzmin were given up by their own men. Kouzmin, unwilling to survive the wreck of their hopes, snatched a pistol from one of his captors, and blew out his own brains.

So terminated this vast conspiracy, a conspiracy in which all that was hopeful or generous or patriotic in Russia was more or less engaged. In the South as in the North the same devoted courage was shown by the few who had conspired from really patriotic motives; the same vacillation, pusillanimity, and fear of acting, marked the many who had either not understood the worth of the Republic or who cared rather for their own selfish interests. So wide a conspiracy well might shake the whole country. Even in the most "loyal" families sons and brothers had tasted the "poison" cup of freedom. Pestel's own father, the Governor of Siberia, a man of most imperial stamp, a pro-consul of the old Roman type, noticeable in his day for his cruelty and depravity, could not bring up his son to follow in his footsteps. Freedom riseth out of strange nests. It is said that when the old man took leave of his condemned son in prison, in order to show his own devotedness to the imperial rule, he cursed him for the sacrifice of his opportunities, bitterly asking him—"What was there left thee to wish for?" "Among other things which you would not understand," said Pestel, "the wish to render it impossible for governors like you to exist in the future."

One hundred and twenty-one conspirators for their share in the attempt were sentenced to death or banishment to Siberia for life, or for twenty to fifty years. The Tzar mercifully carried out the death-sentence upon five : Pestel, Ryléieff, Sergius Mouravieff, Bestoujeff Roumine, and Kachofski. To add to the infamy of their punishment they were hanged instead of decapitated. On the 25th of July, 1826, they were drawn to the place of execution, on the glacis of the fortress of Petersburg, and compelled to witness the erection of their gibbets. They were all hanged at the same moment; but the ropes broke or slipped with three of them, Ryléieff, Mouravieff, and Bestoujeff, who fell, breaking the scaffolding beneath them. Mouravieff was nearly dead, and had to be carried up; the other two coolly reascended the fatal ladder. Ryléieff merely observed that he had been exposed to a double agony; and Bestoujeff exclaimed—" Nothing succeeds with me, even here I meet with disappointment." So perished the first Russian martyrs for Republicanism; and Terror was enthroned as Tzar of All the Russias.

Before the tribunals Ryléieff had taken all upon himself. " I could have stopped all," he said ; " on the contrary, I urged all to action. I am the principal promoter of the events of the 26th. If any one has deserved death for that day, it is I." There was neither flinching nor repentance. Pestel's chief anxiety was concerning his work on Russian Jurisprudence, which he had hidden. He had written much, but not printed. His manuscripts are said to be somewhere buried. When asked what he was writing he used to answer that he was treating of the wretched condition of the Russian soldier; but it was understood that he wrote of the future organization of Russia. His equanimity never deserted him, even at the gallows; and he died with sealed lips, though tortured to wring out his secret. It is the Testament of Pestel that Young Russia would carry out.

On the 25th of January, 1831, Poland in revolution, the Polish Diet pronounced the deposition of the Tzar. On that day they commemorated in Warsaw the martyrdom of the Russian Republicans by a solemn procession. Five coffins, on which were the martyrs' names, were borne through the principal streets under flags inscribed in Russian and Polish with the words—*For our Liberty and yours!*

HERZEN.

R

HERZEN.

"He has talent, observed the President.
"So much the worse! In skilful hands poison is only the more dangerous, added the Inquisitor.
"That is an incorrigible pernicious young man.
"These words were my condemnation."

My Exile.

AUTOBIOGRAPHY.

ALEXANDER HERZEN may fairly have place among European Republicans: not that he was of the European Democratic Committee; not that his socialistic tendencies (there is here an important and special question as regards the Slavonic future) did not often separate him from the Republican policies of Western Europe; not that his caustic irony (unsurpassed by that of Proudhon) was not even sometimes exercised against the always religious teaching of Mazzini; but because, if not his mind, his heart and his active help were ever with us. I would claim him as ours were it only on the authority of these few of his words, rebuking the narrower "socialism" of too many of his contemporaries: "It is the fate of all which is social that no single thing is self-sufficing, that all is drawn into the solidarity of peoples." But I knew him well, and can speak surely.

High-born, and from his birth among the highest in Russian society, brought up in luxury and passing "from the nursery to the university," surrounded by influential friends, influential too in that kind of pleasant education which is so eminently fitted to prevent the misfortunes consequent upon natural integrity and a disposition to self-sacrifice, there was little in his early years to promise a career of patriotism and exile. But nine years had not obliterated the memory of Pestel; and 1834 found the young student at the Moscow University (then just of age) dreaming with his college companions of some yet possible change in Russia; dreaming, and it may be talking with youthful unreserve.

One day in July 1834 he was arrested on suspicion of agreeing with the sentiments of some fellow-students, or, as he was told when at last allowed to have a reason for his arrest, for being present with them (though indeed he was not) at a boys' dinner at which they had unguardedly sung some verses reflecting on the Imperial family.[1]

---

[1] Some verses of the Russian poet Sokolofsky on the death of Alexander, expressing a dread of the accession of the elder brother, Constantine, in terms not too complimentary to the reigning Tzar Nicholas: ending—

". . . To the mighty Tzar,
　　The Lord of earth and heaven,
　　The Russian Tzar departed
　　　　Hath a petition given.

For this boyish escapade, in which he had no part, he was detained in prison from July 1834 to April of the next year, not without the usual efforts of despotic power to induce him to confess to some imagined plot against the Government, and of course to denounce his fellow-conspirators. His account of his first examination, a fortnight after his arrest, may show upon what slight grounds arrests were made, and give some idea of the administration of justice under the drill-sergeant Nicholas. Taken from the prison to the house of the Chief Director of Police, and left waiting in one of the rooms, in about half an hour a stout man entered, with an expression half lazy and half kind. He threw his portfolio on a chair, and gave some commission to the officer who stood at the door (probably that he should not hear the talk with the prisoner). Then turning to young Herzen, he said:

"I suppose you are here on account of N.'s affair." (N. was a young college friend who also had been arrested.)

Herzen nodded assent.

"I have heard some rumours about it," continued the examiner: "a strange and incomprehensible affair."

Herzen replied—"I have now been a prisoner for

"God read, and then reveal'd
 His mercy all divine :
For Nicholas he gave us,
 That king among the swine."

more than a fortnight on account of this affair; and not only do I not understand it, but I absolutely know nothing of it."

"That is right," said the other, looking fixedly at him. "You must not know anything of it. Excuse me for giving you a bit of advice. You are young; your blood is hot; you would easily grow angry; and that would be unlucky. Therefore, mind! you must not know anything of it. That is your only means of safety."

Herzen looked at him with astonishment. His face betrayed no evil meaning. He seemed to guess the prisoner's thoughts, and said, smiling—"I was myself a student at the University twelve years ago."

Hereupon an officer entered, to whom the stout gentleman gave some orders, and with his finger on his lips.

He was taken next before the Police Commission. In a spacious and handsome saloon five persons were seated round a table, all in uniform, with the exception of one decrepid old man in a corner. The five were smoking cigars and conversing merrily; their uniforms were unbuttoned, and they lolled unceremoniously in their arm-chairs. The Chief Director of Police presided, and, when Herzen entered, turned round to the creature in the corner and said—"Father! if you please."

The person addressed was an old priest, with a gray beard and a purple face, half asleep. He yawned, covered his face with his hand, and, in a drawling nasal tone, began an exhortation: of the sin of concealing truth from persons installed in their office by the Emperor, and the uselessness of such concealment, considering the all-seeing eye of God. He did not even spare Biblical texts, such as, "No power save of God," "Render unto Cæsar the things which are Cæsar's," &c.

When he had finished, he told the prisoner to kiss the Bible and the blessed Cross, in confirmation of his having sworn to confess the truth. Not that he had taken any oath: it was not even asked for. That done, he hastily covered up the book and cross. The Director of Police told him he might go; then, turning to Herzen, translated the spiritual exhortation into the official tongue.

"I will add but one thing to the priest's words: you have not the possibility of denying if you wished to do so." And he pointed to a quantity of papers, letters, &c., which were purposely spread upon the table. "Only a sincere avowal can mitigate your fate; and it depends upon yourself either to be set at liberty, or to be sent to Siberia or the Caucasus."

The questions were put in writing: the naïveté of some of them remarkable.

"Are you acquainted with any secret association?"

"Did you not belong to such an one, a literary one or some other?"

"Who are the members, and where do they meet?"

It was easy to answer all these questions in the negative.

"I see you know nothing," said the Director, looking over the written answers. "I have warned you, and you will only aggravate your position by it."

So ended the first hearing. Shortly after he was removed to another prison, in an old monastery converted into barracks, outside the city. "The cells of the monks, built three hundred years before, and half sunk in the ground, had been converted into worldly cells for political criminals. Mine contained nothing but a bedstead without a mattress, one chair, and a small table, whereon stood a jug of water and a large copper candlestick in which a thin tallow candle was burning. The cold and damp made me tremble; the officer ordered the stove to be lighted, and went his way. The soldier had promised to bring me some straw. Meanwhile I lay down on the bare bedstead, with my cloak under my head, and smoked my pipe. In a few minutes I observed that the ceiling of the cell was covered with innumerable wood-lice (*Blada Germanica*). They had not seen any light for a long while, and now came from all sides toward the glare of the candle, swarmed about, pushed each other, fell on the table, and then ran like mad round its edges. I never liked wood-lice, nor in general any of those unbidden guests. . . Three days after, however, the wood-lice retired to the soldier on the other side of the wall, where it was warmer; only now and then one would come, poke out its head, and then quickly return to warm itself.

"By and by I became accustomed to the barracks, conjugated Italian verbs, and read all sorts of books. At first we were treated severely. At nine o'clock in the evening, at the last roll-call, the guard came in, extinguished the light, and locked the door. I had to stay in darkness from nine in the evening till eight in the morning. I never was a heavy sleeper, and particularly not in prison. Without exercise, a few hours of sleep were more than enough. It was a punishment then to have no light. Add to this the cries of the watch, repeated every quarter of an hour in a loud and long-sustained key on both sides of the corridor.

"Some weeks later the calls of the watch were stopped, and candles were allowed, on condition that the window, which was lower than the court-yard, should have no curtain, so that the guard could see everything that the prisoner did. A little later we were granted an inkstand; paper also allowed on condition that the sheets should be counted and remain entire. Yet later we were permitted to walk once a day, in the company of the officer on guard and a soldier, in the court-yard surrounded by a ditch and a line of gensd'armes.

"Life passed monotonously and quietly, and acquired from its military uniformity a mechanical and regular character like the cæsura in poetry. In the morning, with the assistance of the guard, I boiled my coffee on the stove; at ten o'clock the officer on duty made his appearance, bringing in with him

I know not how many cubic inches of cold air, dressed in cloak, helmet, and gloves, with tremendous epaulettes, and his sword clanking as he moved; at one o'clock a soldier brought me a dirty table-napkin, and a dish of soup which he held by the rim, so that his thumb was perceptibly cleaner than his fingers. The food was tolerable; but it must not be forgotten that it cost me two roubles daily; which in the course of nine months' imprisonment amounted to a rather considerable sum for a man without a fortune.

"The father of a prisoner once declared that he had no money. He was coolly answered that in that case it would be stopped out of his pay. Had he no pay to receive, it is likely that he would have been imprisoned with his son.

"I must observe here also, that the colonel commandant received daily a sum of public money for the sustenance of each prisoner."

After some months' incarceration (on the excellent principle that even if he should turn out innocent there would be no undoing that) it was thought worth while to examine him again. By this time they had seized letters which he had written to his friends, papers of compositions, theses, &c. The examination lasted four hours. The first questions were as to the opinions of himself and friends, his own plainly enough expressed in the papers seized; but the inquirers needed farther explanations. In one letter had been discovered the following sentence:

"All constitutional charters lead to nothing, they are merely contracts between the master and his slaves: the task is not to ameliorate the condition of the slaves, but to prevent the existence of slavery."

Called upon to explain what he meant by writing this, Herzen with ready wit replied that he saw no necessity for defending a constitutional form of government, seeing that it might have been made a charge against him.

"But," said the examiner, "it can be attacked from two sides. You are not attacking it from the monarchical side, or you would not speak of slaves."

"Then," coolly rejoined Herzen, "I should commit the same fault as the Empress Catherine, who ordered her subjects never to call themselves slaves."

After a little more of this carte and tierce, there was a pause. Glancing round the room (the examination was in the library of Prince Galitzin, the President of the Commission of Inquiry), Herzen's eyes fell upon an edition of the works of St. Simon. He turned to the President. "What injustice! I am under accusation on account of reading the writings of St. Simon, and here in your library, Prince, are more than twenty volumes of his works." The good old gentleman had never read anything since the day of his birth, and did not know there had been another quite innocent St. Simon in the days of Louis XIV.

As a counterpart to St. Simon, when the police-officer searched N.'s papers and books, he laid aside a volume of Thiers' *History of the French Revolution*, then a second, then a third; at a fourth his patience failed: " What a mass of revolutionary books ! " he cried; "and there is another," as he took down Cuvier *Sur les révolutions du globe terrestre.*

The second series of questions had another current. All kinds of police-tricks were employed to entrap the accused, to entangle them in contradictions. Hints were given of confessions of friends, &c., &c. When the last question had been put to Herzen, he was left alone in the room to write his answers. One of the Commission, wearing a sad and thoughtful countenance, came in to him—" to speak to you before the close of your trial. The acquaintance my deceased father had with yours for many years inspires me with a particular interest in you. You are young; a brilliant career is before you; but for that you must get clear of this business, and fortunately to do so depends only on yourself. Your father has been deeply affected by your arrest. He will not outlive the moment in which he sees you in the gray soldier's cloak.[1] We are disposed to serve you. But to obtain the imperial pardon (as we have nothing whatever against you except our suspicions) we must have proofs—of your repentance. Through a false sense of honour you spare people of whom we know more than you do, who have not

---

[1] For proved offences men went to Siberia. In anticipation they were sometimes only condemned to enter the army as privates, to die in harness in the Caucasus.

been so discreet as you. Write a simple letter of penitence, naming those who have led you astray : a small price for your father's life and your own happiness."

"I know nothing," replied Herzen, "and I will not add a single word to my explanations."

"It is not our fault," said the Commissioner, and so ended the trial.

In January or February 1835 Herzen was for the last time brought before the Commission : this time only to read his own answers and to alter or sign them. Reading them, he demanded how they could sustain any accusation against him. Under what provision of the Code was his offence ?

Oh, the Code was intended for crimes of another kind, they told him.

"But when I read these mere literary productions, it seems impossible that they can be the only cause of my imprisonment for seven months."

"And do you really think," they answered him, "that we believe you, that we do not know of your having formed a secret society ? "

" Where is that society ? " he asked.

"It is your good luck that the traces have not been discovered ; that you had not time to begin; that we prevented you in time, and so saved you."

While he signed his name to the answers he had given, a priest was called, who certified that they had been made voluntarily, and under no constraint. The priest had not been present at the examination, knew nothing of the answers, did not even for sake of a decent appearance ask a single question. It was a form.

Two more months passed. Being convicted, his relations were allowed to visit him. Toward the middle of March his sentence was determined; and, after time to torment him with suspense, he was called up for judgment: then for the first time meeting his companions in misfortune, among them the poet Sokolofsky, arrested for some verses. He, asked to whom he applied the "detestable words" at their end, replied: "Certainly not to the Emperor, but to God. I beg particularly that you will note this extenuating circumstance."

Judgment was pronounced. Sokolofsky with two others, Ibayeff and an artist named Utkin, was ordered to the Casemates. Utkin died there; Sokolofsky was then sent to the Caucasus, where he died; Ibayeff was transported to Perm on the border of Siberia. Their conviction was of high treason. The poet was guilty of a song; the others had never taken part in anything political, but had perhaps expressed opinions. To the less guilty the Commission read their sentence. His Imperial Majesty, in consideration of the youth of the criminals, commanded that they should not be handed over to the courts of justice; but that, although the singing of revolutionary songs was high treason punishable by death, a punishment only to be commuted for lifelong labour in prison, his most gracious Majesty pardoned the least offensive of them, and permitted them to return to their homes under the surveillance of the police. The rest of the less guilty were to be subjected to such punishments as might serve for their reformation; to be sent therefore to distant provinces for an indefinite time, in the service of the State, under safeguard and overseeing of the local authorities. There were six to be so reformed. One Lachten, who knew first of his offence when he received his sentence, died in exile three years later. Herzen was the second. Remanded back to prison, he remained there until the 9th of April, during the last two days allowed a parting interview with his family. He was then carried off to where, by the imperial mercy, he might at least be kept out of mischief; first, to Perm; then, a little later, to Wiatka, not so close to the Asiatic line, where under the eyes of the police he was permitted to have as much liberty as was compatible with the enforced duties of a clerk in the Governor's office—duties which brought him into hourly contact with dirty people of low ideas and coarse habits, the necessity of conversing with whom almost made him regret the German lice and gensd'armes of his prison cell.

" The office "—quoting his own words—" was beyond comparison worse than the prison. The labour was not great; but what made it intolerable was the air of the infected spot, suffocating as a kennel, and the absurd way of wasting time. Alenisia (the head of the office) did not oppress me; he was even more civil than I expected. He had studied in a school at Kasan, and this made him respect a student of the University of Moscow.

"There were about twenty clerks in the office, for the most part people without the least instruction and without a trace of morality. Sons of clerks and secretaries, accustomed from the cradle to look to the service as a profitable way of getting money, and to regard the peasants as a mine from which to dig it, they were to be bribed with twenty or twenty-five kopecks, sold documents for a glass of wine, altered others, and degraded themselves in every possible way; in short, committed every meanness. My servant ceased to play at billiards because, he said, the officials cheated more than anybody else; and he could not even chastise them for it, because as officials they had military rank. With these people, whom only their rank prevented my servant from beating, I was obliged to spend every day, from nine to two in the forepart of the day, and from five to eight in the evening. . . Sometimes, when I had passed the day in this hell, I returned home in a sort of intellectual stupor, and threw myself on my couch, feeling miserable, weakened, degraded, incapable of any kind of work or occupation. . . And when I recollected that I had to go again to-morrow and the morrow after, I was sometimes seized with a fit of rage and despair, and drank to lose myself."

Doubtless with a full prevision of the chances of his rehabilitation, either by being so brutified or by becoming reconciled to the corruption of official life, the Imperial Father had so placed him at Wiatka.

After a time the insupportability of his position was somewhat lessened, owing to the lucky accident of his being wanted for other employment. The Imperial Government had a statistical fit; and the whole country was to be inoculated with the virus. No funds were appropriated for the purpose; only orders were sent out, and the clerical force must do it. Do it!—they could not attempt it at Wiatka. Herzen volunteered, and so was relieved from the worst part of his captivity. He wrote a grand introduction, which so impressed the Governor that he gave him charge of the whole work, allowing him as a reward to work at home. . . " Henceforth I was no longer forced to perform the horrible task of copying papers, and my drunkard of a president almost became my subordinate. For appearance' sake I had to go to the office for a short time every day.

"The only unhappy consequence of that same statistical labour, which saved me from office-work, was my personal intercourse with Tufeyeff"—the Governor of Wiatka.

This worthy was a brutal disgusting *débauché*, whose luxurious banquets, which Herzen was now forced to attend, were a real punishment. His dining-room was like the office, only in another way; less dirty, but more loathsome, for apparently people went there not by compulsion.

s

"Tufeyeff knew his guests perfectly, and despised them; showed them his fangs from time to time, and treated them in general as a master treats his dogs, sometimes with too much familiarity, sometimes with illimitable rudeness. Yet they came, half from fear, half willingly, humbled themselves, gossiped, spied, flattered, smiled, bowed. . . . My friendship with him was not of long duration. He soon guessed that I was not fit for the highest society of Wiatka. After some months he became discontented with me; a few more and he hated me. I not only did not go to his dinners, but I never entered his saloons. A journey of the Tzarovitch through Wiatka saved me from his hatred.

"Not that I had done anything to attract either his invitations or his anger. But he could not bear to see a man behave independently, though without impertinence. . . He wanted to be flattered. He loved his power, and demanded not only submission, but the show of it. Unfortunately this is national.

"A landed proprietor is accustomed to say to his servant—'Be silent! I will allow no answer.'

"The chief of a department pales with anger, and replies to an inferior venturing to oppose him—'You forget yourself; do you know to whom you are speaking?'

"The Tzar sends people to Siberia for their opinions, tortures them to death in casemates on account of a few verses.

"And all these are more willing to pardon theft, bribery, murder, than the boldness of human dignity, or the audacity of free speech.

"Tufeyeff was a true Imperial servant; was esteemed as such, but not sufficiently. Byzantine servitude and official authority were in rare harmony with him. The annihilation of his own self, the renunciation of will and thought before the supreme power, went perfectly with the harsh yoke under which he kept his inferiors. He was well adapted to become a second Kleinmichel, and could have said with him—Zeal overcomes all difficulties. Like him he could have built the walls of the Winter Palace at the cost of men's lives and dried the building with the workmen's lungs. He could equally well have beaten the engineers who would not become informers.

"As a consequence of his own bitter experience, Tufeyeff nourished in his mind a deeply-rooted hatred against everything aristocratic... When he served as military intendant the officers persecuted him, and a colonel had once flogged him in the open streets of Wilna. All this had sunk deep in the heart of the clerk, and the fruit had ripened. Now as governor it was his turn to oppress.

"One of the most lamentable results of the reforms effected by Peter I. is the development of this caste of officials" [*My Exile*, London, 1855].

Against the expected visit of the Tzarovitch an exhibition had been got up by Tufeyeff. Got up, but when the Grand Duke arrived Tufeyeff was too ignorant to conduct him through the place, and Herzen had to do the honours. This led to some little interest being taken in him; and as a consequence, in the beginning of 1838, he was suffered to approach Moscow so near as Wladimir. There he was employed as a writer on the official journal, a yet more irksome occupation, one would think, for a young enthusiast of not only independent but daring thought, than that which latterly had been his business at Wiatka. Still it was nearer home; and for the rest he solaced himself by a stolen visit to Moscow, bringing back with him a wife, a cousin to whom he had been engaged before his exile. Personal liberty was permitted within the limit of the town; and of money, his father being wealthy, he seems never to have known any serious want.

In 1839 he had leave to go to Petersburg, on business for his father, and in order to be introduced to Count Strogonoff, with whom interest had been made to give him a place in the Chancery of the Ministry for Home Affairs. The next year he received the appointment, and removed with his family to the capital. It would seem that throughout, owing to family influence, he was treated with more consideration than was ordinarily shown to the suspected. As Castelar remarks, "This revolutionist, always persecuted, was always an *employé*. His exiles were singular ones. He was treated like a prodigal son of a monarchical or aristocratic family."

Perhaps too, his talent already noticed, it was thought that he might eventually be broken into useful habits of servility. Still a close watch was kept upon him. On his first visit to Petersburg, wishing to see the city, he had been driven to Isaac's Square, where stands the statue of Peter the First, the place of the massacre of the insurgent regiments in 1825. Returned to his hotel, he met a cousin, and after usual greetings made some casual remarks about the Square and the 26th of December. His cousin, hiding his emotion, looked warningly toward the hotel-servant busy in lighting a fire in the stove, and apparently absorbed in his occupation. When the man left the room the cousin rebuked Herzen for his imprudence in talking of such a subject, and in the Russian language. Calling the next day on his father's agent, the agent drew him aside, and, after satisfying himself that they were beyond hearing, besought him while in Petersburg not to speak of his past. "Just now," he said, "you spoke some words about exile, and the cook was in the room." The next year (he had been some months in the Home Office) he was one day notified to accompany a Commissary of Police to the Emperor's own Chancery, the office of the Secret Police.

"We drove over the chain-bridge through the Summer Garden, and turned into the house once belonging to Kutchabei, on one side of which the worldly Inquisition of Nicholas was established. People once entering at the back door, where we now stopped, did not always go out of it again, or they perhaps went out of it in order to go to Siberia or to perish in the Alexei ravelin.

"We went through all the great and little courtyards, and arrived at last at the Chancery. The guard at the door paid no attention to the Commissary, but called out one of the officials to take from him a paper. The official led him into the corridor, and engaged me to come with him. He led me to the Director's room. Behind a large table sat an old, solitary, haggard, gray-headed man, with a prophecy of ill-luck on his face. He first read a paper which he held in his hand, looking all through very important; then he stood up and approached me. On his breast was the star of some order, from which I concluded that he must be the chief of a spy-division.

"'Have you seen General Dubitt?' [One of the heads of the Police.]

"'No!'

"He was silent; then, looking into my eyes and contracting his eyebrows, he asked in an almost suffocated voice—

"'It seems it is not long since you got permission to return to the capital?'

"'Last year.'

"The old man shook his head. 'You profit badly by the Imperial favour. It seems that you depend upon going again to Wiatka.'

"I looked at him with astonishment.

"'Yes!' he continued, 'you show a noble gratitude to Government for your freedom.'

"'Indeed I do not understand,' I said, losing myself in conjectures.

"'You cannot understand what this means? That is very bad. What connections have you? What occupations? Instead of showing an extraordinary zeal to wash off the spots left on you by youthful error, instead of employing your capacities for the public welfare, you continue to occupy yourself with politics and to oppose the Government. Has experience taught you nothing? How then are you sure that in the number of those with whom you converse there is not always some rascal knowing no better than to come the same minute here with a denunciation?'

"'If you can explain to me what all this means you will greatly oblige me. I am torturing myself to understand what you are talking about, or to what you allude.'

"'What I am talking about? Hm! Well, tell me, did you hear that near the Blue Bridge a policeman murdered a man the other night?'

"'I did hear it,' I answered, quite naïvely.

"'And you repeated it?'

"'It seems so.'

"'Reasoning upon it?'

"'Probably.'

"'And with what reasonings? There is always the same disposition to blame the Government. I tell you openly it does you honour that you confess it so frankly, and it will be taken into consideration by the Court.'

"'But for heaven's sake,' I said, 'what do I confess? The whole town talked about this story; they talked about it in the Chanceries of the Minister for Home Affairs as well as in the shops. Is it to be understood that I talked about it in the same manner?'

"'To spread false and pernicious rumours is a crime by law.'

"'It seems that you accuse me of having invented this tale?'

"'In the account made to the Emperor it is only said that you helped to spread this pernicious rumour. But thereupon ensued an Imperial resolution for your returning to Wiatka.'

"'You only mean to frighten me,' I answered. 'Is it possible for such a trifle to exile a man with a family to a distance of a thousand wersts, and moreover to judge and condemn him without ever asking if it be true or not?'

"'You confessed it yourself.'

"'But the account was given and the affair terminated before you spoke to me!'

"'Read it yourself!'

"The old man went to the table, searched in a heap of papers, drew coldly forth one of them, and gave it to me. I read it, and scarcely believed my eyes. I was silent. Methought even that old man felt a little the absurdity of the case, so thought it better to defend it no more. After being silent also for a little while, he asked—

"'You said you were married?'

"'I am married.'

"'What a pity that we did not know that before. If, however, there is anything to be done the Count[1] will do it. I shall repeat to him our conversation. You will have to leave Petersburg in any case.'"

Next day he was taken before General Dubelt, who treated him in similar style for the imprudence which had again deserved the anger of his Majesty. A paternal Government could not allow the public to be frightened with tales of policemen committing murders. Was it not true that he had written about it?

"'I deemed the case of so little importance that I did not think it necessary to conceal it. And so indeed I did write of it, to my father.'

"'The case of course was not at all important; but you see of what consequence it was to you. The Emperor immediately recollected your family name, and that you had been to Wiatka, and ordered that you should be sent back there. And for that purpose the Count wishes me to let you know that he expects you to-morrow morning at eight o'clock, in order that he may communicate to you the supreme will.'

"'And so then it seems settled that I am to

[1] Count Benkendorf, then at the head of the Secret Police.

return to Wiatka, with my sick wife and sick child, on account of an affair which you yourself say is by no means important?'

"'But you are in the Service?' asked Dubelt, looking attentively at the buttons of my undress uniform.

"'In the office of the Minister for Home Affairs.'

"'Since when?'

"'Six months.'

"'And all that time you have been in Petersburg?'

"'The whole time.'

"'I had no idea of that.'

"'You see,' I said smiling, 'how modestly I behave.'

"Sartinsky (the examiner of the previous day) did not know that I was married, Dubelt did not know that I was in the Government Service; but both knew what I talked of in my own chamber, what I thought, and what I wrote to my father. The real reason of the proceeding was that I had become acquainted with some Petersburg literary men and had printed articles in reviews; and above all, that I had been permitted to return from Wladimir to Petersburg through the intervention of Count Strogonoff without the police having to do with it, and that after my arrival in Petersburg I had not presented myself to Dubelt, as prudent people had advised me to do.

"'You see,' Dubelt finished with, 'your misfortune is that the report was delivered to the Emperor before all the circumstances were known. So go away you must. But I think that another town might be named instead of Wiatka.'"

The third day he had to see Count Benkendorf. "He thus addressed me—'His Imperial Majesty has been acquainted with your taking part in the propagation of rumours mischievous to the Government. His Majesty, seeing that you are little changed for the better, deigns to order your return to Wiatka. I however, according to the request of General Dubelt and to the references I have received concerning you, informed his Majesty of the bad state of your wife's health, and his Majesty the Emperor was so gracious as to alter his determination. His Majesty interdicts to you the capitals. You will be again under the surveillance of the police; but your place of abode is to be fixed by the Minister for Home Affairs.' He added—'The third time you would not get off so easily.'"

The Minister for Home Affairs played his card next; asked Herzen where he would rather go, and a week later sent in his name to the Senate for the place of Councillor to the Regency of Novgorod: in fact promoting the man whom the police were required to watch,—a subtle mixture of fear and favour to work for his conversion. The winter passed without farther notice taken of him; and it was not until the following June that the conspirator-councillor left the capital for Novgorod, his place of preferred exile. No happier in this employment than in former ones, his only business to sign papers and witness the cruelties, the caprices, and the corruption of the satrapcy, he bore the yoke of service for half a year, and then asked leave to send in his resignation. The Senate not only granted it, but also gave him the rank of an aulic councillor: the police, however, forbidding him to leave Novgorod. Powerful and persevering friends at length obtained leave for him to go to Moscow.

"I had not at the moment money for the journey. To wait for it from Moscow would have been too long for my impatience. I commissioned my servant to procure me 1000 roubles (£60). A few hours later he returned with the master of the post-hotel where I had lived for a few days. Gebia, a stout man, with an expression of great kindness, bowing, gave me a roll of bank-notes.

"'How much per cent. will you require?' I asked.

"'If you please,' Gebia replied, 'I do no business of the sort; I do not lend on interest. I heard from your servant that you want money; and as we are very well satisfied with you, and, thank God! have money, I have brought it.'

"I thanked him, and asked if he wanted a bill of exchange.

"'That is quite superfluous,' he said; 'I believe more in your word than in a written paper.'

"'But I may die.'

"'Well!' shaking with laughter, 'losing the

money will add nothing to the pain I shall feel at the tidings of your death.'

"I was moved, and instead of writing the bill for him, I pressed his hand warmly. He, embracing and kissing me, after the old Russian fashion, said—'We observe everything and understand much. We know that you have served against your will, and that you have not been like the others, but have always supported the cause of our poor brethren, the black people. Now, you see, I am happy in that chance has given me an opportunity of doing you a service.'

"When we left Novgorod, late in the evening, the postilion stopped his horses at the hotel-entrance. Gebia stood there with a pie of the size of a wheel. That pie was my medal of honour for the Service."

It was in July 1842 that he returned to Moscow, once more to live among the friends and companions of his youth, so many as remained. At that time the thoughtful part of Moscow society was wild with enthusiasm for the philosophy of Hegel, introduced into the University by Pavloff, a distinguished professor there. All political opportunity debarred, even the discussion of political principles impossible, it was natural that the mental activity of the young should seek employment in other channels. If they might not think of political, they could at least discuss the elements of intellectual, freedom. Belinsky was as that time editing his *Patriotic Annals*. To him the Hegelian philosophy was a question of life and death. Truths there taken into consideration were to him no mere abstractions or scholastic games; sincere, and ardent as sincere, he cared to save nothing from the fire of analysis and negation, and revolted against all half-solutions as timid and cowardly concessions. Herzen followed on the same track. Of what importance he thought these early studies is plain from his remark—"The man who has not gone through the study of the *Chronology* of Hegel and the *Contradictions of Political Economy* by Proudhon is not a complete man, is not up to the level of his age . . . the philosophy of Hegel, a revolutionary algebra, delivers man in an extraordinary way, and takes away one stone after the other from the Christian world, from that world of traditions which have outlived themselves." In this sentence is the key to the peculiarities of Herzen's thought. With such studies, and with the study also of the Russian poets, Pouchkine, Lermontoff, Koltzoff, the novelist Gogol, &c., Herzen was preparing himself for the hoped-for time of his escape from under the ban of the police.

Meanwhile his father died, and he succeeded to a rich inheritance. Years passed, and with them the vainly-repeated endeavours of friends at Court to obtain leave for him to travel. At length, on account of his wife's health, he was allowed a passport, that he might visit the German baths. In 1847 he crossed the Russian frontier, and was free.

VIVOS VOCO.

I DO not know how soon after leaving Russia Herzen lost his wife, to whom he was tenderly and devotedly attached. He was alone when I first made acquaintance with him, calling on him in Paris, in 1850, on the day when I last saw Lamennais. I was returning from Lausanne, where I had been some days with Mazzini arranging for trustworthy correspondents for a new newspaper, the London *Leader*, which at its inception was intended to be the organ of the Republican Party. Mazzini gave me letters of introduction, among others to Maurizio Quadrio at Geneva, and to Herzen in Paris. Herzen received me cordially, willingly accepted the office we wished to impose upon him; and when he came to England, at the end of 1852, we resumed acquaintance, and soon became warm friends. His work *On the Development of Revolutionary Ideas in Russia*, by which he can well afford to be judged, written in French, of which language he was a master, appeared first in Paris, I suppose before the *coup d'état*. A second edition, also in French, was printed in 1853 by the Centralization of the Polish Democratic Society at the printing office, 38, Regent Square, London, where aiding and aided by them Herzen established his own Free Russian Press. On beginning to print in London he wrote, in a letter to the Editors of the *Polish Democrat*:—

"Nicholas has stopped our speech, at the moment when for the first time we have something to say to the people. Shall we suffer this mutism, and rest with the gag in our mouths? If we can be silent, what we have to say is not so very important.

" Upon us Russian emigrants devolves the duty of opening out of Russia a free tribune for Russian speech.

" Russian emigrants have written enough, but speaking rather to Europe than to Russia. It was necessary, even indispensable, to make Russia known under all its aspects, and from the most different points of view. But we have another and a more important vocation : to continue the propaganda *in Russia*, and to make it accessible to Russia. This is what I am now endeavouring to do.

" The establishment of a Russian printing office in London is the most revolutionary action a Russian can commit, while waiting for something more."

True Russian, and believing in the future of his Russia, he none the less repudiated that spurious " patriotism " which winks at whatever may increase the Empire.

The never-dying right of Poland was deeply felt by him, and he let no occasion pass without acknowledging it. He introduces the second edition of his *Idées Révolutionnaires* with these words :—

" My friends of the Polish Democratic Centralization desire to bring out a second edition of my work. I attach special importance to this fact. This edition will be a new public witness of the brotherly alliance of revolutionary Poland with the revolutionary Russians."

When the Poles in London commemorated their insurrection (of 1830) on the 29th of November, 1853, at the time when the expectation of the Crimean war brought new hope for Poland to the exiles, Herzen stood beside them (with Arnold Ruge for the German Republicans, Dr. Ronay for the Hungarians, Ledru Rollin for the French, and Colonel Pianciani in place of Mazzini, too sick to be present) to speak for war, war not futile, but decisive against the aggrandisement of Russia, and for the liberty and independence of Poland, could the Powers but dare to take so wise a course.

Nor did he only fraternize with the Poles politically; his personal friendships took the same direction, and the promptings of his warm and pitiful heart were ever leading him to services of kindness and generous giving in which Poles and Russians were sharers without distinction. On leaving Russia he had been prudent enough to invest a considerable sum, perhaps as much as he could with secrecy, in Western hands. When, on his refusal to return to Russia, Nicholas would have confiscated his property, it was found that a lien was held by one Rothschild, and the Tzar was estopped.

He was the one rich man of the knot of European Republicans at that time in London. For some years he resided at Teddington, a few miles from

T

London, in a pleasant country mansion (Elm-field House) on the side of the river Thames, not far from the residence of the Orleans family. His house was the rendezvous of the Republican party. I remember a day there, the day on which we received the news of the death of the Tzar Nicholas. His rooms were crowded with political friends, Russians, Poles, French, Germans, Italians, English. It was a modern Babel, a feast of polyglot congratulations, a confusion of men wild with a fierce delight as in the Saturnalia of old : in the death of the old drill-sergeant they saw and greeted the accession of a new era. Herzen himself could set no bounds to the overflow of his joy. The implusiveness of his Slavonic nature had free manifestation : so unchecked that, while strolling in the grounds, which reached to the river, at one point where they were but slightly fenced off from the public road, he flung money among some boys attracted there by our uproar, merely to have them shout—"Nicholas is dead!" It was the frenzy of the just emancipated serf, child-like, not malevolent : he seemed to have need of uttering the jubilant feeling of a whole race.

A little later, in 1857, we were fellow-mourners, with Ledru Rollin and Mazzini, at the grave of Mazzini's dearest friend in exile, Stanislas Worcell, the venerable and beloved chief of the Polish democracy. When, after the first part of the funeral service in the chapel of the cemetery, the coffin was being lifted up to be carried to the grave, Herzen, tears coursing down his cheeks, stepped forward and placed himself beneath as one of the bearers. It was not only the impulsive action of a friend's love, it meant also homage to the noble Pole, an acknowledgment of the debt of the Muscovite to Poland. "Poland amnesties us!" he had said, beginning his speech at our meeting, three years before.

Yet this man, the rich-blooded barbarian, impulsive, child-like, carried away by enthusiasm where his feelings were concerned, could be wise and diplomatic; was a profound and subtle thinker, choice of speech as well as ready, clear and concise as well as impressive, with remarkable power of apt illustration, witty too, and a "lord of irony." Ever with some lightning flash withering the flowers of poetry and religious fervour in others, he was himself a poet, not only at heart but in expression. Emilio Castelar well describes him in writing of *The Republican Movement in Europe* (*Harper's Magazine*, 1876). "In person he was short of stature" (latterly inclined to corpulency), "with a large head, long fair hair like a Goth's" (fair in the eyes of a Spaniard, rather chestnut than fair), "clear complexion, light beard" (chestnut too), "small luminous eyes like those of the Huns, which according to Fernandez so terrified the degenerate Romans,—all the traits of the Northern races; but he had at the same time, in the vividness of his speech, in the warmth which animated it, in the strong emotion by which he was agitated, in the sudden transitions from the sublime to the grotesque, in marvelous variety and inimitable grace, all the warmth and *verve* of the men of the South."

Removing afterwards to London, with his children, a boy (since, I believe, a physician) and two younger daughters, of whom he was passionately fond, he kept up the same hospitality. At his house I met Bakounine, who had been in a Russian casemate, chained by his neck to the wall for eight months, afterwards sent to Siberia, thence escaping down the Amoor to the Pacific, and returning through America to Europe: a stalwart unbroken giant (six feet two or four), cheerful and humorous for all his sufferings, and laughing heartily when I told him of having written of his death some years before.[1]

The name of the Amoor recalls another of the dreams of Herzen, perhaps no wilder than seemed that of emancipation of the Russian serf, due so much to the influence of his writings. All hopes and presentiments and prophecies of the Future are but idle dreams to the only practical statesman, the

[1] In the *English Republic*, 1851. Bakounine, Herzen's friend at Moscow in 1843, was after that in Paris, well known among the Poles, and much esteemed by them for his endeavours to bring about an alliance between the Polish democrats and the Russians. He fought also on the barricades at Dresden in 1848, for which, arrested in Saxony, he there suffered two years' imprisonment before being given up to the Tzar to be punished for his offences as a Russian Revolutionist. In Petersburg it was reported that he had died of dropsy occasioned by the dampness of his dungeon; but the general suspicion was that he had been poisoned; till he startled and gladdened his friends by his return.

manipulator of to-day. And yet sometimes, witness Italy and Germany, the dreamers may be farther-sighted than the wide-awake. Herzen pleased himself with visions even for Siberia. "Siberia," he writes, "has a great future. As yet (1855) it is only looked upon as a reservoir which contains much money, furs, and other products of nature; but which is cold, covered with snow, poor in provisions and means of communication, and thinly peopled. All that however is not correct. The Russian Government, which kills everything, which produces nothing but by force, by the stick, does not understand how to give that impulse of life which would bring Siberia forward with American rapidity. We shall see what astonishing results will happen when one day the mouth of the Amoor is opened for navigation, and America meets Siberia on the confines of China." Professor Pumpelly's *Across Two Continents* confirms the views of Herzen.

At his house too (Herzen had then returned to Teddington) Garibaldi was a visitor in 1864, when all England was so strangely seized with enthusiasm for the Liberator of the Two Sicilies, that the Government had to smuggle him away for fear of some unprecedented catastrophe. Who could say but that the hero whose entrance into London was an ovation surpassing every royal precedent, who was acclaimed by the highest and the lowest, peers and people, who held the hearts of the mob, and rowed or was rowed by Duchesses in his boat on the Thames,—who could say but that he might be taken with the whim of proclaiming a Republic in constitutional queen-loving Britain ? and then—— So our most prescient Gladstone persuaded him to take himself off in time, and Britain was not revolutionized. But he was permitted to visit Herzen; and here is the account of his visit from a London evening paper (not the Court paper), the *Standard* of April 20, 1864 : " Account of a visit paid by Garibaldi to M. Herzen, a Russian exile, and editor of the *Kolokol*, at Teddington." It is worth quoting if only to show the relations of the men spoken of :—

"A select party of English and foreign friends was assembled to meet the General; amongst them Signor Saffi, Signor Mazzini, Signor Mordini (a member of the Italian Parliament), &c. As usual crowds had assembled to greet the General, who was enthusiastically cheered on his arrival and at his departure. M. Herzen, accompanied by his friend and fellow-editor of the Russian democratic journal *La Cloche*,[1] Mr. N. Ogareff and Mrs. Ogareff, received the General at the garden-gate and led him into the house; but the cheering outside was so vehement that Garibaldi was compelled to return for a moment to the garden. After lunch Mazzini rose and proposed the health of General Garibaldi in the following words :—

"'My toast will include all that is most dear to us, all those things for which we have fought and striven. I drink to the liberty of the peoples, to the association of the peoples, to the man who is the living incarnation of these great ideas, Joseph Garibaldi; to that poor, sacred, heroic Poland, whose sons have been silently fighting and dying for more than a year; to that Young Russia whose desire is land and liberty, that new Russia that will at no distant day hold out a sister's hand to Poland, acknowledge her equality and independence, and cancel the remembrance of the Russia of the Tzar; to those Russians who with our

---

[1] That is the *Kolokol*, or *Alarm Bell*, called *Tocsin* by Castelar.

friend Herzen at their head have most wrought and laboured toward the creation of this new Russia; to that religion of duty which will give us strength to strive and to devote ourselves even unto death for the realization of these ideas.' The toast having been drunk, Garibaldi rose and said :—' I am about to make a declaration which I ought to have made long ago. There is a man amongst us here who has rendered the greatest services to our country and to the cause of liberty. When I was a young man, having nought but aspirations toward the Good, I sought for one able to act as the guide and counsellor of my young years. I sought such a man even as he who is athirst seeks the spring. I found the man. He alone watched when all around him slept; he alone fed the sacred flame. He has ever remained my friend; ever as full of love for his country and of devotion to the cause of liberty. This man is Joseph Mazzini. To my friend and teacher!' The General rose again, and said:—'Mazzini has uttered some words with regard to unhappy Poland, to which I adhere with all my heart. Now let us drink to that Young Russia, which suffers, struggles, and shall triumph like ourselves, and which is destined to play a noble and important part in Europe.'"

Herzen's first serial issue from his Russian press was the *Kolokol* (the *Alarm Bell*, with the motto *Vivos Voco*—I call the living), which was succeeded, I should rather say supplemented, I think in 1857, or it may be later, by the *Polar Star*, a name recalling a former publication by Ryléieff and Bestoujeff. The *Kolokol* passed the Tzarian frontiers, the Poles aiding in the transmission, spread rapidly through Russia, reaching even to the Imperial presence, not without direct effect upon the actions of the Government. Read everywhere with enthusiasm, it did its work of propagandism, and efficiently prompted the course of revolutionary thoughts which after the reverses in the Crimea could only be stayed by the ordonnance of the 2nd of December, 1857, which decreed the emancipation of the Russian serfs.

That was the day of Herzen's triumph ; and well might he be proud of his not inconsiderable share in the enfranchisement of 22,000,000 of human beings.

It is said that since then his influence has declined ; Young Russia regards his name, but his party is narrowed and its hopes are on the wane. It may be so : since reaction for a time is everywhere dominant ; or rather since men not too deeply impressed with republican principles are content to take brief advantage of reforms wrung from the fears of the ruling powers, and to leave for a future generation the founding of a new organization of society. The ordonnance of December 2nd is sufficient epitaph for Herzen. Regarding other reforms allowed for the present by absolutism, whether calculated only to dull the edge of republican criticism or to supersede the re-organization for desiring which republicans are blamed, there may be some truth in earlier words of Herzen, spoken with reference to reforms before his day.

" Peter III. abolished the Secret Police and Torture-Chamber.

" Catherine II. abolished torture.

" Alexander I. abolished it again.

" Answers extorted by brutality are not valid before the law. Any official who tortures an accused man is himself subject to the most rigorous punishment.

" And yet people are tortured through the whole of Russia, from Behring's Straits to Tauroggen" [*My Exile*].

Joseph Hume was one of the most moderate and (which is the same thing) practical reformers of most practical England: a man of shrewd common sense, unsuspected of poetry or genius. He confined himself to a persistent struggle for the pennies he set himself to save, and was content with the cheeseparings of political success, basing his position as a truly moderate reformer on the Scotch proverb— " A little and a little makes a mickle "; not heeding the modern perversion of another proverb—" Scotch a snake, but do not kill it!" He spent a long and earnest life in the pursuance of economical reforms, not valueless, only too readily appreciable. Before he died he was led to confess that but a small percentage of the time and energy he had devoted and seen devoted to these concessions from the Powers would perhaps have sufficed to transfer power to the petitioners, and so have been even more economical in the end: the end not being the continuance of the Powers from whom we have to beg. Herzen was not a reformer of the Hume stamp. He proposed no programme of chartered favours or bit-by-bit reforms; he sought to overthrow the Tzar and to establish, instead of the most beneficent absolutism, the simple and safe rule of a Russian Republic.

He died in Paris on the 21st of January, 1870.

He has been accused of being anti-national; of

seeking to graft Western institutions upon those natural and necessary to the Slavonic race; of Panslavism; of contempt for all Western ideas; and of looking for the only salvation of Europe in a new irruption of the East, parodying in his creed Béranger's song of *The Cossack to his Horse—*

> .... "Efface in our new ride
> Towers, temples, laws, all history's sacred things!
> Neigh, O my faithful courser! neigh with pride,
> And trample underfoot the peoples and their kings!"

That he was anti-national is altogether untrue, though he did not believe that all which the *empire* had absorbed or conquered became therefore an integral part of the *nation;* and though he was, I think, not unwilling to allow the possibility of the sometime growth of separate nationalities even within the bounds of what might at present be fitly called one country; though also he respected and consistently insisted upon the nationality of Poland, not deeming a mere brutal annexation to be an act of God. That of itself disposes of his "Panslavism." For the rest, the party *par excellence*, the Slavophiles themselves, would reject the man who plainly accused them of wishing only to exchange the collar of German slavery for a Slavo-Byzantine collar, who attacked them for being retrograde instead of progressive.

"The Slavophiles hurled themselves furiously against all that Peter the Great had done, and, in fine, against whatever was Europeanized, civilized.

One may comprehend and justify this attraction as an act of opposition, but unfortunately the opposition went too far, and found itself strangely placed on the side of the Government against its own aspirations for freedom.

"After having decided *à priori* that whatever came from the Germans was worth nothing, that whatever had been introduced by Peter I. was detestable, the Slavophiles went back to an admiration for the narrow forms of the Muscovite state, and, abdicating their own reason and their proper lights, ran with fervour for shelter beneath the Cross of the Greek Church. . . . They, the Slavophiles, strangely deceived themselves as to the Muscovite organization, and lent to Greek orthodoxy an importance which it has never had. Full of indignation against despotism, they arrived only at a slavery political and moral; with all their sympathies for the Slave nationality, they went out by the opposite door from this very nationality. Greek orthodoxy dragged them toward Byzantinism; and, in fact, they rapidly directed themselves toward that abyss of stagnation, in which have disappeared the vestiges of the ancient world. If the forms and the spirit of the West were not suitable to Russia, what was there in common between her and the organization of the Lower Empire? Where is manifested the organic tie between the Slaves, barbarians because of their youth, and the Greeks, barbarians through decrepitude? And, in fine, what is this Byzantium if it is not Rome, the Rome of the decadence, Rome without glorious reminiscences, without remorse? What new principles has Byzantium brought to history? Is it Greek orthodoxy? But that is only apathetic Catholicism. The principles are so exactly the same that it has taken seven centuries of controversies and dissensions to make believe in some differences of principle. Is it the social organization? But that was based in the Eastern Empire upon absolute authority, on passive obedience, on the complete absorption of the individual by the State, of the State by the Emperor.

"Is it such a condition that can communicate new life to a young people? The Western Slaves of the South have been sufficiently long in contact with the Greeks of the Lower Empire: what have they gained by it?

"Have we already forgotten what were those herds of men packed by the Greek emperors under the benediction of the Patriarchs of Constantinople? It is enough to throw a glance upon their laws of *lèse-majesté*, recently so well imitated by Nicholas and his jurisconsult Hube,[1] to appreciate this casuistry

---

[1] In the Russian Catechism:—

"... What duties does religion teach us, the humble subjects of his Majesty the Emperor of Russia, to practise towards him?

"Worship, obedience, fidelity, the payment of taxes, service, love, and prayer: the whole being comprised in the words worship and fidelity.

"... Does religion then forbid us to rebel and overthrow the Government of the Emperor?

"We are interdicted from so doing at all times and under any circumstances.

of servitude, this philosophy of slavery. And these laws concerned not only the temporal; came afterwards canonical laws which regulated movements, form of dress, food, and laughter. One may fancy what became of the man caught in the double net of the State and the Church, continually trembling and threatened, here by the judge without appeal and the obedient executioner, there by the priest acting in the name of God, and by the epithemies which bound him in this world and the next.

" Where can we see any beneficent influence of the Eastern Church? What people has it civilized or emancipated among all those who have accepted it from the fourth century to our own days? Is it Armenia, Georgia, the scarcely to be called peoples of Asia Minor, the poor inhabitants of Trebisond? Is it the Morea? We shall be told perhaps that nothing could be done with these peoples, used up, corrupted, without future. But the Slaves, a race sound in body and in soul, have they gained anything? The Eastern Church was introduced into Russia at the serene and flourishing epoch of Kiew,

---

". . . What examples confirm this doctrine ?

"The example of Jesus Christ Himself, who lived and died in allegiance to the Emperor of Rome, and respectfully submitted to the judgment which condemned him to death. We have, moreover, the example of the Apostles, who both loved and respected them, suffered meekly in dungeons conformably to the will of the Emperors, and did not revolt like traitors and malefactors. We must, therefore, in imitation of these examples, suffer and be silent."—*Catechism (promulgated in* 1832) *for the Use of Schools and Churches in Russian Poland.*

under the grand prince Wladimir. It has led her to the sad and abject time described by Kachikine[1]; it has blessed and sanctioned all the measures taken against the liberty of the people. It has taught Byzantine despotism to the Tzars, and to the people prescribed a blind obedience even when they attached them to the land and bowed their necks to serfdom. Peter the Great paralyzed the influence of the clergy: it was one of his most important acts. And they would revive that influence.

"The Slavism which looked for the salvation of Russia only in the rehabilitation of the Byzantine-Muscovite *régime* did not emancipate, but bind; did not advance, but recoiled. The 'Europeans,' as they were called by the Slavophiles, did not wish to change a German collar for a Slavo-orthodox collar; they desired to free themselves from all possible collars. They were not forced to erase the times that had elapsed since Peter I., the efforts of a century so hard, so full of fatigues. That which had been obtained by so many sufferings, by torrents of blood, they were not willing to resign, to return to a narrow order of things, an exclusive nationality, a stationary Church. It was very fine for the Slavophiles to say, like the Legitimists, that they could take the good side and leave the bad. It was a grave error; and they committed another common to all reactionists. Adorers of the historic principle, they constantly

---

[1] A Russian diplomatist of the time of Alexis, the father of Peter I., who wrote of the condition of Russia in those days.

forgot that all which had passed since Peter I. was also history, and that no living force, to say nothing of mere ghosts, could efface accomplished facts, or eliminate their consequences." [*Développement des Idées Révolutionnaires.*]

No Panslavist, nor yet a Nationalist in the sense of selfish patriotism being the sole rule, he was yet a Russian to the core, a believer in the destiny of his country, and despite her faults her passionate lover, although, nay ! even because none exposed her faults more earnestly than himself. The charge of forcing Western modes upon her is met by the counter accusation of his contempt for the West. This last count in his indictment alone has show of truth. That he was no admirer of the effeteness and negative results of Western civilization, nor impressed with the all-sufficiency of Western democratic or other recipes, is true enough; it is also true that his objections went the length of pointing out, with no apologetic circumlocution, the differences between the natural characteristics of East and West, and that he would insist that medicines not yet successfully exhibited in the one were not proved specifics for the other. Political, like other, doctors and dogmatists are not infallible. Who shall decide when they disagree ? Lord Palmerston would have flung all national life into one constitutional mould (certainly to the great convenience of constitutional governments), utterly regardless of differences of nature, history, or environments. So some of our "Republican" friends (but the word-distinction has lost strength since anything monarchical, only ceasing to be called so, now claims, as in America and France, to be republican),—so some "Republicans" would fit each and every nation to the Procrustean bed of their own conceits, in that forgetting the very meaning of the nationality taught by Mazzini, the opportunity for growth of distinctive characteristics. It was to such pattern-plates of Western fashions that Herzen applied the dissolving acid of his irony; and, Socialist himself, refused assent no less to the "socialisms" of the West. May not he have been right (I believe he was) in his opinion of the opportunity yet held by the Slaves to escape the pitfalls and stumbling-places which have been necessary for the education of the Latin and Teutonic races? What becomes of the solidarity, of the growth and perfectibility of Humanity, if every people (why not every man also?) must tread continually in the false steps of others, if the blind must ever be led by the blind, and history be condemned eternally to repeat itself? He writes to me in 1854:—

"You ask me what will be the future of Russia? I answer you with another question—Is Europe capable of a social regeneration?

". . . It seems to me that Europe, such as it now is, has played its part; its dissolution has advanced since 1848. These words frighten, and are disputed without much judgment. Certainly it is not the Peoples who will perish, but the States and their

Roman, Christian, feudal, and *juste-milieu* institutions, no matter whether monarchical, parliamentary, or 'republican.'

". . . Until these days the European world has undergone only reformations; the bases of the modern States have remained intact; only some of their details have been ameliorated. Such was Luther's Reformation, such the Revolution of '89. The Social Revolution will not be like this.

" We have gone to the utmost extent of plastering. It is impossible to move among the old forms without breaking them. Our revolutionary idea is utterly incompatible with the existing condition of things. The State, based upon the Roman idea of the absorption of the individual by Society, of the sanctification of accidental and monopolized property, of a religion consecrating the most absolute dualism (even in the revolutionary formula, God and [1] the People), can offer nothing to the Future but its carcase, the mere chemical elements set free by death.

". . . All the relations between society and individuals, and between individuals themselves, must be totally changed. Now the grand question is, whether the Germano-Roman peoples will have the force to undergo this metempsychosis, and if they have it at this present?

" The idea of the social revolution is European. That does not prove that the peoples most capable of realizing it are the peoples of the West.

[1] Unless the *and* be conjunctive instead of disjunctive.

"Christianity was only crucified at Jerusalem.

"The social idea may be only a testament, a last will, a limit beyond which the Western world cannot pass. It may also be the solemn entry into a new existence, the acquisition of the manly toga.

"Europe is too rich to risk her all: she has too much to take care of, is too highly civilized in her upper regions, and too little in her lower, to throw herself forlornly into so complete a revolution. Republicans and monarchists, deists and jesuits, shopkeepers and peasants,—they are all conservatives in Europe. There are no revolutionists but the workmen.

"The Workman can save the Old World from a great shame, and from great misfortunes. But saved by him the Old World would not survive a day. We shall then be in full socialism militant. And the question will be positively solved.

"But also the Workman may be overthrown, as in the days of June. The repression will be yet more cruel, and more terrible. Then the destruction of the Old World must enter in at another door, and the realization of the social idea have to be brought about in another world.

"Look at these two immense platforms which from the sides of Europe touch each other at their extremes! Why are they so great?—or what are they preparing? What is the passion of activity and aggrandisement which devours them? These two worlds, so opposed one to the other, to which however it is impossible to refuse some analogy, are the United States and Russia. No one doubts America being the veritable continuation of the development of Europe, and nothing but that continuation. Denuded of all initiative, of all invention, as she is, America is ready to receive Europe, to realize her social ideas, but she will not come to finish the old edifice, she will not quit her fertile plains.

"Can the same be said of the Slavonic world? What is the Slavonic world? What would this silent world which has traversed the ages from the migration of races even to our days in a continual *aside*, without unclosing its teeth?

. . . . . .

"It would seem that the time of these peoples has not come, that they wait for something, that the state in which they live is but provisional.

. . . . . .

"It was the Slavonians who first began the great struggle against the Papacy, and who afterwards, in the revolt of the Taborites, stamped upon it a character so strongly social.

. . . . . .

"It was at Moscow that the Byzantine and Oriental absolutism of the Tzars was formed. It was through that the last franchises of the people perished. Everything was sacrificed to the idea of a State of immense frame.

"After accomplishing its work of welding, Moscow stopped. It knew not what to do with the forces it had evoked, which remained without employ. The issue was found afterwards. Where there is force enough the issue is always found. Peter I. made of the Russian State an European State.

"The ease with which a part of the nation united itself to European manners and renounced its old habitudes is a palpable proof that the Muscovite State was by no means a veritable expression of the popular life, but only a transitory form. Wherever the really national elements were touched the people defended them with obstinacy. The whole peasant class accepted nothing of the reforms of Peter I. And it was the real depositary of the national life. And the base of this life (as the historian Michelet has said) was *communism;* that is to say, the continual sharing of the land among the whole number of working-men, and the absence of any individual landed property.

. . . . . .

"From the moment in which Europe at Paris, at Vienna, at Aix-la-Chapelle, and at Verona, recognized, *nolens volens*, the leadership of an Emperor of Russia, the work of Peter was terminated, and the Imperial power saw itself in the same position in which the Tzars of Moscow were before the time of Peter.

. . . . . .

"The Reformation and the Revolution went not beyond the walls of the Church or the precincts of the Monarchical State; they were evidently unable to pull down the old edifice. The Gothic roof sank in, the throne leaned over; but the ruins stood. And neither the Reformation nor the Revolution had any prise upon them.

"It is very well to be reformed, evangelic, Lutheran, Protestant, Quaker : the Church exists still,—that is to say, liberty of conscience does not exist, or is only an act of individual rebellion. It is very fine to be parliamentary, constitutional, with two houses of parliament or one, with a limited suffrage or with universal suffrage : the lop-sided throne always remains, and, though every minute the kings tumble off, new ones are found. In default of a king in a 'Republic' they have a man of straw which they set upon the throne, and for which they keep the royal parks and palaces, the Tuileries and St. Cloud.

"Meanwhile a secular and rationalist Christianity pushes against the Church, not knowing that itself will be crushed by the falling vault; and a monarchical republicanism pushes down the throne to seat itself all royally upon it.

"The breath of revolutionary life is elsewhere. The torrent has changed its course, and leaves these old Montagues and Capulets to continue their hereditary struggle in another place. The standard is no longer uplifted against the priest, no longer against the king, no longer against the noble,—but against the heir of all these, against the *Master*, against the patented monopolizer of the tools of toil. And the revolutionist is no longer either Huguenot, or Protestant, or Liberal: he is called the *Workman*.

"And lo, Europe, her youth once, nay! twice renewed, halts at a third limit; not daring to pass. She trembles at that word *Socialism* which she reads upon her door. She has been told that Catiline will open the door. It is very true. Perhaps the door may not be opened: but if opened it will be by Catiline, and a Catiline with too many friends for all of them to be strangled in prison. Cicero, the conscientious and civil assassin, had easier work than his colleague Cavaignac.

"This limit is more difficult to pass than the others were. All these reformations kept the half of the Old World, which they covered with new drapery. The heart was not all broken, nor all quite lost: some part of what we loved, of what had been dear to us from infancy, of what we reverenced, what was traditional, remained to console the weak. Adieu, ye nursery songs! Adieu, ye recollections of the paternal home! Adieu, great habit! whose force, says Bacon, is greater than the force of genius!

"Nothing will pass the custom-house during the storm; and will they have patience to wait the calm?

. . . . . .

"A most natural question would be to ask if Russia must pass through all the phases of European development, or if it shall have a revolutionary development altogether different? For me, I altogether deny the necessity of these repetitions. The different painful, difficult phases of the historical development of our predecessors can and must be gone through by us, but only in the same way in which the fœtus passes through the inferior degrees of zoological existence. A work once done, a result obtained, is done and is obtained for all who can understand it. This is the solidarity of progress— this is the humanitarian inheritance. I know well enough that the result of itself alone is intransmissible, at least useless: it is real only when assimilating itself to the whole logical genesis. Every scholar discusses over again the propositions of Euclid: but what a difference between the toil of Euclid and that of the boy of to-day!

"Russia has done her revolutionary embryogeny in her European class. The nobility with the Government forms the European State in the Slavonic State. We have passed through all the phases of liberalism, from English constitutionalism to the worship of '93 and '94. We have done it, as the aberration of the stars repeats in little the path of the earth in its orbit.

"Our people has no occasion to repeat this sad work. Why should it pour out its blood to arrive at those half solutions at which we others have already arrived, whose only importance is that they have set us *other* questions and awakened *other* inspirations?

" We have done this painful heavy service for the

people; we have paid for it with the gibbet, the hulks, the casemates, by exile, and by a cursed existence, yes! by a cursed existence. There is little thought in Europe of what we have suffered during two generations.

. . . . . .

"The facts related by us are published *in extenso* by Haxthausen.[1] I will not again repeat all that I have said of the rudimentary organization of self-government in the communes, where all is elective, where every one is a proprietor, although the land belongs to no one, where the proletarian is an abnormity, an exception. You know enough of it to understand that the Russian people, unhappy as it is, crushed partly by serfdom, and wholly by the Government which despises and oppresses it, could not follow the example of the peoples of Europe in those completely urban phases of their revolutions which would have immediately attacked the very base of the communal organization.

. . . . . .

"To preserve the commune and render the individual free; to extend the self-government of the commune and the district to the towns and to the whole State, and maintain the national unity, to develop personal rights and maintain the indivisi-

[1] Who published in 1847, in French and German, three volumes concerning the rural commune in Russia: Haxthausen, Catholic and Prussian, a writer on agriculture, and so radical a monarchist that he finds the King of Prussia too liberal and the Emperor Nicholas too philanthropic.

bility of the land—here is the revolutionary question for Russia.

"The State and the individual,—authority and liberty,—communism and egotism (in the wider sense of the word),—these are the Herculean pillars of the great struggle, of the grand revolutionary epic.

"Europe offers a solution mutilated and arbitrary; Russia another mutilated and savage.

"The Revolution will complete the synthesis. Social formulas never exist except vaguely before their realization.

"The Anglo-Saxon races have arrived at the emancipation of the individual in denying the community and isolating the man. The Russian preserves the community, and denies the individual, absorbing the man." [*Letters on Russia and the Old World* in the *English Republic*, vol. 3.]

He was a believer in the socialism which seemed to him native and adapted to his race; not in the socialisms (whose name is Legion) or the communism of the French schools. Yet he could do justice to them and acknowledge the debt owed to every one who sincerely endeavours to solve a necessary problem. He writes—

"St. Simonianism, vague, religious, and at the same time analytic, went marvelously well among the Muscovites. After having studied it they passed quite naturally to Proudhon, as from Hegel to Feuerbach. Fourierism rather than St. Simonianism suited the studious youth of Petersburg : Fourierism, which looked only for immediate realization, which desired a practical application, which dreamed (Fourier also dreamed, but he propped his dreams upon arithmetical calculations, hiding his poesy under the title of industry and his love of liberty under his brigadement of workers), Fourierism could not help finding an echo in Petersburg. The phalanstery is nothing else than a Russian commune with a barrack for the workers, a military colony on a civil basis, an industrial regiment. It has been remarked that the Opposition which in the struggle faces a Government has always something of its character, though in an inverse sense. And I can well believe that there was some ground of truth in the fear that the Russian Government began to have of communism : communism is Russian autocracy overthrown. . . . The House of Holstein-Gotorp is too German, too pedantic, too learned, to throw itself frankly into the arms of a half-savage nationalism in order to put itself at the head of a popular movement which at the beginning would desire only to settle its accounts with the nobility, and to extend the institutions of the rural commune to all properties, to the towns, to the whole State.

"We have seen a monarchy 'surrounded by Republican institutions,' but our imagination refuses to conceive an Emperor of Russia surrounded by communists." [*Idées Révolutionnaires.*]

Is this a too overweening trust in Russian capability of action, or too contemptuous treatment of Western theories? Nevertheless he writes:—

"The Russian Government after having travailed for twenty years, has arrived at allying Russia in an indissoluble manner to revolutionary Europe. There are no longer frontiers between Russia and Poland. . . . Confounding Poland with Russia, the Government has raised an immense bridge for the solemn passage of revolutionary ideas, gathered by the Poles during their exile in the West: a bridge which begins at the Vistula and finishes at the Black Sea." [*Idées Révolutionnaires.*]

Again:—"For the Western man one of the greatest of those misfortunes which help the maintenance of slavery, the pauperism of the masses and the powerlessness of revolutions, is moral servitude (*l'asservissement*); it is not the want of the sentiment of individuality, but the want of clearness in this sentiment, falsified as it is by historical antecedents which limit individual independence. The people of Europe have given so much of soul and so much blood for past revolutions that they are always present; and the individual cannot take a step without shocking his souvenirs, *fueros* more or less obligatory and acknowledged by himself. All questions have already been half-solved. Principles, the relations of men with one another, duties, moralities, and crimes: all is determined, and that not by superior force, but in part by the assent of men. It follows that the individual, instead of preserving his freedom of action, has only to submit or be insurgent. These norms without appeal, these ready-made notions, traverse the ocean, and are introduced into the fundamental pact of a republic altogether new; they survive the guillotined king, and tranquilly seat themselves on the benches of the Jacobins and at the Convention. This mass of half-truths and half-prejudices has long been taken for solid and absolute foundations of social life, for results immutable and beyond doubt. Each of them indeed has been a veritable progress, a victory for its time, but collectively they have built little by little the walls of a new prison. Thinking men perceived this at the beginning of our century: but they saw at the same time the thickness of the walls, and what efforts it would take to break them.

"Russia is in another position. The walls of her prison are of wood, raised by mere brute force: they would yield to the first shock. One part of the people, renouncing all its past with Peter I., has shown what power of negation it possesses; the other, remaining a stranger to the actual state of things, has bent to but has not accepted the new *régime*, which appears to be a temporary bivouac. They obey because they fear, but they do not believe.

"It is evident that neither Western Europe nor Russia can go much farther on their way without completely rejecting the fashions of their being, political and moral. But, like Europe, Nicodemus was too rich to sacrifice his great having for a hope: the fishermen of the Gospel had nothing to regret—it was easy to exchange their nets for the beggar's wallet. What they *had* was a living soul able to comprehend the Word." [*Idées Révolutionnaires.*]

And of the Commune, the Russian Commune, on which his hope of the future was based, at all events for Russia itself, thanking Europe for having enlightened them concerning it, he writes, again condemning the Slavophiles:—

"They shut themselves up in the period of Kiew,[1] and held only to the rural commune. The period of Kiew did not hinder that of Moscow, nor the loss of all liberties. The commune did not save the peasant from serfdom. Far from denying the importance of the commune,[2] we tremble for it, *because in reality there is nothing stable without individual liberty.* Europe, not knowing this commune, or having lost it in the vicissitudes of past ages, yet understands it; and Russia, which possesses it since a thousand years, did not at all understand it till Europe came to tell her of the treasure hidden in her bosom. They began to appreciate their Slave commune when socialism began to spread." [*Idées Révolutionnaires.*]

"Eternally looking toward Europe, and attentive to struggles and questions beyond our frontiers, we were very little acquainted with our own Russian people. It was only after understanding socialism [3]

[1] The same error, though inversely, as that of the Paris Commune in 1871, which went back to the urban communes of early Gaul, ignoring the changes and the lessons of after history.

[2] It would seem he was accused even of that.

[3] As elaborated in Western thought. He is speaking of the

that we comprehended the immense bearing of our rural commune, autonomic and communistic, sharing the usufruct among all its members, and permitting no individual possession. It was only then that we appreciated the strange genius of this people, which stepping forth from its rural commune forms on the instant a community of workmen so soon as men of the same calling meet in the same place. . . . It was then that we remarked that this people, which has so well preserved its communes, has never undergone the influence of the Roman law, of feudal institutions, of Catholic priests or Protestant preachers, of a shop-keeper code (*code bourgeois*); that it has only been oppressed by a force altogether material, which has rendered it very unhappy, but which, thanks to the commune, has neither crushed nor corrupted it." [*Polish Democrat*, 1853.]

So he did believe, this Russian, in something to be learned from the West, though he valued the freshness of his own yet uncivilized race, and counted on some untried strength of youth which in the career of human progress might speed them beyond their tired preceders. He thought that his Russia might have her turn in teaching something to the world,— perhaps the true application of this same communistic idea. Methinks his prayers will find some echoes, and the hopes he fostered, however choked with

---

Russian students and littérateurs, great readers of Western socialistic and philosophic publications, while profoundly ignorant of their own people.

weeds, imperial or other, yet grow and ripen for the harvest.

With the genius of a Gibbon, writing of the decline and fall of the exotic empire of the great Peter, brought up under the shadow of the Winter Palace, his very hopes are not without a recollection of the darkness and doubt in which they had been nursed; but he scoffed only at what appeared to him as ghostly fallacies, at a religion which no longer actuates men's daily lives, which statesmen and publicists have ignominiously dismissed from politics, and of which the world's rulers, by grace of God or imposition *motu proprio*, are even more sceptical than he was. He, a disciple of Proudhon, a rebel against the divine Tzar, might also undervalue the religious aspirations of Mazzini; but he accepted with his whole heart, and promoted with the unspared strength of a consistent life, the religion of *continuous duty*, nor bowed, even in the house of Rimmon, to any dogma which would divorce the life of the individual or of the people from that. An escaped serf, in the intoxication of his freedom mocking at the tyranny of forms, as idols everywhere, analytic rather than synthetic in the character of his intellect, in heart and soul and mind he was eminently a searcher after truth, a believer in the Gospel of Well-doing, a zealous and most devoted worker for the future of mankind.

Shall not the Emperor also have some credit for the Emancipation of the Serfs? Surely he shall have his due, such as Bismarck and his Emperor may claim also for the unification of Germany, or Cavour for his successful Piedmontese campaigns. But without the faith and more statesman-like because prophetic capacity of Mazzini, Italy might yet have to be contented with Cavour's great scheme of a federation of Italian or Italianized princes; German unity owes something to the barricades of '48, something too to Hecker, Robert Blum, Arnold Ruge, and others of the Frankfort Parliament; and but for the initiating labours of Pestel and Ryléieff and Herzen, and the dread of another Polish insurrection, Russian Emancipation might have been——how long deferred? Honour to whom honour is due, even though they be Republicans!

Among Herzen's many writings, in earlier days appearing with the signature of Iscander (Alexander), may especially be mentioned his letters on *Dilettantism in Science*, and the *Study of Nature*, written in Russia; *My Exile*, an account of his banishments from Moscow and Petersburg; his book on the *Development of Revolutionary Ideas in Russia;* and *The Russian People and their Socialism*, a letter in defence of his country, replying to Michelet's *Poland and Russia*. His articles in the *Kolokol* and the *Polar Star* are too numerous to be here named.

KONARSKI—DARASZ—STOLZMAN—
WORCELL.

X

KONARSKI.

"Soldat fidèle, j'ai achevé ma faction : qu'un autre me relève ! "

"He went forth wandering over the earth. God guide the poor exile ! "
Certain Polish envoys, says Michelet, in his *Legend of Kosciusko*, being at Rome, asked the Pope for some relics to place in their churches. They got this answer from him : " Why come here for relics ? Have you forgotten the song of your own land ?—O Poles ! Poles ! dig where you will the earth of Poland —everywhere is martyr dust."

SIMON KONARSKI, by birth a "gentleman," and brought up in the Protestant persuasion, was twenty-two years of age at the breaking out of the Polish Insurrection of 1830. In that holy war he served first as an ensign ; but his bravery and military talents soon obtained for him the rank of captain and the cross of honour. After sharing in all the battles of that not less glorious because unsuccessful campaign, he, when compelled in common with thousands of his fellow-countrymen to emigrate, took refuge in France. But his soul was too fervent, his need of action too imperious, to allow him to remain at rest. In 1833, under an assumed name, and pretending to be a traveling clockmaker, he and thirty-nine others of the Emigration, under the leadership of Zalivski, almost moneyless, and without passports, penetrated through Germany to Poland, with the intention of inciting the people to a guerilla warfare as prelude to another national insurrection. The enterprise failed. Most of those who took part in it fell into the hands of the enemy, and were shot or hanged, or buried in the mines of Siberia or the Austrian dungeons of Kufstein. Konarski had the good fortune to escape the indefatigable pursuit of the Russian Government, in spite of spies, innumerable hordes of Cossacks and large detachments of the regular army occupying the newly-conquered country, and the populations of whole villages turned out (with not much of enthusiasm on the part of these last) to hunt down the emigrants. For months he hid himself in the forests, half-clothed, and scarcely supplying himself with food to support life. Once he owed his safety to a Russian officer, who called out the master of the thouse in which he had for the time found shelter, to tell him that his house was about to be rigorously searched, and to conjure him to care for his friend's safety. Of course the man protested that there was no stranger there; the officer repeated his warning, adding: "I too am of the party of Mouravieff, save your friend!" That was enough: the search was unsuccessful. At last, at Eylau, where he thought himself out of danger, his ignorance of some technicality of clock-making awakened the suspicions of the local police; he was arrested ; but the Prussian authorities contented themselves with sending him to Dantzic and there putting him on board a ship for Antwerp. Mazzini was then preparing for the expedition into Savoy, and Konarski hastened to join him. Failure again, but he was not disheartened. His zeal but seemed to be inflamed with new ardour at every obstacle; his courage grew with danger. Before making a new endeavour, however, he set himself as an ordinary workman to obtain some farther knowledge of clock-making, in order that resuming his old disguise he might be secure from a recurrence of the dilemma in which he had found himself at Eylau. Then, commissioned by the Association of "Young Poland," of which he was a member, he in 1835 betook himself to London, thence to Cracow to confer with the co-religionists there, and thence, toward the end of the same year, passing into Russian Poland, traversed under various disguises, with death ever at his elbow, all the Polish provinces subjected to the Muscovite knout. Wonderfully active, he spread everywhere his republican faith, distributed tracts, organized associations, revivified the old patriotic spirit, and kindled the fire of new thoughts in quarters even the least suspected. The Youth of the Universities of Kiew and Wilna heard him, and answered with promises of adhesion to the alliance of the peoples; he penetrated even into the ranks of the Russian army, not yet forgetful of Pestel and 1824, enlisting the soldiers' sympathy for the Republic and for Poland. It is remarkable, as an indication of the spirit then leavening Europe both in the West and in the East, that among the many soldiers and officers of the Russian army whom Konarski admitted to his confidence, never one betrayed him. Even the consummate spy-system of Nicholas failed against him, for it had to cope with a man uniting perfect coolness and presence of mind with a genius always fertile in resources. For nearly three years he persevered in his apostolate, baffling all the skill and craft that dogged him from place to place, until at last, in May 1838, in the neighbourhood of Wilna, he was denounced by a German who had overheard a conversation, and was arrested. Taken to Wilna, the Governor before whom he was brought had the baseness to strike him. Konarski lifted up his fettered hands and smote him down. For nine months he was in prison, so long detained in the vain hope of extorting from him revelations that might implicate others and help for the overthrow of his work so far accomplished. All he endured during this terrible period will never be known; but it was known that when he remained silent under the knout, they, trying other orthodox recipes, fed him on salt provisions to produce thirst, and then placed drink before him tempting him to confess. As in the Italian prisons, they deprived him of sleep. They made incisions in his flesh (perhaps only the usual unpremeditated result of the knout), and into such raw places dropped boiling wax, not wanting to kill him, then spirits of wine to which they set fire. It would seem incredible, did we not know that during the later barbarisms of Neroic Rome, during the dark ages of succeeding Christianity, nay! it is said, even as part of the holy offices of the Christian and Roman Inquisition, such varieties of torment, whether for sake of the State or of the soul of the unhappy individual, such Red-Indian-like appliances were neither uncommon nor remarkable. The spirit of a Christian martyr upheld Konarski. Their appliances availed not. Nothing could be got out of him. The Russian Governor, superintendent of the means of grace, could not withhold his admiration : "It is a man of iron!" Two Russian officers refused the office of shooting him, in spite of the judicial sentence. One of them, Koravaeff (may his name be remembered!), an enthusiastic, devoted youth, sought to save him by contriving his escape. He had prepared all when his turn on guard should come, but was betrayed, and sent to Siberia to expiate his perception of a duty superior to military discipline. Of him there is no more known.

At length, no use to keep him alive, and he might escape, they brought him out for execution. Three days before, in their disgust at his obduracy, they had brutally driven out of Wilna his mother, who asked only to take leave of him. The 27th of February, 1839, was a day of bitter cold : they had left him in his summer clothes ; and he asked to be allowed a warmer dress. "My shivering limbs may tremble, and I would not seem to fear death." The jailer could do nothing without authority, and could only assure him that the way was not long. A few hours before his setting out a monk was permitted to visit him. "My good father," said Konarski, taking his hand, "I am sure that God will remit my sins so bitterly expiated: I have suffered both for my Country and for Humanity. I am a Calvinist: yet your benediction will be as welcome as that of a minister of my own creed. Bless me then, as thy son, one like thyself, a believer in the Cross, and I shall die happy." The monk wept, and blessed him, without attempting his conversion. A Greek monk probably: a Roman had been less—passive. Afterwards a Protestant minister was admitted to his cell. With him he breakfasted, conversing of God and immortality, till the time came for him to ascend his sledge to be carried to the place of execution outside the city walls. The streets were crowded. Women, children, and rude men, all were in tears. But he, lifting his fettered arms, cried to them—"Weep not for me! a little while and I shall be free: weep rather for yourselves!" Turning to the minister, who was with him in the sledge, he said—"How many monarchs might envy me a funeral procession so numerous, so spontaneous!" His one request was that his eyes might not be bound. So to the last he looked death in the face, not merely with firmness, but with the assured serenity of one who saw beyond death the Future, and whose unshaken faith prophesied to him of Poland's freedom and hereafter certain glory.

The *Augsburg Gazette,* reporting his execution, let

slip the phrase—"Konarski has been shot; and has died with a firmness worthy of a better cause." A Russian General, present at his death, could not refrain from crying out—"From this time I abhor my epaulettes." Later, Russian officers procured his chains, and had them forged into rings, to be worn however secretly in memory of his sufferings and the cause for which he suffered. But the Polish population of Wilna waited not. Hardly had he fallen when the agonized crowd burst through the Russian ranks, eager to touch the body of the Saint, to possess some relic, even a handful of the earth upon which he lay, of him who had so loved them, who for them had dared, had suffered, and had died.

ALBERT DARASZ.

To suffer nobly for one's country and Humanity: this is martyrdom, whether the death be in battle, or by the executioner, by slow prison torture, or the more merciful sentence of exile. To Albert Darasz exile was but a synonym for death. Shut out from Poland, forbidden to tread the soil of imperializing France, not admitted into Switzerland, he had but the choice between England or Belgium and some milder climate in which he might check the consumptive tendency which threatened him. He chose the place in which he could best work; came to England, sickened, and died.

Born at Warsaw in 1808, he was of the same age as Konarski. When only nineteen he had completed, with distinction, his course of law and administration,[1] and taken the degree of M.A. at the Warsaw University. An official career was open to him, but 1830 came, his country wanted him as a soldier, and he volunteered. Belonging to one of the best Polish

[1] The course through which a student in the colleges of Russian Poland had to pass to qualify him for any place under Government.

regiments, he took part in almost all the great battles, was promoted to a lieutenancy, and when the fight was over, passed with the rest into exile. Even there, military rank formed a sort of lower aristocracy; but Darasz had deep at heart a love of equality, had also profoundly studied the history of his country: he took his place then in the ranks of the democracy, declaring war à outrance against all privilege or aristocratic assumption, a war from which he flinched not while he had life. Elected on the Committees of the various local Polish Associations, to which he successively belonged, acting as secretary to most, he soon joined the secret societies in France which were endeavouring to find the ground for working out the problems of social progress; and when the monarchical Czartoryski party among the Poles was proved not only incompetent, but traitorous, and the Polish Democratic Society appeared to be the only possible form of organization for the party of the future in the Polish Emigration, he promptly entered its ranks, and identified himself with it: living, acting only for it, in accordance with its noble programme—"Through the Democratic Society for Poland, through Poland for Humanity."

His influence rapidly increased, becoming generally known and appreciated; and when, in 1833, at Poitiers, the Democratic Society re-organized itself and framed a definitive constitution, Darasz was chosen as a member of its principal committee, called the "Centralization." The history of the Polish Centralization is the history of Darasz.

When the Centralization undertook to conduct the *Polish Democrat*, a journal which soon found its way into the most secluded corners of Poland, stirring the country to its veriest depths, the direction was confided to Darasz. And when his labours in the Committee compelled him to give up his editorship, he still continued to be its inspiration, and to enrich it with his contributions: contributions soon remarked in the Emigration for the clearness of their language, their close, sharp logic and implacable reasonings. It was here that he wrestled with and overthrew the double-headed giant that stood in the way of every truly patriotic endeavour,—the double party of monarchical pretence and Jesuitism, personified in the Czartoryski faction and the Society of the "Redeemers." At length the propagandism of the Centralization bore its fruit. From all parts of Poland came the demand for aid in behalf of a new movement. Then the Committee, setting forth to join the patriots at home, left to Darasz the charge of collecting and forwarding the exiles. They had reserved for him one of the most important commissions in Poland, when the arrest of the chiefs in the Prussian Grand-duchy of Posen, and the execrable massacre, by Austria, of the patriot nobles in Galicia,[1] frustrated the attempt at a general uprising,

[1] The Austrian Ministers, Metternich and Brandt, aware of the projected insurrection, conceived the atrocious project of

one episode of which attempt, however, the insurrection of Cracow, in 1846, was enough to awaken the dormant revolutionary spirit in Europe, gleaming like the aurora of the republican dawn of 1848. The French members of the Polish Committee in aid,

massacring all the Polish landowners and gentry suspected of patriotic leanings. For this purpose, having first disseminated reports that the landowners intended only to farther enslave the peasantry, they set at liberty a peasant named Szela, in prison for horrible crime, and employed him as leader of other convicts, disguised soldiers and such peasants as could be induced to join them, to bring in the heads of the nobles and gentry, at a price of so much a head if alive, and so much additional if dead. From an incomplete list, bearing 1484 names, I take almost at random four or five,—not desiring to shock the reader, but because it is necessary to show by what means the Party of Order in Europe has, *within the last generation*, endeavoured to keep down the Republic.

"Theodore and John Bromiski were butchered in their own houses. Theodore had his ribs, arms, and legs broken, and was then killed with flails. John had his ears and nose cut off, and his head skinned. His wife was forced to hold a light while they tore out his eyes.

"Charles Kotarski, often mentioned in the journals as the benefactor of the country people, had his jaw-bones taken out before they killed him.

"Sokulski was thrown into a trough, and minced up for food for pigs.

"Madame Kempinska (born Countess Dembicka) was killed with a dung-fork. She was with child; they took the unborn twins to get the Government price per head."

"Why unearth such horrors? It is so long since 1846."

In 1849, Ugo Bassi, a priest who escaped from Rome with Garibaldi, fell into the hands of the Austrians. To preserve the tonsure from profanation, they would not kill him till he had been scalped. And in 1871, Thiers was shooting women in Paris.

of 1846, Ledru Rollin, T. Flocon, Francis Arago, Armand Marrast, Goodchaux, Guinard, etc., became in 1848 the Provisional Government of France.

Darasz had already reached Poland before the failure was known. Sent back to France, he was again on his way to Poland, when the bombardment of Cracow put an end to every hope, and drove the chiefs of the movement back to exile, to conspire afresh.

The editorship of the *Polish Democrat*, suspended during more active measures, was now resumed by Darasz, and continued until 1849, when Ledru Rollin's manifestation against the French expedition to Rome was made the ground for expelling from France the Polish Republicans, in particular the two most prominent members of the Centralization, Darasz and Worcell, the latter the close and dear friend of Mazzini.

They came to England, Darasz ignorant of the language, and warned against the climate. But there was work to be done, and he would not be deterred. In the beginning of 1850 he, with Mazzini, Arnold Ruge, and Ledru Rollin, formed the Central European Democratic Committee (see *Appendix*). That they were proud of him and chose him as their colleague is enough to show what manner of man he was.

But the seeds of consumption were ripening, and his life was wearing away. Such change of air as could be obtained in England, such attentions as the love of all who knew him insured,—these could but alleviate, scarcely delayed, the progress of the disease. Not even the love and skill of his brother, Paul Darasz (since also dead), a physician, who escaped from a Russian prison to tend his sick-bed for some weeks before his death, had power to save him. His grave was ready. He might see the Promised Land from the height of faith, but his bones must lie in the place of exile. He died in London on the 19th of September, 1852.

Twelve hundred mourners, exiles like himself, followed his funeral car, on which lay his sabre and his Polish cap, to Highgate Cemetery, on the outskirts of and overlooking the great city. Heading the procession as chief mourners with his brother were his two colleagues in the Centralization, MM. Worcell and Zabicki, and close to them the members of the European Committee, Mazzini, Ledru Rollin, Bratiano,[1] and M. Goegg (president of the German Republicans, who took the place of Dr. Ruge, absent on account of sickness). Behind them came first the French Republicans in ranks of five abreast, bearing their red flag with the inscription, " République démocratique et sociale"; the Italians followed with their tricolour; then the Germans; and last of all the Poles under their national flag, the white eagle on a sanguine field.

[1] Bratiano, a Wallachian, the agent in Paris of the revolutionary party in the Danubian Principalities during their attempt in 1848. He had been added to the European Committee.

Zabicki, a man of singular simplicity and integrity of nature, had fought under Bem in the Hungarian War.

CHARLES STOLZMAN.

I HAVE little to say of Stolzman. The life of exile has not much variety: inaction alternating with fruitless endeavour, deferred hope, disappointment, poverty, sickness or broken health, premature old age, and death. The history of one of the exiles is the history of all. Yet Stolzman deserves remembrance as one of the signers of the pact of Young Europe, as a zealous member of the Polish Centralization, and as the close friend with Worcell of Mazzini, who esteemed him for his nobility of character. Through Mazzini I first knew him, Stolzman's letters (my own also) being among those opened in the English post-office by order of the Home Secretary, in 1844; and our three names, Mazzini's, Stolzman's, and my own, affixed to the petition to Parliament for inquiry. At that period Worcell also was in England. To know those two friends was to esteem and love them: Worcell for his rare courtesy and gracious manners, the manners of the old noble, the expression yet more of a beautiful and gentle nature, for the dignity of his sentiments and the wonderful variety of his knowledge; Stolzman for his simple, soldierly uprightness and goodness of heart. I can but speak of the two men together, for they were inseparable: brothers not only in political faith but in intimate affection. And Mazzini equally loved and was loved by both. The one only occasion in which (so far as my knowledge went) Mazzini's most remarkable self-command gave way was in relation to Stolzman. Poor they all were: Mazzini by his writings barely providing for his own most simple wants and the claims upon him of other Italians; Worcell dependent upon occasional and irregular remittances from Poland, some remainder of his large estates, so much as was not confiscated, in the hands of members of his family, who if not patriotic did not like to leave him in absolute want; Stolzman living I know not how. One day when Mazzini called to speak with me, I noticed something unusual in his manner: pressing him for the reason, he at last told me that he had just come from Stolzman; he had for some time seen that all was not well with him, and that morning by accident had discovered that he was starving, for some days without food, keeping silence, uttering not a murmur lest he should rob his friends by taking of their scantiness. It was my first glance into the lower depth of the miseries of exile. God knows I have looked into that gulf but too often since: nor wondered that all sufferers had not the heroism of this one.

Stolzman was born at Warsaw, in 1793. He was but a lad when he entered the army in the Grand Duchy of Warsaw, which under Napoleon had part in the invasion of Russia. With the remains of Napoleon's host Stolzman went to France, where, I believe, he was for some time in the Imperial Guard: a tall athletic soldier, of irreproachable conduct, a good swordsman, and not wanting in military talent. After Napoleon's fall, and on the establishment of what was called the "Kingdom of Poland," he returned home. In 1830, he was captain of artillery in the Polish army, and, conspiring with other officers, took part in the rising of Warsaw on the 29th of November. He also defended Warsaw when besieged in October of the following year; and for his gallant and able conduct during the war was promoted by the Polish General Bem to the rank of lieutenant-colonel. Poland fallen, he went back to France.

During the revolution he had belonged to what may be called the patriotic or popular party, to distinguish it from the party of diplomacy, Prince Czartoryski's party, which depended rather upon foreign Courts and foreign intervention than on the efforts of the people themselves. In exile he joined his friend Lelevel, the historian, and the democratic section of the Emigration. In 1833 he acted with Colonel Zalivski, who with Konarski hoped to prepare a guerilla war in Poland. German help was promised through a rising in Frankfort. Stolzman's part was to collect the exiles in France, mostly settled at

Dijon and Besançon, conduct them to Switzerland, and wait events. Zalivski's expedition failing, the Frankfort help was useless. Stolzman remained in Switzerland, to join Mazzini in the projected attempt on Savoy. When this was frustrated by the treachery of General Ramorino, and, hope failing of immediate renewal of action, Mazzini formed the Association of "Young Europe," Stolzman took part as representative of "Young Poland," of which he was a leading member. At the same time the Polish Democratic Society was preparing a more general organization of the emigrants, Lelevel seeking to establish the "Polish Union," embracing all parties. In this latter society Young Poland became merged. Meanwhile Stolzman and his companions, expelled from Switzerland and forbidden to enter France, took refuge in England. There he was chosen on the Committee of the Union; and when General Dwernicki, its head, went over to the aristocratic faction, occasioning the break-up of the Union, Stolzman led his friends into the Democratic Society, the principles of which indeed he had always held.

In 1844 he published a work on *Partisan* (guerilla) *Warfare*, which was extensively circulated through Poland; intended to encourage the people by showing them how to depend on their own resources, and how best to apply them.

In 1848 he endeavoured to reach Poland, hoping to give aid in Posen; but, discovered, and unable to cross the frontier, returned to England, baffled and sorrow-stricken, an altered man. His faith remained, his energy was broken. In 1852 he left London to reside with me at Brantwood, on the side of Coniston Water, in the house now owned by Ruskin. For a time he rallied; then his health gave way. In the course of not many months he had become a feeble old man. In the autumn of 1854, for the sake of sea-bathing, he went to a little village, Haverrigg, on the Cumberland coast. He had just been elected to the Polish Centralization, to replace his friend Worcell, older and yet more feeble than himself; and he was anxious to recover some strength for his work, and for the long-desired return to Poland, if England, in that Crimean war, might yet be forced to change her policy, be wise enough to summon Poland against the Tzar. On the 18th of September he had a paralytic fit, and in three hours was dead.

In the little country churchyard of Millom, under the shadow of the English mountains, one single mourner, an Englishman, laid the body of the Polish soldier; a man not of genius or world-note, but than whom the world has known none truer, manlier, more upright, more soldierly, more patriotic, or more worthy of honourable recollection.

STANISLAS WORCELL.

ONE will look in vain through contemporary history for the name of STANISLAS WORCELL. To him might be applied the words of Landor concerning the old Greek philosopher—" He neither lived nor died with the multitude : there are, however, some Clazomenians who know that Anaxagoras was of Clazomenai." Some Republicans may yet remember that Worcell was of our best, say our best had there not been Mazzini to stand beside him.

I know not whether he was with Mazzini in Switzerland. He may have been the friend for whose sake Mazzini came to England; for when I first knew him they were as brothers, Mazzini treating him with the affection and respect due to an elder brother. It seemed as if the love which in earlier days he had for Jacobo Ruffini had been transferred to the beloved Pole. Beloved indeed he was, and not by Mazzini alone, but by all who came into his presence. Beloved and revered : he was the Nestor of the Republican camp.

I know not how old he was. He never spoke of

himself, nor of his family,—wife, son, and brother, who probably looked on him as a patriotic fool, but from whom or of whom I think he occasionally heard, when some tithed percentage of what had been his own reached him, to keep him from want of bread, or to help, through his most unselfish generosity, some other exile wanting also.

In 1830, Count Worcell, related to the royal Czartoryskis, was owner of large estates in his native Volhynia, that part of Poland the spoil of Russia. At the beginning of the insurrection, he armed a troop on his own lands, and putting himself at the head of the insurgents of his district, joined a corps under the command of Colonel Rozycki, which fought its way through the enemy's forces till it reached the national head-quarters at Warsaw. There he was elected a member of the National Diet, and took his seat as representative of Volhynia. Wandering afterwards in exile, through Germany and Switzerland to France, he joined the Polish Union under the presidency of Lelevel. In 1833, on the requisition of the Russian ambassador, he was expelled from France and took refuge in Belgium. Thence he went to England. In 1845, he returned to Belgium, being elected on the Committee of the Union, and in the following year reëntered France as a member of the Polish Centralization. In 1849, he was again expelled under pretext that he had been concerned in the republican manifestation of Ledru Rollin, Considérant, and others, on the 13th of June, protesting against the French invasion of Rome. Of course as a republican he was concerned. He then with his friend Darasz found shelter in England.

Like Herzen, belonging to a high family, brought up in luxury, his tastes literary and artistic, well cultivated, accomplished, gentle, courtly, almost fastidious, a patrician in all but patrician exclusiveness and selfishness, this man left all his estates, and he had great possessions, to follow the shadow of patriotism; gave up all, home, wife and child, fortune, ease, the student's calm for which none were better qualified, the pleasant pursuits of peace, at the call of duty. Such devotion prophesies even yet of the Poland that has to be. And never in his extremest destitution, never under any suffering, was word of complaint or of regret wrung from that most saintly, most devoted heart. Never accent of lament for himself profaned the lips of that most serene of martyrs : though he knew the depths of poverty, poverty of the affections (two photographs, one of his child, brought up as a Russian—this all instead of home), material poverty also, for of the little that came not regularly to hand there were always sharers. So poor was he (and yet so uncomplaining, with the pride of a gentleman, that one rag of prosperity preserved), that a friend who wanted to be of help had to take a lodging in the same house, under pretence of having to consult him on political matters, in order to have the opportunity of asking him to dinner, and so insuring him some better sustenance, for at least a while. Yet poor as that, when almost in his latest days, the remittance from abroad failing, he had to ask a loan, and he of whom he asked it would make a condition that the money should be applied only to his own personal needs, and not wasted for perhaps some new political occasion, or in help to some other political sufferer, he indignantly refused to accept assistance on such degrading terms. For the honour of the friend who for the moment so mistook him, let it be also said that he promptly acknowledged his mistake, and was only the more delicate and unremitting in his after kindness.

Suffering continually from asthma, aggravated by his having to live in London, I do not recollect a day in which he seemed at ease, save one when, being in the North for some political object, he came to see his friend Stolzman and myself at Coniston. There, climbing with some difficulty the fells at the back of my house, as he reached a height and rested, the pure mountain air seemed to revive him, and made him feel, he said, like a new man. But weak, or out of health, or in pain, he was ever ready at any inconvenience, at any suffering or risk, to meet the constant calls upon him for advice or exertion from the whole body of the Polish refugees, who looked to him as to a wise father. I might write on, not knowing where to stop, of this man, whom indeed I loved as a father, of whose love for me I am as proud as I was sure. Perhaps I speak fondly, and but too partially. Herzen, who knew him too, may take my place, and speak for me his funeral oration: it will only be a change of words, his better than mine.

The following is from the *Polar Star:* "on the death of Stanislas Worcell"—

" The 3rd of February, 1857, in a little street in London, Hunter Street near Russell Square, in a poor chamber on the ground floor, ceased, hardly remarked, a holy existence.

" Poland counts one martyr more. She will not refuse to lend his martyrology to us. We need it for the teaching of our Russian children.

" Worcell was a *Saint.* I use this word with intention : it best expresses his dominant characteristic. The whole existence of this man was an act of devotedness without bounds, of complete self-abnegation, of incessant travail. All that most strikes us in the legends of the Saints we find in him : trait for trait, with more of love, with a more human element.

" Born in opulence, in the midst of the Polish aristocracy, he died poor and a democrat. He flung away his titles and abandoned his fortune when his country was struck down. I say this but in passing : for never has any people more readily sacrificed their fortunes than the Slaves, especially the Poles. And in leaving Poland he did not betake him to repose, as did the weary Romans who, throwing away their titles and their wealth to escape from a world crumbling beneath their feet, sought in the deserts of the Thebaid to make of the completest indolence a religion of despair. It was in exile that the great work, the travail of Worcell began. Lone, poor, abandoned by his wife, by his own child, he laboured twenty-six years in exile for the organization of the democratic and republican party in the Polish Emigration. Overwhelmed with misfortunes, privations, maladies, he was day and night at his work, with that calm serenity, that resigned gentleness, that candid simplicity, which a faith not to be shaken gives to a great heart.

"No one ever heard a single plaint from his mouth. Of that I am sure. He was sometimes more sad: that was all. I would know if any one of the friends who lived intimately with him was ever witness to one of those moments of bitterness and indignation when wrath, overcoming faith, drags from us those cold and biting words with which a man would revenge himself for the agonies he has felt. Never have I heard such from Worcell's lips: and I was closely allied with him; there was a time when I saw him almost every day.

"His was one of those integral natures,—I would say more, one of those fanatical natures, which, dominated by one grand thought, having one grand and only end in view, reach the calm of a perfect resolution, an imperturbable tranquility, and through that to a great gentleness as well as an inflexible will.

"Such were for the most part the martyrs of science, the heroes of religion, at the epoch of the

Renaissance and at the Reformation. For such men there is no stop, no fatigue, no return. The principal thing has been absolutely decided for them in the forum of their own souls. The rest, the mere happening, does not occupy their thought. They have only to continue, to march on, *ora e sempre*, keeping their way. Misfortunes, poverty, abandonment, the sobs of the feeble, the cries of those who would hang back, the groans of the dying, prison, chains, the gallows,—shall they halt on their way for that? Not they! They keep the same step, calm, austere, inflexible.

" That was the step of Worcell. It is the step of one of his friends whom he passionately loved—Joseph Mazzini.

" Faithful soldier of Poland, he was always at his post, even to the hour when his hand, stiffening at the approach of death, traced the touching words that Ledru Rollin quoted in his speech.[1]

" These words remind me of another time. Nine years ago, some days after the Revolution of February, Lamartine (like those husbands in some savage countries who lie in state when their wives are brought to bed) was receiving congratulations on occasion of the birth of the Republic. Among the deputations one group held themselves apart, a

[1] Ledru Rollin spoke over his grave, the grave in which Darasz had been laid little more than four years before. " When he could no longer speak he made signs for a pen, and wrote these words: *Soldat fidèle, j'ai achevé ma faction ; qu'un autre me relève !* " (My watch is over; let another take my place !)

group among whom were men with white hair and grizzled moustaches. On their manly faces, furrowed by misfortune, one saw the severe intrepidity of the old soldier and the sadness of the exile. Their spokesman (if I mistake not, it was Worcell) said to Lamartine, or rather to the French Republic: 'To every appeal of the peoples in the years of struggle and distress, Poland has been the first to answer— HERE! for she saw in every struggle for Liberty a struggle for Poland. She is here now.'

"There was in these words something most sadly solemn, as it were the involuntary reproach of a generous people which had been sacrificed.

"The Polish Emigration, Worcell their sentinel in advance, were indeed under arms and ready. But there was no appeal. The peoples slept. Order, that of Warsaw, reigned in Europe. The faithful soldier fell at his post, and the heavy wheels of the reaction passed over his bones.

"The destiny of the Polish Emigration has been very remarkable. Conquered only by superior force, betrayed by the Governments of Europe, the Polish patriots retreated fighting, and, holding themselves erect, passed the frontier, carrying their country with them. Europe respectfully made way for this solemn triumphal march of the vanquished. The peoples came out to meet them; kings stood aside to give them room. For an instant their step awakened men's nobler sympathies. The old world had tears, money, and dared to give them. It was as if a sudden remorse had crossed its soul, as if this martyr-soldier, this crusader of independence, the Polish Emigration, represented in its eyes the expiation of a mean and pusillanimous century. Since then all is changed: it is in vain that expatriated Poland answers to every call in the days of struggle and danger; it is in vain that in the vanguard, in every battle for Liberty, the Pole is always found who sheds his blood for others while dreaming of his country. They have done nothing for Poland. A misfortune that lasts too long uses up our sympathies.

"But let the shade of our friend send down milder thoughts and peace into our souls.

"Let me speak of him!

"Toward the end of 1852, coming from Italy, I met Worcell in London. The time was sad, under the weight of calamities. The Continent was being irresistibly dragged toward that state of senile barbarism which it has fallen into now. Everywhere a brutal and ferocious reaction had the upper hand. I tried to turn from the gloomy spectacle of this agony, and fancying I saw the dawn on another side, I concentrated all my powers for the organization in London of a centre of Russian propagandism. I spoke of it to Worcell. The eagerness, the joy, the friendship with which he prevented my words, were admirable: it was he, the representative of the Polish Democracy, who took the most active part in the foundation of an independent tribune for Russian speech. Poor dear friend! I see him now, with that face so full of suffering, that intelligent look, those white hairs, that voice feeble from sickness, holding in his hands the first sheet printed in Russian at London; and hear him saying to me: 'My God! my God! a free Russian press! . . . Ah! how much of the sad happenings of these last days is effaced by this bit of paper!' Afterwards, taking both my hands in his, he repeated: 'Yes! we ought to march together; we have the same enemy; we ought to be united.'

"The Russian printing office was at first attached to the office of the Polish Centralization. Worcell placed at my disposal all the means of which he and his friends had control, to send our papers through Poland into Russia. They reached there, as you know.

"The *Polish Democrat*, announcing the establishment of the Russian press, and giving at the same time translations of my articles, inserted also a sympathetic appeal to the Russians. 'What hate has a right to persist,' wrote Michelet then, 'when the Poles ally themselves with the Russians?'

"During the Crimean war hatred and fear found room for a recrudescence of animosity against us. Atrabilious maniacs revenged themselves for their fears by confounding every Russian, were he a Pestel or a Mouravieff, with official Russia. Worcell, whom the war did not deceive, came forward publicly against the infamous pretence. He took up with indignation the defence of our friend Bakounine, still remaining (1857) in the dungeons of the clement Alexander II.; and defended me also when my turn came to pass through the filthy douche.

"It is however a very remarkable fact that this animal hatred against the Russians has scarcely any existence among the Poles, who alone have an indisputable right to detest us. *They* do not require of us to betray our country in witness of our good citizenship; nor that we should undervalue our Russian people in proof of our sincerity. When a Russian approaches the Poles, his heart afflicted with the thought of what his Government has done against Poland, reddening with shame for his own fetters, and labouring to break them, *they* receive him as a brother. Bakounine and many others found this: I also. 'We love you,' said Worcell to me one day, when we were speaking of this, 'precisely because you love your country: otherwise you would not be with us; you would be a man to whom we should be indifferent, one who had expatriated himself only for his own pleasure!'

"So, before his eyes were closed in death, Worcell had at least the joy of seeing the complete success of the Russian propaganda, the extent to which it went, and the continually increasing demand for our writings. He spoke with me of this only some weeks before his death.

. . . . . .

"Worcell was of a nature eminently religious. That certain mysticism which we almost always meet with in the Polish poets had strong roots in the soul of Worcell, without however having power to trouble the great lucidity of his mind. His genius was logical, wide-sighted, but at the same time delicately subtle (*d'une grande finesse*). Highly endowed with the faculty of abstract reasoning, he naturally became a profound mathematician. His active and ardent mind, however, stopped not at geometry and astronomy, but studied in turn all the natural sciences. His erudition was prodigious. He occupied himself with everything, was interested in everything, and forgot nothing. Speaking, not only well but elegantly, French, English, and German, he was thoroughly acquainted with modern literature. I often addressed myself to him as a living cyclopedia; and the answer was always ready. Conscientious in everything, if he afterwards thought that he had been wrong, he would next day write in correction. This mass of varied knowledge, with a reflection of mysticism thrown upon it, gave a peculiar originality to his conversation, and to his way of looking at things.

"And all this, science and mysticism, history and mathematics, was only on the lower plane of his life. Above all was his religion, the thought of his whole existence, his faith in Poland. The rest was only recreation, relaxation (*délassement*). His powers, his dreams, his faculties, his being, his whole soul was there. Having sacrificed to that cause his home-happiness, his fortune, his entire life, he wished to make even his death of service to his country. Feeling himself near his end, he sent for Mazzini and two or three other friends. Feeble, exhausted, hardly breathing, he lay on his bed scarcely able to speak. He made a sign for Mazzini to approach. The grave and austere expression of his face became yet more solemn, as with a voice almost gone he asked of him his sacred promise not to forget Poland in the great day of the future awakening of the peoples. It was the Swear! (as in Hamlet) of the manes of a great people sacrificed. Mazzini took a pen, wrote some lines, and read and showed them to him. Overcome with emotion, the old man could not speak; but his whole appearance was transfigured, his eyes brightened with a superhuman brilliance; he thanked him with a look in which content and ecstasy were as strong as death.

"Ten days after, Mazzini, much moved, spoke to me of the expression of the dying man. And I thought of St. Jerome receiving the last sacrament (Domenichino's picture in the Vatican): the same faith, passing beyond the tomb, the same sacrifice, the same tranquility at the last."

On the 9th of February, the sad company of the wrecked, the nations' refugees in London, and those English friends who knew and respected them and him, met before the house in which he died. He had not left sufficient to pay for his funeral. His friend Mr. P. A. Taylor, the member of Parliament, took on himself the expenses. Mazzini and Ledru Rollin followed the hearse on foot: two Russians helped to carry the coffin to the grave; Ledru Rollin and Mr. Taylor spoke over it. It was a day of almost Spring weather, a rare day, with cloudless sky, clear and hopeful as the youth in that old man's soul.

Faithfullest soldier! who shall take thy place?

I have chosen these names from among the Dead. Were there none others, perhaps equally worthy of remembrance? Many, ah! many: FORESTI (whom some Americans may remember), Silvio Pellico's companion in Spielberg; the PISTRUCCIS, father and son; LAMBERTI; ROSALINO PILO; PISACANE; MANARA; PIANCIANI; FELICE ORSINI; yes! and PIANORI. The names of the last two shall not be erased from the Scroll of Honour because, like Ehud in Holy Writ, or like Brutus whom in our youth we were taught to admire and emulate, they aimed directly at a crowned head instead of attacking the eunuchs at the palace-gates. Was that a crime? Walter Savage Landor shall answer for me—

> "Most dear of all the Virtues to her sire
> Is Justice: and most dear
> To Justice is Tyrannicide."

These I would name among Italians. How many more have given their lives as devotedly if not for Italy and the Italian Republic, yet for the Republican Future of Mankind? I have spoken of those of whom I was best able to speak. Else I had not omitted to wreathe such words as were well deserved for LEDRU ROLLIN, the staunch, the generous, the eloquent advocate of the Republic; for BAUDIN and ROSSEL; for DELESCHIZE also, dying heroically, however mistakenly, on the ruins of Communal Paris. Of Poles the martyr-name is LEGION. Of Germans also have been brave men. Surely I did not forget ROBERT BLUM: the poor untaught tinker's apprentice of Cologne, the self-educated bookseller and citizen leader at Leipsic, the member for Leipsic in the first German Parliament, in 1848; who might have been prime minister of Saxony, but preferred a patriot's grave beneath the barricades of Vienna.[1]

Neither in Germany, nor elsewhere throughout continental Europe, has there been any lack of Confessors of our republican faith, the faith as taught us by Mazzini and Lamennais, not the "republicanism" of Thiers.

And of the living [1867], some since dead: AURELIO SAFFI, the Triumvir, good and true, always persevering in his well-known path toward the Republic; good old MAURIZIO QUADRIO; FABRIZZI; Dr. BERTANI, Mazzini's friend and physician: how many more whose names I know not? Little need to mark the unstable crowd, falling off, like Medici

[1] So had he chosen; but was taken prisoner and sentenced to be hanged, the sentence commuted to shooting from fear of his popularity. Having heard the sentence, he only said—"I expected it." He wrote to his wife—"Be resigned! bring up our children so that my name be never tarnished by them!" And so died, "for the freedom of my country."

under temptation of a smaller success, or like Gallenga through envy and poor-heartedness, from the hopes and aspirations of their wiser years. Let them pass! But of the true I would not leave unnamed Dr. ARNOLD RUGE, the German colleague of the European Committee, honoured both in Germany and England.

Italy cannot lose sight of Mazzini. The Poles are scattered through all lands, but, be they where they may, with the undying memory of Worcell and Mazzini must live the fruitful germs by them implanted. The Polish Republic is sure. In England the fowls of the air have not picked up every seed. If few or none to be fairly called disciples, Mazzini left loving friends in England (none personally knowing him could be other than loving); and if his fiery zeal was too enthusiastic for our colder climate, his name and character are at least above misunderstanding or dispute. But he was singularly unfortunate in the class in which alone he had the opportunity of association. At the time of his first sojourning in England, the only liberal and progressive party in politics was mainly composed of and almost identical with the religious sect called Unitarian; and in the cold dead formalism in which they lived and moved and had their being (their political creed also the pale reflection of the philosophy of the French Revolution —the Rights of Man under restriction), there was little fertility of soil for the growth of a religious faith. Of those who listened to him I would hesitate to name one of public prominence really adhering to him or even understanding him. Some were politic enough to use him as a stepping-stone, thinking at the same time that they loved him, and ready in all kindness privately to make life pleasant to him, willing even at times to stand not too inconveniently beside him in public. Save to the very few he is still only the sublime dreamer; the rest, even some with whom he took loving pains, have fallen off; some returning to the mere atheistic materialism of English politics, others straying away on any vague philosophic or pseudo-Christian errand. Only among our English working-class, men loving him for his goodness, out of the very warmth of simple hearts comprehending his devoted patriotism, and with the natural logic of unbewildered minds able to comprehend his humanitarian views, would I look (save as before said for some few exceptions) for men able to perceive that the teachings of our own wisest, of Vane and Milton and Eliot, lead directly to the completer and farther Gospel which by word and life Mazzini has announced, and of which the first apostles have been among the men whose memories are here before the reader.

Have I spoken too enthusiastically, too affectionately of them? Some were my dearest friends. Also I had to speak of men calumniated during life, forgotten or calumniated since their death. How else should I speak of those who are despised and rejected of men because the world knoweth them not?"

"Ils sont partis!" They are gone: the apostles and the martyrs of a new faith, the friends with whom I gladly walked and was most proud to work in days when life was bright with the aurora of the Republic, when the Future seemed within our grasp.

There is a time between the sowing and the harvesting. The husbandman must wait.

APPENDIX.

A BASIS OF ORGANIZATION.

(From the Manifesto of the Central European Democratic Committee, London, 1850.)

WE believe in the progressive development of human faculties, and in the direction of the moral law which has been imposed upon us.

We believe in association as the only regular means which can attain this end.

We believe that the interpretation of the moral law and rule of progress can not be confided to a caste or an individual, but ought to be confided to the people enlightened by national education directed by those among them whom virtue and genius point out to them as their best.

We believe in the sacredness of both the individual and society, which ought not to be effaced nor to combat, but to harmonize together for the amelioration of all by all.

We believe in Liberty, without which all human responsibility vanishes;

In Equality, without which Liberty is only a deception;

In Fraternity, without which Liberty and Equality would be only means without end;

In Association, without which Fraternity would be an unrealizable programme;

In Family, City, and Country, as so many progressive spheres in which man ought to successively grow in the knowledge and practice of Liberty, Equality, Fraternity, and Association.

We believe in the holiness of Work, in its inviolability, in the Property which proceeds from it as its sign and its fruit;

In the duty of Society to furnish the element of material work by Credit, of intellectual and moral work by Education;

In the duty of the individual to make use of it with the utmost concurrence of his faculties for the common amelioration.

We believe, to resume, in a social state having God and His Law at the summit; the People, the universality of the citizens free and equal, at its base; progress for rule, association as means, devotion for baptism, genius and virtue for lights upon the way.

And that which we believe to be true for a single people, we believe to be true for all. There is but one sun in heaven for the whole earth; there is but one law of Truth and Justice for all who people it.

Inasmuch as we believe in Liberty, Equality, Fraternity, and Association, for the individuals composing the State, we believe also in the Liberty, Equality, Fraternity, and Association of Nations. Peoples are the individuals of Humanity. Nationality is the sign of their individuality and the guarantee of their liberty : it is sacred. Indicated at once by tradition, by language, by a determined aptitude, by a special mission to fulfil, it ought to harmonize itself with the whole, and assume its proper functions for the amelioration of all, for the progress of Humanity.

We believe that the map and organization of Europe are to be remade, in accordance with these principles. We believe that a pact, through a congress of the representatives of all nationalities, constituted and recognized, having for mission to serry the holy alliance of Peoples and to formulize the common right and duty, is at the end of all our efforts.

We believe, in a word, in a general organization, having God and His Law at the summit, Humanity, the universality of nations free and equal, at its base, common progress for end, alliance for means, the example of those peoples most loving and most devoted for encouragement on the way.

．　　．　　．　　．　　．　　．

We have not now to say what this organization should be. It suffices to-day for us to establish its urgency and possibility. We are not giving a programme; we make an appeal.

To all men who share our faith;

To all the Peoples who have a nationality to conquer;

To all those who think that every divorce, even for a time, between thought and action is fatal;

To all those who feel stirring within their hearts a holy indignation against the display which is made in Europe in the service of tyranny and falsehood:

We say—come to us! Sacrifice to the one great object your secondary disagreements, and rally yourselves on the ground we are pointing out to you!

．　　．　　．　　．　　．

For the Central European Democratic Committee.

LEDRU ROLLIN.   JOSEPH MAZZINI.
ALBERT DARASZ.   ARNOLD RUGE.

THE END.

www.ingramcontent.com/pod-product-compliance
Lightning Source LLC
Chambersburg PA
CBHW032356230426
43672CB00007B/717